Sri Garib Dass Oriental Series No.241

THEORIES OF KNOWLEDGE

A Critique

Book -II

Veluri Subba Rao

Sri Satguru Publications
A Division of
Indian Books Centre
Delhi, India

Published by :
Sri Satguru Publications
A Division of :
Indian Books Centre
Indological and Oriental Publishers
40/5, Shakti Nagar,
Delhi-110007
(INDIA)
Email : ibcindia@ibcindia.com

ISBN 81-7030-575-6

First Edition : Delhi, 1998

Published by Sunil Gupta for Sri Satguru Publications a division of Indian Books Centre, 40/5, Shakti Nagar, Delhi-110 007, India and printed at Mudran Bharti, Delhi-110007

To

My Wife

Sitā Sundarī

The author of the work, Prof. Veluri Subba Rao passed away in April 1994. Dr. Veluri Ananta Ramam, the author's son took up the rough manuscript and got it press ready. In this connection Dr. Ramam would like to thank profoundly the academic and the technical assistance provided by Dr. G.A. Sarma, Head of the Department of Sanskrit at the Andhra University. The encouragement given by Prof. V. Gandhi Babu in the initial stages is also acknowledged.

Shri Naresh Gupta of the Indian Books Centre is thanked for publishing this work on Indian theories of knowledge in the present form. The publishers have done an excellent job and executed the work in a record time.

- Veluri Ananta Ramam

Contents

List of Abbreviations
List of Works in Sanskrit Consulted or Quoted

S.No.	Abbreviations used	Name of Work	Sastra	Author	Publisher
1	2	3	4	5	6
1.	Ad. Bh.	Adharva Samhitabhāṣya	Veda	Sāyana	Edited by Sankara Panduranga Pandit, Government Central Book Depot, Bombay.
2.	Ad. Par.	Advaita Vedānta Paribhāṣā	Vedānta	Dharmarājā-dhvarīndra	Khemaraj Srikrishna Das, Chetty, Bombay
3.	Ad. Sid.	Advaita Siddhi with Sarala	Vedānta	Madhusudana Saraswathi	Bombay
4.	Br.	Brhati	Prabhākara Mīmāmsa	Prabhākara	Madras University Sanskrit Series No. 3, Part II.
5.	Bh. Cin.	Bhātta Cintāmaṇi	Bhatta Mimamsa	Gaga Bhatta	Chowkhamba Sanskrit Series.
6.	Bh. Di.	Bhātta Dīpikā with Cintāmani	Bhatta Mimamsa	Khanda Deva	Edited by Venkata Subrahmanya Sastri
7.	Dee. Sar.	Dīpikā Sarvaswam on Tarkasaṃgraha	Tarka	Kuruganti Sreerama Sastri	K. Srinivasa Sastri, Tenali, Guntur Dt. (A.P.)

1	2	3	4	5	6
8.	Gu.-Kau.	Gurusammatapadarthahkaumārila	Mīmāmsa	–	Trivandrum Sanskrit Series, No. 171
9.	Jai Tar. Bh.	Jaina Tarka Bhāsā	Jaina	Yaśovijaya	Sanchalak Singhi Jaina Granthamala, Calcutta.
10.	Mad. Kar.	Mādhyamika Karikāḥ	Buddhist (Mādhyamikā)	Nagarjuna	Andhra Sahitya Parishat, Kakinada, Andhra Pradesh.
11.	Man. Mey.	Mānameyodaya	Bhātta Mimamsa	Narayana	Theosophical Publishing House, Madras.
12.	Mim. Dar.	Mīmāmsadarśana with Sābarabhāṣya	Mīmāmsa	Jaimini and Sabara	Jai Krishna Dass Hari Dass Gupta, Chowkhamba Sanskrit Series.
13.	Muk.	Kārikāvali with Siddhanta Muktāvali	Tarka	Viśwanātha	
14.	Nil.	Nilakantha Prākāśikā	Tarka	Nīlakantha	S. Chandrasekhara Sastrigal Triplicane, Madras.
15.	Ny. Bin.	Nyāya Bindu	Buddhist	Dharmakirti	Chowkhamba Sanskrit Series.
16.	Ny. Bin. Ti.	Nyāya Bindutika	Buddhist	Dharmottara	Bibliotheca Indica Asiatic Society of Bengal, Calcutta.
17.	Ny. Chan.	Nyāya Candrikā with Nyaya Prakaśikā	Advaita Vedanta	Ananda Purīna	Government Oriental Series, Madras
18.	Ny. Kau.	Nyāya Kaustubha	Tarka	Mahādeva Punatamaraka	Prince Wales, Saraswati Bhavan Series

1	2	3	4	5	6
19.	Ny. Ku.	Nyāya Kusumānjali	Tarka	Udayana	Chowkhamba Sanskrit Series.
20.	Ny. Ko.	Nyāya Kośa	Lexicon	Bhīmācarya Jhalkekar	Bhandarkar Oriental Research Institute, Poona.
21.	Ny. Mak.	Nyāya Makaranda with Com.	Vedanta	Ānandabodha Bhattaraka and Com. by Citsukha	Chowkhamba Sanskrit Series.
22.	Ny. Man.	Nyāyamanjari	Tarka	Jayanta Bhaṭṭa	E.J. Lazurus & Co., Banaras
23.	Ny. Par.	Nyāya Parisuddhi	Visistadvaita Vedanta	Venkatanatha	Chowkhamba Sanskrit Series.
24.	Ny. Rat.	Nyāyaratnamāla	Bhatta Mimamsa	Parthasarathi Misra	Babu Hardass Gupta, Banaras
25.	Ny. Sid. Man.	Nyāya Siddhanta Manjari Prakāsa with Com. Brhaṭṭīkā	Tarka	Janakinatha Nilakantha	Ambikacarana Chattopadhyay
26.	Ny. Sid. Man. Sa.	–do–	Tarka	Com. by Yādava-cārya	Bhagavati Prasad Lazurus & Co., Banaras.
26(a).	Ny. Sid.	Nyāya Siddhāñjana	Visista-dvaita	Vedānta Deśika	Ed. by Nila Meghacharya, Pub. by Director, Research Institute, Varanasya Sanskrit Visva Vidyalaya, Varanasi.
26(b).	Ny. Su.	Nyāya Sūtra	Nyaya	With Bhāṣya	Bhagavati Prasad Lazurus & Co., Banaras.

1	2	3	4	5	6
27.	Par. Mu.	Pariksamukhasūtra with Laghu Vṛtti	Digambara Jaina	Manikyanandin	Bibliotheca Indica, Asiatic Society of Bengal.
28.	Pat. Dar.	Patañjala Darśana with Vyāsabhāṣya	Yoga	Patanjali (Com. Vyasa). Sub Com. of Vacaspati	
29.	Pra. Kim.	Pramāṇa Mīmāṃsa	Jaina	Hemacandra	Sanchalak Singh Jaina Granth-mala, Ahmedabad, Calcutta.
29(a).	Pra. Var. (with Bhāṣya)	Pramāṇa Vārtikā	Bauddha	Dharmakīrti	Ed. by G. Rahul Samkrtyayana
29(b).	Pra. Var. (Vṛtti)	Pramāṇa Vārtikā	Buddhist	Dharmakīrti	Ed. by G. Rahul Samkrtyayana
30.	Pra. Pan.	Prakaraṇa Pañcika	Prabhakara Mimamsa	Salikānātha	Vidya Vilas Press, Banaras.
31.	Pr. Rat.	Prāmāṇya Ratnāmkara	Jaina	Abhinavacaru-kirti Pandita-cārya.	Oriental Research Publications.
32.	Sam. Kar.	Sāṃkhya Kārikā	Sāṃkhya	Iswaraḳrsṇa	Chowkhamba Sanskrit Series.
33.	Sam. Kau.	Sāmkhya Tattvakaumudi with the Com. Samkhyatattva Vibhakara	Samkhya	Vacaspati	Chowkhamba Sanskrit Series.
34.	Sim. Pr. Bha.	Vijnanabhiksu	Samkhya	Vijñanabhiksu (Ed. by Garbe)	Harward University Press.
35.	Sam. Pr. Su.	Sāmkhya Pravacanasūtra with the Com. of Vijnanabhiksu	Samkhya	Kapila	New Sanskrit Press, Calcutta

1	2	3	4	5	6
36.	Sar. Dar.	Sarvadarśana Samgraha	Mixed	Sayana Madhava	Ananda Press, Poona.
37.	Sas. Dee.	Sāstra Dipika with Yuktisneha Prapuraṇi	Bhatta Mimamsa	Parthasarathi Ramakrishna	Chowkhamba Sanskrit Series.
38.	Sid. Bin.	Siddhanta Bindu	Advaita Vedanta	Madhusudana Saraswati	Advaita Manjari Series (V. Sambasiva Ayyar)
38(a).	S.S.L.S.	Śāstra Śiddhanta Lesa Saṃgraha	Sankara Advaita	Appayya Diksita	Srimad Appayya Dikshitendra Granthavali Prakarana Samiti Secunderabad.
39.	Sy. Vad.	Syadvādamañjari	Svetambara Jaina	Mallisena Suri and Hemacandra	Bombay Sanskrit and Prakrit Series
40.	Sl. Var.	Mīmāmsa Ślokavārtika with Kasika	Bhatta Mimamsa	Kumarila	Trivandrum Sanskrit Series
41.	Tar. Bha.	Tarka Bhāsā with Com.	Buddhist	Moksakaragupta Com. by E. Krishnamacarya	Oriental Institute, Baroda.
42.	Tar. Rak.	Tārkika Rakṣa	Nyaya	Varadaraja	Benaras Sanskrit College Series
43.	T. Sam. Sar.	Tarka Saṃgraha Sarvaswaṃ	Tarka	Kuruganti Sri-rama Sastri	K. Srirama Sastri, Tenali Guntur District (A.P.).
44.	T.C.	Tattva Cintāmaṇi	Tarka	Gangesa	Sudarsana Press, Kanchi
45.	T.S.	Tarka Samgraha	Tarka	Annambhatta	Nirnayasagara Press, Bombay

1	2	3	4	5	6
46.	T.C.D. T.C.D. (Gad.)	(a) with Didhiti and Gadadhari (Different Khandas)	Tarka	Raghunatha & Siromani and Gādādhara	Sundarsana Press, Kanchi.
47.	T.C. (Rah.)	(b) With Cintamani Tarka Rahasya	Tarka	(b) (1) Mathura-natha	Asiatic Society
	T.C. (Aloka)	(2) with Aloka on Tarka Anuvya-vasaya and Nirukalpaka etc.	Tarka	(2) Jaya Deva	Bibliotheca Indica Series.
48.	Tat. Pr.	Tattva Pradīpikā (Citsukhi)	Advaita Vedanta	Citsukhācārya	Nirnaya Sagara Press, 1931 Bombay
49.	Tat. Sam.	Tattva Saṃgraha with Com. Pañcika.	Buddhist	Santaraksita Kamalsila	Gaekward's Oriental Series
50.	Ved. Pan	Vedanta Pancadasī with Com. by Sri Rayaprolu Linganna Somayaji	Advaita Vedanta	Vidyāranya and Com. by Sri. R. Linganna Somayaji	Sri Rayaprolu Linganna Soma-yaji, Advocate, Guntur (A.P.)
51.	Yat.	Yatīndramata Dīpikā	Visistadvaita	Srinivasadasa	Sri Ramakrishna Math, Mylapore, Madras.

In addition to these, works like the Nyāya Bhāṣya, Khaṇdana Khandakhādya, Vaiśeśika Sūtra etc. have been consulted and referred to in relevant places.

1	2	3	4	5	6
		WORKS IN ENGLISH Etc.			
52.	Hist. Log.	History of Indian Logic–A	Nyāya	Mm. S.C.V. Bhusan	Motilal Banarasidas, Delhi.
53.	Phil. Sen.	Philosophy of a Sentence and Its Parts	Mixed	V. Subba Rao	Munshi Ram Manoharlal, Delhi.
		WORKS IN TELUGU			
54.	At. Bo.	Ātma Bodhāmṛtamu	Vedānta	M. Somasundra Rao and V. Venkateswara Sastri	M.V. Lakshminārayana Rao Homeo Doctor, Arundalpet, Guntur.
55.	C.K.	The Concepts of Knowledge Indian Theories	Mixed	Debabrata Sen	K.P. Bagchi & Co., 286, B.B. Ganguli Street, Calcutta.

Chapter 1
A Critique on the Theories of Knowledge

Epistemological Theories – A General Survey

Now let us examine in detail the relative claims of each of the theories of knowledge with a view to a nearer approach to the true nature of knowledge, its production, its cognition, its properties, its varieties and its means. This critique is expected only review and criticise the general theorics of knowledge, with the help of disputations extant in the different theories. The very subtle and complicated arguments and counter-arguments in works like the Citsukhi, Advaitasiddhi etc. have been left over for detailed debate in learned councils. Knowledge is a complicated and largely disputed process a study of which is far from easy.

Nevertheless, casting a general glance at the theories of knowledge advocated by the different schools of Epistemologists and not taking into account the many subtleties confronting the theories, the Buddhist's theory of knowledge appears to be the most simple (next to the Cārvaka's) and the Sankarite's (Advaita – Vedantin's) theory the most complicated. In between these two the other theories appear to have taken notice of the use congruities and difficulties involved in them and appear to have developed their own theories with their own rational approach. If the Yogācāra felt that knowledge is the only real entity in the world and all else is non-existent he admits only two means of valid knowledge Pratyakṣa and Anumana and all knowledge obtained by the other means according to others is either included in the above two Pramāṇas or is considered false knowledge. No objects except those in the consciousness are disallowed. Even the relationships are restricted to two – Tādātmya and Tadutpatti. The Śāṅkarite on the other hand though he accepts that consciousness is the only reality in the world, pleads for the falsity of all objects much against practical life. His theory of oneness of the reality, Māyā or and Avidyā as the causes of the falsity of world appearance the falsity of falsity itself, the threefold reality of the world, the issue as to whom the Māyā or and Avidyā envelops, their beginningless existence, Jiva and Īśwara, they as Sākṣins, the admission Vṛtti as a cause of knowledge, its going out, the mind not being a sense organ, Ekajivavada, Anekajīvavāda and a host of such problems have complicated the theory to the point of brain fag. The Sāṃkhya and the Naiyāyika (Logician) appear to have made a purely rational approach to the subject admitting only those means of knowledge which are essentially required for valid knowledge. The Mīmāṃsaka required more means of valid knowledge which otherwise would not account for certain legitimate categories. The Jaina started and developed an entirely new theory of non-absolutism even in the case of knowledge. The others of the Vedāntins like the Viśiṣṭādvaitins and the Dvaitin leaned to the side of non-monism incorporated in the Logician's theory.

Mainly, there appear to be two theories of knowledge one advocating that all knowledge or pure knowledge exists and is covered by a veil of Ajñāna and the veil is removed on that part of the Ajñāna when the mind comes in contact with it. The Śaṅkarite and the Jaina are its adherents. The Sāṃkhya also appears to think on similar lines but requires that Cit should be reflected in the intellect (Buddhi) without which no sentence can be attributed to knowledge.

It is also another point to note whether there exists pure consciousness (Suddha Caitanya) as opposed to object consciousness (Viṣaya-Caitanya). It has also to be decided whether the pure Cit means the faculty of knowing or a bundle of all knowledge pieces permuted and combined so as to be identified when ordered for. If all knowledge were not present in any one locus is it that knowledge is produced every now and then with the help of sense organs impressions etc.? It is better to hold knowledge is produced and destroyed.

Another big question is whether it is only knowledge that cognises objects as the Śaṅkarite and the Buddhist hold or is it the locus of knowledge which cognises by acquiring knowledge. Is a permanent self-like entity needed to store knowledge, impressions etc. or is it possible for the Epistemologist to get on with momentary knowledge pieces? How could memory, recognition and ultimate salvation be achieved without a permanent conscious agent? What is knowledge? If one school thought that bliss is all pervading and pain is only false and could be removed, the other school thought that everything in the world is misery and it could be removed by right knowledge. On similar lines the second theory of knowledge is what is advocated by the Logician, the Mīmāmsaka etc. It holds that knowledge of the objects of the world have to be acquired by means of Pramāṇas and it is this valid knowledge that affords all the goals of life.

All these problems are a hard nut to crack, for any theorist and all the Epistemologists tried their best to know the truth not only of the universe but also of knowledge in their own way. To criticise these views adversely is neither easy nor constructive in nature but to establish a non-controversial catholic theory of knowledge appears to be a Herculean task. That is why probably on such matters our people turn to super-human agencies, Holy texts, prophets and others in bitter dejection.

What Category is Knowledge and How are We to Define It?

Before going into the details of some other questions, let us try to ascertain extent what 'Knowledge' is. Then we can think of its definition. The word Knowledge (Jñāna) is derived from the verbal root (Jñā) to know.[1] The word Jñāna can be derived in more than one way from the root Jñā by adding the Kṛt suffix Lyuṭ. This suffix Lyuṭ generally comes in three meanings – 1. instrument (Karaṇa) 2. Locus (Adhikaraṇa) and 3. the act (Bhāva) but it is enjoined in other meanings as well by the Sūtra of Pāṇṇi kṛtyalyuto bahulaṃ. Thus if we take into account the first meaning jñā + lyuṭ[2] (=Jñāna) jñāna may mean '*the instrument of knowing*' (Avabodhana karaṇa) through Karaṇavyutpatti. That is to say in this sense Jñāna means the instrument (Karaṇa) (*the one after the action of which the result* 'knowing' is produced). In such a case it would mean the sense-organ (through contact with the object) in the *case of perception and consideration* (Parāmarśa)[3] in the case of inference etc. But we are not presently concerned with the meaning of this word 'Jñāna' as it is very well-known and discussed. The second meaning of Lyuṭ as 'Locus.' Here by 'Jñāna' is meant *the locus of knowing* (a rare meaning). Thus it will be the self (Atman) in the Logician's view for, the locus of all knowledge is Ātman for him.[4] To the Śāṅkarite and the Buddhist, on the other hand, there is no 'locus' for actual cognition but the locus of the secondary Vṛttijñāna (mode of the mind) for the Śāṅkarite and the Sārupya (assumption of the form of the object by the mind) for the Buddhist and they are the instruments (Karaṇa) of knowing. But since these two are clearly noticeable and are themselves insentient it is not even the second meaning of Lyuṭ that we discuss here. The third meaning of Lyuṭ is bhāva. It means the *'act of knowing.'* It is with this meaning of the word 'Jñāna' we are presently concerned. By 'act' here is meant the (basic meaning of the) verbal root Jña (to know). Thus our effort now is to understand what is meant by the *act knowing* or cognising (Jñādhātvartha). Of course, in many places even on the oriental view Artha Prakāśa (the illumination of the object) Arthaparicchitti (determining the object) etc. have been propounded as the meaning of Jñāna. But the words 'illumination' etc. are either synonymous with knowing or approximations of the root-meaning which cannot help us to clearly define 'knowledge.' If we make a division of knowing epistemologically there are also some related words relating to Jñāna-like Jñātā, the Jñeya (which two of course cannot be the general meanings of the suffix Lyuṭ). Thus if we can weed out from our definition of Jñāna, all the above meanings except the root-meaning we may be in a position to define Jñāna, the act of knowing, Prabhākara in his Triputi-pratyakṣatāvāda speaks of Jñāna, Jñeya and Jñātā. We know Jñeya (the known) is the object of knowledge.[5] The word Jñāta means the agent of the act of knowing. Who is this Jñātā. According to the Logician the 'self' is the agent (substratum of the act of knowing). According to the idealist Buddhist it is the Jñāna itself that knows as it only is sentient.[6] If thus the cognition (Jñāna) itself be the cogniser (Jñāta) and also the act of knowing, then there is the contingency of the noun *knower and the verb meaning knowing* becoming one. Same appears to be the case with the Śāṅkarite as there is nothing else but knowledge (consciousness) for him in this world. Here we should question the two above said theorists whether knowledge is a category (like a noun word which is said to know) or an (act), which means knowing. But surprisingly for both there is nothing but knowledge in the world and hence they both cannot use ordinary sentences like 'he knows' or 'he knows this object' (as object also is knowledge for the Buddhist) (and the objects does not really exist for the Śāṅkarite). They cannot even say 'act of knowing knows' or the act of knowing is also a knowledge.

Hence the Logician accepts the view that knowledge is not an activity (Karma) but a property (Guṇa) of the individual soul (Jīvātman). This property called knowledge which inheres in the soul. That is to say as long as the knowledge lasts it will be in the self only and nowhere else and hence the relation of inherence between the two, the self and the knowledge. Thus his 'knower' is the self and knowledge (property called knowledge) is in him and that is why the self is called the knower (Cetana). Though the Logician like all other Epistemologists does not clearly say what 'knowing' or 'knowledge,' by itself is, he says 'knowledge' is produced in the self when the causes like sense-contact with the object etc. are all present just as hot touch is produced with the contact of fire. He says the object is the known 'Viṣaya' because knowledge like 'desire' (Icchā), effort (Kṛti) etc. cannot help having an object for it.[7] The Sanskrit grammarian holds that Jñāna is an activity (Kriyā) and an effort is necessary to undertake the activity. But what it is he may not be able to say.[8] But the Logician avoids all this nuisance and says that knowledge is a property of the soul generated by the presence of necessary causes.

We don't find strict definition of knowledge in many treaties on Buddhism, as probably, they have in mind knowledge as conceived in common parlance of the word seeing Mokṣākaraguptā considers knowledge (Jñāna) for the Sa Kāravādin as that which happens to be the common usage of external object (Bāhyārthā vyavahāra) of the people at large.

The Śāṅkarite thinks that knowledge, consciousness or Brahman is indefinable. It is cognised with the help of negative statements like 'knowledge' (Brahman) is not this, not that etc.[9] I think it is better to accept this view as what knowledge actually is, nobody is destined to know. He posits that it is the only category existing in the world and nothing else. All other categories with all their objects are simple hallucinations.

According to Bhaṭṭa Knowledge we have seen, is a *Super-sensuous or transcendental object* which is cognised with the help of an inference where known-ness is the reason (Liṅga). It is doubtful here whether knownness which should be the reason in the concerned inference presupposes knowledge itself in which case the question will have to be begged.[10]

For the Advaita Vedāntin knowledge is of two types. One is knowledge or cognition in the real sense of the word which is not different from Brahman and is eternal and indeterminate. The other type of knowledge called Vṛttijñāna is also called knowledge in a secondary sense inasmuch as it is of the form of the mental modification (Vṛtti) and is the determinant of cognition (Jñānāvacchedaka). Unless the modification of the internal organ into the form of the object is produced the ignorance relating to that object is not removed. Now the point here is that the Vedāntin does not try to distinguish between the knower (Jñātā) and the knowledge (Jñāna) as in that case the knower without knowledge would be an insentient object like a piece of wood which is absurd as he holds. Hence in stead of assuming two knowledge and its locus–he accepts knowledge alone as the ultimate reality. This of course, is concealed or veiled by ignorance (Ajñana) and hence is not manifest. Thus to Śāṅkara knowledge in the real sense (Jñāna) is eternal (Nitya) and as such cannot be attained by effort (is not produced) consciousness Jñāna is manifested only when the last mental modification of the form of Brahman is formed with the attainment of consciousness implied (Upalakṣata) (Brahmākārā vṛttiḥ). All efforts made in this direction is only to ward off ignorance or Avidyā. Thus to Śāṅkara Jñāna is not a product (Kārya) but an eternal substance, whereas Vṛttijñāna is of the form of a transformation (Pariṇāma) of the Antaḥkaraṇa into the form of the object. This also is called Jñāna only in a secondary sense as it determines Jñāna. Here also it may be noticed that the insentient Vṛttijñāna requires the help of the reflection of consciousness in it for its manifestation as in the Śāṃkhya view.

Thus to Śāṅkara Brahman, Caitanya or knowledge is the only reality only explainable as 'not this' 'not this' (Neti Neti) and it has no other form. It has neither content nor any property. In the world of experience however, knowledge of individual objects is gained as the veil of ignorance is removed (Āvaraṇābhibhāva) or as the necessary painting of the object (Arthoparāga) is effected by the internal organs mode. That is how occasional knowledge is explained away by him.

Rāmānuja also divides Jñāna into two kinds. One is called the Dharmijñāna and the other the Dharmabhūtajñāna. It is only the latter that is of the form of a (Dharma or) property of the soul and is capable of contraction and expansion (Samkoca and Vikāsa) and as such it is stated to be produced and destroyed. This is self-effulgent and hence comes under the non-insentient category (Ajaḍa). The Dharmijñāna also is self-effulgent but the difference between this and the Dharmabhūtajñāna is that while the former like a lamp reveals itself the latter reveals itself and another also like its light (Prabhā). Thus in Rāmānuja's view it is a substance as well as a property (Dravyātmakaguṇa), a peculiar category.

Even the Sāṃkhya (and the Śāṅkarite)[11] avoids a strict definition of knowledge and states that the inert Buddhi (intellect) appears to become sentient by the reflection of the sentient self in it. But he says that the self is the knower (Cetana). What then is knowledge?[12] The Buddhist also doesn't define pure knowledge but says it is the only 'existent.' The Śāṅkarite, though he accepts insentient Vṛtti (mental mode which assumes the form of the object) argues that consciousness (Cit) is reflected in the Vṛtti. But he too does not definitely say how this reflection becomes sentient. But he makes a distinction (of course in the Vyāvahārike plane) between Drṣya, the object and Dṛk, the knower. He also rigidly contends that the knower cannot be known. The moment he becomes known he becomes an insentient object. That is his objection. Thus he finally concludes that consciousness alone is the one entity in the world and it cannot be defined (Avāṇgmānasagocara). This appears of course, to be somewhat satisfactory as there is no other precise way of defining knowledge. The Upaniṣhad also holds the same view.[13] That is why probably the Śāṅkarite views that Jñāna is the Jñāta in the final view and the only existent.

The Viśiṣṭādvaitin defines knowledge (Buddhi) as 'mani festation which has an object' or manifestation which has an agent (Kartā). But these definitions stress only on the point that cognition is an activity referring to an object but do not exclude desire etc. which also fall under same class. Even the permanent emotions like Rati, Hāsa are only forms of knowledge for him. But we find that it is only after a knowledge of 'This is pot' we experience a knowledge of pleasure, pain etc. as 'This pot' gives me happiness, experience etc.

Though in this way a strict definition of knowledge is avoided by almost all philosophers it appears that the attempt made to define knowledge indirectly is the only way. 'Knowledge' is the uncommon causes (Asādhāraṇa Kāraṇa) of desire (icchā) or detestation (Dveṣa) or disinterestedness (Upekṣā). Indeed desire (for an object) is produced with help of and soon after the production of Jñāna (knowledge) a property as its noninherent cause. We know that desire for an object inheres in the self, according to the Logician. So the self is the Samavāyikāraṇa (inherent cause) of 'desire,' knowledge (of the object) is its uncommon cause. It seems to me it is the only way in which knowledge can be defined. It has been defined in a similar way in some logical treatises. Knowledge is the uncommon cause of all usage of words (Sarvavyahārāsādhāraṇa-kāraṇam). We cannot give a better definition for knowledge than this. Here it may be noted that in the case of knowledge, the self is the inherent cause, the self-mind contact is the non-inherent cause and mind etc. are the Nimitta Kāraṇas.

As we have seen knowledge has been defined in a similar way as the uncommon cause of all usage of words (Vyāvahāra). The word uncommon cause (Asādhāraṇa Kāraṇa) is used in the definition to avoid its over application on time (Kāla etc.) which are also causes but they are only common causes (not uncommon). If it be urged that even after the production of knowledge person may not make use of words 'This is a pot etc.' To avoid contingency the definition is modified as 'knowledge is one that has the genus (Jāti) which they determine not being the producer of the usage of words.[14] This enables us to bring indeterminate knowledge also under the scope of knowledge.

This definition mutatis mutandis is accepted by many other theorists also.

Knowledge, The Knower and The Known (The Śaṅkarite Buddhist Views)

We know knowledge always comprises the knowledge part, the knower part and the known part. The idealist Buddhist speaks only of knowledge as the real existent and contends that the knower, the known etc. are fictitious abstractions. The Śaṅkarite also holds a similar view with some deviations. The view of these theorists appears to be that, when knowledge itself is capable of knowing why should a knower be accepted and when beginningless impressions or nescience (Ajñāna) is accepted why should the (known) object be accepted. Further both the Śaṅkarite and the Buddhist (idealist) are of the view that knowledge is the only existent which appears as several object-forms due to the above mentioned impressions etc. So Śaṅkara holds (pure) knowledge is Brahman itself and is eternal, while for the Buddhist it is the momentary knowledge that is the real existent and all else is false.

Now a question arises here what pure knowledge is and whether it could be defined at all and why it should be called knowledge at all where there is no object attached to it and where the eternity of knowledge is not perceived in experience. Further who is the one that attains salvation finally in the Buddhist view? Is it the momentary knowledge that attains it in which case salvation also is momentary. Further on this view impressions cannot be momentary as they are to produce knowledge pieces one by one.

With some of such difficulties knowledge may not be maintained as the only real existent.

It appears more feasible to hold that knowledge is the act of knowing and the locus of knowledge is the knower and object known is the object of knowing. In practical life we call a pot a non-knower as it has no knowledge of any kind. We call men (with a self, sense-organs etc.) as knowers and it is a fact also since they react to knowledge situations by desiring the object or avoiding it. It should not be urged, however, that the knower would be insentient if knowledge is removed from him for, knowledge impressions etc. we accept, are inherent in him just as a pot has an inherent colour though of course, knowledge it may be obstructed in the case of deep sleep etc. Without a known object also there can be no knowledge (even in a dream state where impression are aroused) as there is no evidence for such a stand. So we should posit that the knower (like the self) knows with its activity of knowledge and the object is the known. During salvation it should be the knower who finally knows the falsity of his earthly miseries etc. and attains salvation. Without a permanent entity like the self the Buddhist cannot speak of salvation (of beings). If knowledge were to get salvation it should be experienced in life. Even if impressions are destroyed who is to gain by that destruction? These are questions which have to be satisfactorily answered. Further what we want is *our misery* to go and the object determining 'our' here has to be established by the idealist who has no permanent entity. Even if there is an occasional break in the momentary knowledge it is not of interest for us. It may be remembered that a permanent entity like a soul is necessary precedent for the acceptance of eternal bliss or avoidance of misery.

According to the Buddhist knowledge is produced from knowledge. Knowledge (cognition) begins at birth and continues to be produced even at death. Knowledge is produced with the help of impressions of old and desires or Ignorance (Avidya) in the Buddhist view. The previous knowledge produces another knowledge and gets destroyed. Thus knowledge, according to the Buddhist is beginningless. It is not produced with the help of the internal organ (mind) as the orthodox thinkers hold. Thus it is the object that is responsible for the knowledge. In fact we say the object is known. (The object may be an internal one or an external one according to the domination of the Buddhist). He does not speak about the different types of causes producing knowledge.

Here a question arises as to how one knowledge produces another knowledge without some relation. In perception it is only the Svalakṣaṇa that is cognised. This Svalakṣaṇa is unique in itself and is characteristic of the particular object (say cow) seen. Then again in a different place and time suppose a cow is perceived and again another Svalakṣaṇa is perceived – at the time of the second perception. The Buddhist holds that the Svalakṣaṇa is later made determinate (Savikalpaka) by the association of name etc. mentally. But how is this possible for him? For, the latter Svalakṣaṇa is different from the previous Svalakṣaṇa as each cow has its own characteristic features and there is nothing common between the first and the second Svalákṣaṇa because the Buddhist does not accept genus (Jāti) as a category at all. As the Buddhist holds the percipient perceives the cow and recollects the cow of the same genus seen before. But there is no genus for him nor is it cognised earlier. Then how could even another cow be perceived (as cow)? If he holds that it is due to similarity with the previous cow even a pot is similar to a cow in consideration of some similarity like something existent etc. If, on the other hand, exclusion (Apoha) is coronated in the place of Jati in his view, even then as Apoha may be of the type of exclusion of the non-cow, so also Apoha may be of the type of exclusion of the non-that (cow) – object (this has reference to the previous cow) in which case the Apoha, excludes even cows other than the one already perceived earlier. Thus Apoha will not be able to decide a second perception of the object (cow) as cow. This contingency cannot be avoided. Hence it is better to hold that genus (Jati) is cognised at the time of perception and this genus existing in the cow later seen at a different place or time also produces a knowledge of 'cow.' We know children see a cow in one place and time for the first time (as named by their elders) and in another place where they see an object of the same genus conceived earlier they comprehend it as a cow. If genus is not accepted even inference will be at stake.

The Buddhist, we have seen, holds that one knowledge produces another knowledge. This series (continuation) of cognition goes on even at death and the last of the series is responsible for the cognition in the next birth of an individual. Painting (Raga) of the cognition is responsible for the knowledge after re-birth. Now let us see whether one knowledge can produce another knowledge without some other accessory cause. Every knowledge has its object when produced. How could it produce a knowledge with a different object (by itself)? A cognition of pot cannot be said to produce a knowledge of mat though knowledge pieces may come one after the other as (1) the former knowledge gets destroyed soon after it is produced and (2) during the time of cognition it is endowed with the form of the former object and (3) later destroyed. Hence knowledge (even in continuation). Further who is to decide whether the two knowledges are to be in the same series or a different series. There is no agency for the Buddhist except the unseen Vāsana.

Then again where is knowledge produced according to the Buddhist? He holds that pot etc. are insentient (Jada) in which case he should hold that knowledge is not present in a pot. Then he should accept certain varieties of objects (not cognitions) which have knowledge. Such objects should be distinguished from the others by means of a mind or soul which is not possible otherwise. Further due to desire knowledge is produced according to him. What is the agency that desires a particular object and the agency that directs the knowledge towards the knowledge of the object.

Here a doubt arises as to how the means, the capability of knowledge to secure the object for us as it exists (Sarūpasat) can produce a valid knowledge (Samyagjñāna) as the Tarka-Bhasa of the Buddhist may hold; for, even in the Vikalpa stage it is only a definite knowledge (Avadhāraṇa) of the means that is produced and practically it may not get the right object for us as even a definite knowledge may be valid or invalid. In case it is invalid it cannot be correct knowledge (Samyagjñāna). Thus the means of valid knowledge should be stated to be a definite knowledge capable of securing the right object forms. Not having a definite knowledge capable of securing the right object though it is capable of prompting one to activity it should be only invalid and thus it cannot be a Pramāṇa. But the Buddhist holds that only prompting to action (Pravṛtti) is the result of the means of knowledge (probably not Prama) and that is secured by a knowledge of the means (i.e. knowledge which presents to us the object as it comprehends (Yathāvabhāsam) and thus there is no bar to inducement to action. But if the actual activity is not achieved it is only due to some hindrance. Thus not disagreeing with the object (Avisamvaditvam) means for him only securing the object as it is presented by the knowledge. It cannot be objected, however, that the yellow conch is not secured wrong as long as yellow is not different from conch.

In the view of the Vaibhasika and the Sautrantika though they accept the external existence of objects, their theory of knowledge holds that the external object (secured by Pratyaksa or inference as the case may be) gives its form to the knowledge. Now a question arises here as to when the form is assumed by the knowledge – if it is before the knowledge is produced, how could knowledge not produced at all get its form? If it is after the formation of knowledge how could knowledge in its state of destruction take the form of the object (that is why probably the Vaibhasika accepts a five minute existence of objects). The knowledge on the other alternative, cannot assume the form of the knowledge as the knowledge process if progressing and not completed. Hence in the view knowledge cannot assume the form of the object. Thus the Buddhist has to accept a mind or an equivalent object for knowledge to assume the form of the object.

The same is a clearer case with the Yogācāra idealist also who does not accept any external object at all. Thus in his case it is due to impressions of old that the colours blue etc. are cognised. This is a clear violation of an experience not accepting the object seen and accepting a Vāsana not seen for the perception of a particular object. Object perception in the waking state could be explained with the help of the existing external objects. But dream-state objects need not be compared to these waking state objects as the conditions in the two cases are different.

Again the Buddhist holds the view that knowledge (Citta) and the different particular states of Citta are self-revealed (or more accurately revealed by nothing else but by knowledge itself) is not sound, for, first by taking the case of cognition or knowledge as self-revealed how could the Buddhist argue that the knowledge of blue (the Pramāṇaphala in knowledge) is cognised by nothing else but the knowledge itself. It cannot be established by inference, that knowledge of a knowledge of blue (I know blue) is produced by the knowledge of blue (This is blue) as no relation can be established between the two. Even accepting the possibility, it must be accepted that the knowledge of the knowledge of blue is again cognised by a knowledge of the knowledge of the knowledge of blue and so on ad infinitum and thus no other knowledge is possible later. Thus this stand of the Buddhist cannot be accepted.

The Yogācāra Buddhist who argues that the same knowledge which was the means becomes the end-knowledge also wherein it appears to be external in the form of an object, cannot establish validity for perception as it only appears as an external object (which is not to be treated as valid knowledge).

Again identity (Tādātmya) and causation (Tadutpatti) alone cannot cover all the marks in inferential knowledge. For in an inference like 'The mango must be sweet as it has a yellow colour,' it cannot be held that taste is produced from yellow colour. If knowledge were not an object of another knowledge (judgment) how could we account for statements like 'This my knowledge is correct' 'this is incorrect.' 'This is his knowledge not my knowledge' and so on as correctness of knowledge etc. are revealed by verification with object activity in another knowledge.

If the Śaṅkarite makes an inference and establishes the self-luminosity of knowledge his knowledge would be having some characteristics features which theory goes against his doctrine that it is indeterminate. It also makes a piece of knowledge (This is a pot etc.) revealed or known (self-luminous). Thus the objectivity (Viṣayatā) of knowledge cannot be ruled out by him.

Further as already stated 'this is a pot' is a knowledge (of the object); here though the object pot is known in the knowledge the knowledge only exists (Svarūpasat) but it is not known (Jñātā). Hence knowledge itself is not revealed in a knowledge but the object alone (along, of course, with its relation etc.) but not the knowledge, sense organ or ego or light etc. Even if the knowledge of knowledge is not known (as stated above) there is no impediment for inducement to activity (Pravṛtti). But when it is sought to be known for establishing its correctness etc. it becomes an object and thus the theory of apperception gains ground.

Again the Śaṅkarite thinks that Vṛtti is only for the sake of removal of ignorance (Avidyā). What is this? When the veil on the object is removed the object (as known) is its effect. What is the use of Phala[15] in that case? If it is for the sake of knowing knowledge (by the Sākṣi) it is too prolix and not necessary for practical purposes.

Further a clear line of demarcation is not possible to be stated between pragmatic knowledge and transcendental knowledge. If knowledge is not an object it cannot be known even immediately.

Again the Advaitin's statement that pure knowledge does not depend upon Phala for its revelation may be doubted as the question 'to whom is it revealed' persists. But if the knower and the known are stated to be absent in the case of this transcendental knowledge there should be neither the knower nor the revealed for, the Sākṣin is himself the consciousness whose adjunct is the internal organ. If the adjunct is said not to have contact with the object without Vrtti what relation does the Advaitin accept between pure consciousness and the adjunct (Upādhi). Adhyasa is beginningless and cannot be an adventitious cause with which it is not in direct contact to assume that colour.

Another difficulty is what is the knowledge that has turned blue in the Buddhist's view? Is it the knowledge of the immediately preceding moment of some other previous object known (object like yellow) in which case as it is destroyed in the very next minute it cannot be a cause. If it were to produce a Santana how can a knowledge of yellow become a Santana with blue (with a different content) in the next minute. If, on the other hand, it is not the same series with yellow, what is the knowledge (without any contact in it) that takes the blue form. In this case a knowledge without content will have to be accepted and its production too from a source without an object. This difficulty arises in his view in all new pieces of knowledge arising in an individual.

If there were no object and activity and the knowledge were blue how is it that the object is called blue? How is the blue colour of the object when changed into red (after heating), when alone it is that the percepients knowledge also becomes red and not independent of the red colour of the object, gained?

Again to hold that knowledge becomes blue or assumes the form of blue (or hot) is against experience. Further it is overburdening the knowledge with properties which it has not got. It cannot be stated that such a stand is unintentable as, otherwise, the experience of blue etc. cannot be explained for, it is enough if it is maintained that the eye with the help of the mind contacts blue etc.

Again what is the contact of the knowledge before assuming the blue colour? The previous knowledge would have been destroyed by the time the blue is to give its form to the knowledge. At this stage what are the components of the knowledge present? The idealist Buddhist owes a reply to this question which is difficult to answer as he has neither a knower, nor any other accessory like the mind. Even the impression of blue etc. should be aroused with the help of some cause like the object present but it is not accepted by the idealist. If it is the impression of the blue around that is the cause, a reason for its arousal is needed.

As already pointed out either the sense perception, (Indriyajñana) or the mental perception (Mānasajñana) need not be cognised (Svasamvedya) for producing perceptional knowledge as it is enough that they are (produced) existent. No purpose is served by knowing the knowledge. What is actually desired to be refuted by the Logician etc. on the Buddhist stand is that knowledge is not cognised by itself (Svaprakāśa) and also, as I think, that knowledge should be known for purposeful activity desired.

The Śāṅkarite's conclusion 'that it is knowledge alone that persists in the case of all knowledges like knowledge of pot, mat etc. 'Knowledge alone is the real entity (as it persists) may not be tenable as in the case of desire also there is the desire of pot, mat etc. and desire etc. also should be real. Further in knowledge pieces like 'I don't know a pot,' 'I don't know a mat etc.' since the absence of knowledge is present (of course as a knowledge itself) 'absence of knowledge also should be real as it persists.' Again in the statement 'Knowledge of pot, mat' etc. it must be noted that they are part and parcel of knowledge itself. There is no knowledge (of pot) without a pot in it and so on. If there is no content 'pot' in the knowledge it cannot be called 'knowledge of pot.' Thus as long as there is knowledge there is an object (though it may change in each case). Hence in a determinate knowledge of object 'knowledge of object' etc. some object also is persistent and hence objects as objects (if not as pot, mat etc.) should be real as they persist as long as the knowledge lasts. To accept that there is a species of knowledge without an object, is beyond one's practical experience. If at all it is there it should be of the form of the 'Faculty of knowing' which cannot be designated knowledge as the object of knowing is not there. Again what is this faculty of knowing? Is it of the form of a Vṛtti and the reflection of it in the pure consciousness (Cit) in which case the object also has to be taken into consideration. The object is a condition precedent for Vṛtti. Even if it be the knowledge the presence of the object is of necessity to be accepted. That is why probably the Śāṅkarite thinks that Brahman or consciousness on pure knowledge is indefinable.

For the Śāṅkarite to argue that the external adjuncts (Upadhis) are responsible for empirical knowledge, we should question here 'What is the origin of the Upadhis.' They should only be objects which are practically seen and used by us in daily life. If the Upadhis are stated by him to be caused by hallucination, whose is the hallucination when he vows that knowledge or Cit alone is the one and only one eternal object. If it is held that hallucination is beginningless it may not be annulled too. But the Holy text admits its destruction.

The view of the Śāṅkarite that pure knowledge has always been there and it is eternal and indeterminate appears to be against common experience. There is prolixity in the view that all knowledge pieces like 'this is a pot, this is a mat etc.' are all present jumbled up in the pure knowledge is too prolix to be admitted. Instead we could admit that particular knowledges are produced with the help of their own causes. An indeterminate knowledge serves no empirical purpose and it is to be proved that determinate knowledge emerges from such a knowledge. To argue that knowledge is eternal strikes a strange note when we find all knowledge as produced and limited in time. If the Śāṅkarites opinion be that it is the faculty of knowing (capability to know things when presented) is what is meant by pure knowledge there is not much objection but it cannot be called knowledge as it has no object of its own (without any attributes at all). Further objection to his theory of knowledge is that knowledge cannot be all pervading as it is found to subsist in only those beings which have the sources of the faculty of knowing – sense organs, power of recollection, generalisation etc. we know that the pot or the mat has no knowledge, yet forms the Śāṅkarites stand point out it is pot-delimited knowledge (Ghaṭāvacchima caitanya). It is not quite clear what is achieved by calling it pot-consciousness instead of pot as far as a knowledge of it is concerned (rather how did that person arrive at a knowledge of the non-existent Upādhi). If it is all due to impressions due to beginningless hallucination how could an impression be formed without an object. If the object is said to be due to hallucination the definition of hallucination is not possible,[16] because the Tat (that) and Atat (not that) are not known before hallucination. The non-existent objects also cannot precede hallucination. If both hallucination and objects are both beginningless, then both objects are real existents. This appears to be the difficulty in the Śāṅkarites theory of knowledge and objects. Thus hallucination and (the existence of) objects appear to be caught in the trap of mutual dependence (Anyonyāśraya) if both of them are beginningless.

The Buddhist also believes that all Cittas (knowledges which cognise only objects) and Caittas (pleasure, pain and indifference which cognise the different states of the mind) are self-revealed and do not require any other knowledge to reveal them just as a lamp reveals itself (by its light) from its own causes. Nor can knowledge be known by another knowledge as it does not help the other or even by a subsequent knowledge as the original knowledge is momentary and is destroyed by that time.

He further argues that our statements like 'the pot is known' (Jñāto ghaṭaḥ) will not be possible if knowledge be not self-revealed because a knowledge of the attribute (Viśesana) is necessary for a knowledge of the substantive (Viśesya).[17] Here in Jñāta (known) the attribute is knowledge and the substantive is the object and hence he argues that without knowledge (the attribute and the object) the substantive cannot be known. This is his argument.

But there is a difficulty here. The knowledge produced in a case is, say, 'This is a pot,' the pot is revealed in the knowledge. In this case there is no need to know the knowledge also (to undertake Vyavahāra or to fetch water etc.) It is simply enough that the knowledge is there (Sat) even not being known. But the case of a knowledge like 'The pot is known or I know the pot' are different where a later knowledge cognises the knowledge as present in the person and as related to the object. The meaning of the word 'known' here is that the pot is the object revealed in the Jñana (which latter need not be known). Thus the pot is known (Jnato ghatah) is a case of apperception where the knowledge (along with the object) is also known. But strictly speaking as I construc 'This is a pot' is the actual form of the original knowledge produced and 'I know that this is a pot' is the form of the apperceptional knowledge (where the necessary attributes and substantives of knowledge can be fully illustrated).

Further the Buddhist resorts to Vyavasthapaka vyavasthāpya bhava instead of Grāhya-grāhakabhava between knowledge and its cognition. Due to the peculiar nature of objects one of them is the peculiar cause which determines (Vyavasthāpaka) the nature (Svabhāva) of the particular entity and the particular nature of the entity is its determined (Vyavasthāpya). Elsewhere it is stated that the Vyavasthāpaka is the blue colour etc. (assured by the mind) and knowledge of blue etc. is then determined. But the Buddhist owes an argument as to how from the assumption of the blue colour (Vyavasthāpaka) by the knowledge the knowledge of blue (the Vyavasthāpya) is produced, for in such cases the Vyavasthāpya should be 'My mind is blue or I am blue' etc.

Thus the Buddhist holds that by its own nature and its own causes (unspecified probably) knowledge like a lamp reveals itself. This is his theory.

But his rival says 'on this analogy how can pleasure, pain etc. are also considered self-revealed when they do not reveal an object as knowledge does. To this the Buddhist replies that pleasure, pain etc. are experienced along with the form (Rūpa) etc. experienced. How they are experienced is not by the experience of form itself as they are innate in the body and form (of an object) is outside. If it be some mental perception the order of knowledge pieces is disturbed. If they are to said to be experienced soon after the Rūpa etc. is experienced it cannot hold good as every object is momentary.

Here it may be observed that the defect is that the experience of the Rūpa etc. of the object and experience of pleasure etc. cannot be simultaneous as the former is the cause of the latter. The cause is expected to be earlier in time. To say that the two experiences go hand in hand is a hallucination as the experiences spread over a length of time and this cause and effect relationship of each individual experience is not taken cognizance of. If knowledge cannot be revealed if not alongwith the object as the idealist argues, then the Nyāya retorts that the object is revealed when the causes of its knowledge are all present – light etc., just so when the causes of knowing a knowledge (sense object contact etc.) are present (desire to know the knowledge, a doubt about the knowledge produced etc.) knowledge is known – not till then. Thus in the knowledge of an object only the object is known 'This is a pot etc.' but not 'This is knowledge' also or 'I have a knowledge' etc. which are superfluous and beyond our experience.

Further the knowledge of the object is a condition precedent for a knowledge of its knowledge. Hence the object and knowledge cannot be simultaneously apprehended.

The word Sahopalambha (simultaneous presence of the object and the knowledge) used by the idealist Buddhist itself implies that the object is different from knowledge. If one were identified with the other where is the scope for simultaneity of both?

When there is the desire for an object say pot, knowledge is produced when only the object is present and the knowledge 'this is a pot' is produced for carrying out some activity. There is no question of 'I' or 'I know' there as it is not desired at all. The object of knowledge alone is known and not all its other causes too (though they may be present).

Again the difference between several knowledges of different persons and a knowledge of multiple objects cannot be explained if objects do not exist.

I am convinced that most of the confusion about the object and a knowledge of it and the latter's self-effulgence is due to the fact that a well calculated definition of knowledge is not given either by the Buddhist or the Vedantin. It is not clear whether they hold that by 'Knowledge' is meant 'the knowing of an object' or it is 'simple knowing without an object.' Let us postpone the meaning of knowing for a later discussion. If it (knowledge) is the knowing of an object (a Saviṣaya) knowing can be effected if only the 'object' is present as a cause and in that case knowledgehood may be accepted to be present in knowledge and objecthood in the object because knowledge is knowing of a general (Sāmanya) object and the knowing of the particular object (Viśesa like pot, mat etc.) is an individual knowledge (Jñana viśesa). We do not call the knowing of any object (unspecified) also as knowledge as it is not found in general experience. If, on the other hand by knowledge is meant knowing without an object (or with the object included in it) it makes no menaing. Without an object there can be no knowledge for anybody. Either a mental object or a physical object must be present). We know something or everything or not at all. So also we don't know a thing etc but there is no simple knowing. Now it may be argued by the Vijñanavādin that the object is identical with the knowledge. He is to be questioned 'Is the object the whole knowledge or a part of the Knowledge?' If it is the whole knowledge the knowledge is of the type 'pot.' It cannot be of the type 'this thing is a pot' (which is also a knowledge) where one general object (this) is known as a particular object (pot) and a relation of these is also to be known in which case the object cannot be held to be the whole knowledge. In the case (if the object is a part of the knowledge concerned) the other parts of it should be specified (like the particular person i.e. impression of the person etc. to the Buddhist) and some sort of Vṛtti too in the case of the Vedantin), in which case relations between the impression or Vṛtti and the object and the relation between them (Impression or Vṛtti) and knowledge which again is a stumbling block for the theorists concerned. Even the theory of the Advaitin that Vṛtti is reflected in the Sentient Consciousness does not satisfy one (though it may be more acceptable) as we don't say who the agent of the reflection process is. The Vṛtti or impression is inert and it cannot take the lead in the activity nor can pure consciousness (or pure knowledge in the case of the Buddhist) can reflect it as in the view of the Advaitin the pure consciousness has no activity at all and the pure knowledge of the Buddhist too admits of no relation with any object at all as it is identical with the object.

From the foregoing account it is difficult to speak of self-effulgence of knowledge too. For, the knowledge to be revealed should be present before its revelation as you say 'Knowledge is revealed.' The knowledge too is not complete without the object. If the object and the knowledge are revealed at the same moment, though the object may be known with the help of knowledge, the knowledge cannot reveal itself till the knowledge, process is completed and alas! the very next minute the knowledge is destroyed for the Buddhist. Hence knowledge cannot be held to be self-revealed by these theorists. We know the object and we also know later that we know that the object is known. This is the experience. But it is not 'I know the object' 'and the knowledge.' None says 'I know the particular knowledge' but not 'I know knowledge.' One says 'I don't know when one does not know the particular object but does not say I don't know knowledge.' The self-effulgence of knowledge has been accepted (says the Advaitin) by the Logician his (the Logicians apperception must precede a knowledge of the original knowledge). But this is not true as the original knowledge as existent (Svarūpasat) is enough to be known in the next moment. It is not necessary that the prior knowledge should be known (Jñata). That is why the former existent (Vyāvasaya) is known in the latter as an object.

The objection of the Śaṅkarite against the Logician that the Vyāvasaya (original knowledge) is destroyed in the third minute and hence its Anuvyāvasaya is not possible may be ruled out on the ground that apperception may not be an invariable sequal of Vyāvasaya. If it is desired to be known it is membered for the purpose. This is my own opinion of course.

Further if knowledge be self-luminous, then 'Is this knowledge of self-luminosity itself self-luminous?' and the latter knowledge again self-luminous and so on and so forth, where is the knower to stop at last? Otherwise self-luminosity of knowledge be the only knowledge that accrues to one and not any other knowledge because a knowledge of self-luminosity of the knowledges goes on repeating itself.

The Yogacara Buddhist is of the view that knowledge is the only real existent in the world. He does not define what knowledge (Jñāna or Vijñāna) is or how it is generated in its specific forms. He doesn't also make a strict distinction between the knower and the knowledge though he speaks of the known (object etc.) sometimes. Whereas most of the orthodox thinkers of India are of the opinion that there are three entities – the knower, the known and knowledge, the Buddhist reserves the act of knowing to knowledge itself. The knowledge or cognition (assuming the form of the object) cognises itself (and its object) just as a lamp illumines itself. Here we have to note that in popular parlance we say 'I know the pot' (where all the three the cogniser, the cognition and the object are referred to) or sometimes, we say 'I have a knowledge of pot' wherein also all the three are expressed. But we never say 'my cognition cognises the cognition (of the object).' Indeed the existence of objects in the world is attributed either to usage of words or to our understanding.[18] Thus this stand of the Buddhist goes against the dictum.

Further any cognition to be designated a determinate one requires a substantive (Viśesya), an attribute (Prakāra) and their relation (Samsarga) which without there can be no determinate congition at all. A mere sensation cannot be a cognition in the real sense. Even indeterminate knowledge has only two of the three components (the Viśeṣya-object and the Viśeṣana-object which are the objects of mere sensational knowledge) but not the relation between the two which latter only accounts for the nature of cognitionhood of cognition in the real sense. We know that in the Logician's view in the first perception of a pot the individual (pot) and the genus (pothood) are cognised (but not as the substantive and the attribute) but not their relation of inherence. That is why it may not be a knowledge in the real sense of the word. If you are prepared to designate that also as 'knowledge' (without the relation) it would not be helpful for undertaking any action in its regard. Nor does such a knowledge (knowledge as you call it) even resolve a doubt about the object concerned. Thus on this view the purpose of knowledge is defeated. That is why the Logician thinks that, if there is some semblance of a cognition in the indeterminate knowledge, then it is only, some fourth kind of objecthood that is present in the object perceived. In this way it is difficult to accept the view of the Buddhist that the sense perception (Indriya jñāna) that he speaks of is not in any way the (complete) perception (but only a sensation) as it does not lead to any Arthakriyā (or eligibility for cognising it) directly. This sensation should be no more than the contact of the inert sense organ with the object (whatever be its form). How could the insentient sense organ cognise even Svalakṣana without the help of a sentient entity. That is why probably the Buddhist holds that it is only of the form of assumption of the object-form by the sense organ. That is also why he is obliged to connect it in a continuous series with the next moment of cognition (calling the previous one, a Samanantarapratyaya) and the object of the same class of the next moment as an auxiliary or helping cause (Sahakārin). The second object is called a Sahakārin as it produces along with the sense perception concerned only one knowledge in the particular series. It is actually (in the second minute) in this latter part that the sensation part of cognition (where the knowledge assumes the form of the object) is completed with the help of the mental cognition with the object of the next minute as its auxiliary. This mental cognition also cognises only Svalakṣaṇa (like the previous one). This mental cognition (Mānasa jñana) is followed by a mental construction (like giving a class, name etc. to the form assumed by the cognition) with the help of recollection and then the full scale cognition of objects like blue or pot is engendered and here is the purpose of cognition really served as it decides the object by Apoha and induces a person to action. Further the Buddhism in the indeterminate stage speaks about Svalakṣaṇa, which is of the Apoha type cognised though it is consummated by Adhyavasāya in the Vikalpa stage. What is the Svalakṣaṇa which the Buddhism accepts? This is the known (Grāhya) because a knowledge of that form is produced. This knowledge limited by the pot is Svalakṣaṇa and is defined in space, time and form, and is devoid of generality (Sāmanya). The other type of knowledge produced in the same series (Ekasantāna) immediately after the activity of the Pramāna is definite knowledge of the pot (which is a product of the Vikalpa pratyaya). Here let us try to see what Svalaksana is. As the Buddhist holds it is which is define forefront (but without qualities etc.) and is the object of our engagement in activity (later) and which is different from all objects of its own class or of another class on what could such a thing be? Though of course the words are not used thus, it should only be a knowledge of pot and pothood only (as the Logician holds) as it is later expected to carry water etc. and is expected to be different from all other classes of objects and other objects of its own class. In order that the object should be different from all other classes or genuses, the genus of the pot (Jati) should be known. In order that it may be distinguished from other objects of its own class the individual pot (Ghata vyakta:[19]) also should be known. For a knowledge of being capable of carrying water etc.[20] also both the individual and the genus are expected to be known. This is not possible on the Buddhist stand as the genus, as genus, pothood and the individual pot as pot cannot be cognised at the time the indeterminate Svalaksana is cognised. Hence it is better to accept Savikalpaka (after the Logicians Nirvikalpa) where pothood and pot are cognised as the attribute and the substantive in the Savikalpaka stage. That is why the Logician holds that indeterminate knowledge serves as the instrumental cause (Karana) in producing determinate knowledge which prompts one to activity (later). Indeterminate knowledge is exclusively like the knowledge of babies, the dumb people and so on. Though it is so it is to be accepted as a cause of determinate knowledge. Though a baby has the sensation of the pot it has no use for it as it cannot use it for any sensible activity. It of course tries to catch the object of sensation and hence it may be designated knowledge, it may be argued. But that is not purposeful activity as the child does not have any purpose in its mind. Thus mere sense perception of the Buddhist cannot be accepted as perception in the real sense of the word as he does not speak of either the attribute or the substantive (pothood, pot etc.) as cognised in it.

Now coming to the form of the object assumed the Buddhist speaks of knowledge assuming the form of the object and not the mind as the orthodox schools hold which latter appears to be the better of the two alternatives and is more sound to be accepted. If knowledge were to assume the form of the object then a knowledge of each object of all the sense organs of the perceiver lays its claim to assume its own form. None of them is superior to the other and hence all the sense-perceptions of colour, taste etc. should be sensed simultaneously as there is no separate controlling agency for it. Further according to the Buddhist the sense perception first assumes the form of the object and this form has to be embedded in the next moment in the mental perception again in the same continuous series. Instead it is better to accept that the sense organ alongwith the mind (and not knowledge as he holds) comes into contact with the object and when all the accessories of knowledge are collected the object is known. The mind (cognition of the Buddhist) assuming the form of the object is to cognise itself and the object too according to the Buddhist. Since the sense organ is insentient it cannot be expected to cognise the object. So he has to find a different special cause to cognise the object. Even the mind of the orthodox schools cannot perceive the object as it itself is insentient and hence some of the orthodox schools have taken recourse to a reflection of the soul (which is ever sentient) in the mind (which is capable of doing so). But the Buddhist takes recourse to a next-minute-cognition to cognise and affirm or assume the form of the object. Here is a difficulty. If a cognition itself be capable of cognising (the form of) the object why not even the sense-perception which he speaks of cognise the form of the object and itself also in one sweep and Kalpana etc. come about in the next minute. Then it will be a single cognition (in a span of two minutes). Why should mental construction creep in between the two as a cause? His idea is that in the mental construction later, the percipient recollects the nature of the same object previously perceived and confirms that the particular object is a pot etc. and nothing else. Unless this Vikalpa is admitted the knowledge concerned is not purposeful in practical life. Further in the Buddhist stand, as already stated above, when an object is perceived by one why should not all the various sense percepts be cognised simultaneously? It cannot be held that the desire of the perceiver is not there for such perception. But to him the perceiver is the cognition itself which is busy with its own cognition but not with the desire (which also is another previous cognition which needs another minute to operate in). Then again what is the mental cognition that arises (in the next moment) in the same series after the sense-perception? Does this perception also have the form of the object or not. If it has one already it cannot cognise the form of another object. If there be no object in it cannot be a cognition. Who is sure of a mere cognition without any content in it? (or a form as he holds). I think this objection is also applicable to the orthodox schools but they explain it away by holding that pure consciousness does not have a content in it. But the Buddhist does not expressly state that such a knowledge exists though he holds that cognition assumes the form of the object. If that also be a pure cognition without content like the one of the orthodox schools it amounts to the acceptance of a soul like entity as the Logician himself holds. Further, to the latter, soul is the locus of all knowledge (the actual cogniser) but to the Advaitin the mind is the actual cogniser when the soul is reflected in the mental modification (Vṛtti). Thus it is better to concede the mind as the invervening agent for all the advantages it affords in the process of knowing. By accepting the agency 'mind' and soul even pleasure, pain etc. can be explained away as objects cognised by the mind (or the soul) directly. Indeed we say 'I experience pleasure, pain etc. which testifies to their being objects of knowledge. Even the statement 'I am happy' involves a cognition of happiness by the (ego or) soul. Further if everything in the world were cognition and none other, does it mean that the cognitions have a content (object) or not? On the former alternative there is the contingency of an object also existing side by side with cognition against the Yogacara Buddhist's stand and on the second alternative the cognition cannot be called as such as it has no form (of the object). To argue that objects are not necessary for cognition as impressions of old are enough for the purpose cannot hold good, as, in that case, between cognition and impression there arises the fault of mutual dependance (Anyonyāśraya). If both are considered beginning-less positive products their nature (Svabhava) cannot be changed and there will be no final salvation (cessation of mental states etc.) according to the Buddhist. To the Vedāntin, however, these impressions etc. (though beginning-less) which are due to hallucination are dispelled when the hallucination is removed along with the last mental state with the help of right knowledge (Vidya).

Again if knowledge or cognition be considered momentary the cognition will have already been lost by the time its causal efficiency is cognised and so the cognition does not reveal the validity of knowledge even when there is a doubt about it. If it be the same series (Santana) of the cognition that serves the purpose, it cannot be so as a series is not a real existent (Vastu, Sat) even according to the Buddhist. Further in a cognition of several trees (a long road etc.) one moment is not enough for, we take one minute each to cognise each individual and add the number up. If the cognition of the earlier tree is destroyed when the second tree is perceived how can the cognition of several trees be produced. If it is otherwise formed somehow by Vikalpa it should be false knowledge.

Again if exclusion of other objects (Anyāpoha) be considered by the Buddhist to take the place of genus (Jāti or Sāmanya) of the Logician, as stated elsewhere herein is a knowledge of the negative counterpart of the object (say a Gauḥ) which depends upon a knowledge of its counter positive (Gauḥ) is impossible, there is also another difficulty. To assess the negative counterpart of the object how many other objects are to be cognised and they too definitely positively (as they are objects themselves). Instead of cognising thousands of known objects for exclusion (leaving aside the case of unknown objects of which the present object may doubted to be one) it is better to hold that the object (Gauḥ etc.) itself is cognised as the particular object by virtue of its genus or class.

In refuting a sentient existent self (or Atman) the Buddhist holds that a sentient and permanent Atman should not produce a piece of knowledge which is momentary as the cause is different from the effect. Hence he suggests that ego (Ahaṃkāra) which is impermanent might be taken to be the cogniser, instead of Ātman. The ego too, he argues is not permanent as it does not function in deep sleep etc. but the argument may not stand as the absence of any one of the many causes of knowledge can bar permanent knowledge and produce momentary knowledge and produce momentary knowledge – causes such as the proximity of the sense-organ with the mind or the mind and the self etc. may.

If knowledge were to cognise itself, the second cognition (I cognise the cognition) also should be self-cognised and such a third cognition should be admitted and so on and so forth ad infinitum. So the Buddhist himself with his self-cognition theory cannot escape the fault of infinite regress which he levels against the views of the orthodox schools.

Further the admission of a second minute of mental perception after his sense perception (Indriya jñāna) in the same series is questionable. How is it that a perception of the same type is produced by the cognition of the next minute? There also he has to admit nature (Svabhava) as the cause. To the realist of the orthodox schools the one perception stretches over the mental aspect also as mind is in communion with the sense organ and the perception is produced in a single minute's duration (after the operation of the necessary causes), whereas the Buddhist has to explore a separate reason for a similar or dessimilar series following in the next minute.

Further, the succession of knowledge (Citte santana) is not possible on the Buddhist view for, in the former minute, the knowledge is produced and instantly lost. How could then, the later knowledge become one Santana with the previous one? When the previous moment was there the later moment was absents. Even if it be held that the intervening space (Deśa) be held responsible for the production, it cannot be so as even space is momentary for him. Hence in his view Santanaikya and Bhinna Santāna appears to be difficult to be established. Even the permanent knower of the succession (Santana) who is the Ahamartha (the ego) is itself transient in his view.

Again the Buddhist thinks that one cognition produces another. We ask him if there is a relation between the former and the latter cognition. If there is one it is only one of his inevitable relations and thus only an inference should follow every cognition and not perception. Further, the theory that one cognition produces another cognition later as advanced by the Buddhist, may not stand to reason, as there is no cogniser who or which has cognised this production. The former knowledge cannot cognise production (of the next cognition) as it would have ceased to exist by the time the latter is produced. The latter cognition cannot cognise its own production from the previous one as it was not there earlier. If, however, it is held that the former knowledge is destroyed while producing the latter knowledge it cannot be admitted that what is already being destroyed in the minute is also producing another knowledge at the same time. No other cogniser is there. But if the theory means that after one cognition another cognition is produced (from its own causes) there is no dispute.

To the Buddhist, as we know, not only pure sense perception but also inference where there is a mental construction, is valid knowledge which determines the way to gain a fruitful action. In such a case he may easily posit that it is not the pure sensational aspect of sense perception but also the mental perception which takes place in the next minute together that together constitute one knowledge which takes two minutes for its production. He cannot maintain that the assumption of the form of the object by the former moment of perception is valid knowledge though it forms such an idea as he holds as it does not lead us to a determination of fruitful action (Prapaka) without the latter. Nor, then the object of both the perceptions could be Svalaksana. Hence there should be no objection to hold the sense perception and the mental perception together as one piece of perceptional Vikalpa knowledge.

Thus we have to posit that knowledge of all types, perception, inference etc. are linked to mental construction (Vikalpa) with the details of name, class etc. and they should be called knowledge. Even the indeterminate knowledge of the Logician can be called knowledge though in it there is non-cognition of the relation between the substantive and the attribute but all the same both are perceived even with the help of the sense organ-object contact. This cognition is not insentient for him as the soul also is involved in the process. But for the Buddhist pure sense perception cannot be a cognition as sense object contact only is there but no cognition-producer. To the Samkhya knowing is the reflection of the consciousness (Cit) in the mental modification (Buddhivṛtti). Here the reflection accounts for a semblance in the insentient Vṛtti. This is admitted by them as Cit (Purusa) is without attachment (Asanga) to any other thing.

Thus the image of the object in the Vrtti accounts for the cognition of the objects. This theory also appears to uphold the hallucinational nature of sentience in the cognition of the object.

The Advaitin holds that the process of perception takes place when consciousness (Cit)[21] and the object (pot etc.)[22] come into the same locus and there is the presentation of the object (Visayapratyaksa). But when the internal organ which assumes the form of the object and consciousness (Cit) are in the same locus it is called the process of perception[23] that ensues. In the case of inference however there is no necessity for the modified internal organ to go to the place of object.

The cognition of negation or absence is only the cognition of the locus of negation as for the Prābhākara.

To the Logician by knowing (an object) is meant the self being the locus of knowledge (Jnanasrayatvam). Knowledge is a property which inheres in the soul when the causal aggregate of it is present. Actually cognition is not an activity for them though the word Jānāti etc. are used with the tense sense also included in the word Jānāti. The actual meaning of the sentence 'He knows' is – 'He is the locus of knowledge in the present time.' When all the causes are present knowledge is produced in a minute's time knowledge has invariably an object (related to it, as an object) (Viṣaya). The (practical) knowledge is only determinate. Indeterminate knowledge is accepted only for the sake of introduction of items like name, class, genus etc. into it later. Without perceiving the attribute pothood and the (individual) pot which are the attribute and the substantive a knowledge of the relation and the pot in particular cannot be conceived. In the case of every knowledge there is always an object – a substantive, an attribute and their relation. Knowledge is also called the object-holder (possessor) since it holds objects in its respective capacities as substantive etc.

To the Jaina by valid knowledge (Pramana) is meant only determinate knowledge, (not indeterminate) without doubt or indecision. Some theorists, I think, would have done better if they had discussed production of knowledge separately and validity separately. Some of them (of course with some differences) speak of knowledge and its validity (Jñanaṃ prāmānyam ca) arising out of the means of valid knowledge. Here there is a confusion whether knowledge and its validity are both cognised from the same sources (i.e. the knowledge itself) in which case there should be no case of invalid knowledge at all. We know that in certain cases some accept knowledge is self-valid. In such cases the validity also must be accepted to have arisen from the same knowledge.[24] Thus accepting no difference between the sources of mere knowledge and its validity in which case the words 'Avisamvadi' Abhrānta or Doṣābhava etc. to shift the responsibility of talking of validity to its negative aspect could be easily avoided. Even otherwise how long is one expected to wait for the validity of knowledge to be cognised and till that time the contingency is that the knowledge acquired should be neither valid nor invalid. Such a knowledge we have never come across. Surely not practically dis-agreeing with the object (Avisamvada) is also to be cognised before the validity of the cognition is decided as otherwise in the case of a doubt about validity if it intervenes, should be dispelled.

For this again another knowledge of cognition should be accepted which he does not speak about. Even if agreement with the object itself is a cognition for him when the connection between the object and its activity are not undertaken practically the knowledge of agreement cannot be cognised. Hence the discrepancy. He has to accept Arthakriya as a separate activity different from knowledge only after the necessary experiment is carried out in practice (which cannot be mere knowledge but is cognised with the help of knowledge activity). Further the Arthakriya knowledge cannot be identified with the knowledge of pot as they are two separate cognitions (at least in the very first time of its cognition).

To the Bhatta Mimamsaka, knowledge is what is inferred from knownness (Jnatata). When a pot is known knownness is produced in the pot. This knownness is also called manifestation (Prākatya) and it is produced from the knowledge (Jnana) and inheres in the object as there is the statement in practice 'this pot is known.' That is to say in other words in a cognition like 'this is a pot' as the two causes knowledge of the pot (the efficient cause) and the pot (the inherent cause) are present and hence our statement in vogue the 'pot is known.' It may be noted here that no non-inherent cause is necessary in the Mimamsaka's view with regard to a positive product. With the help of this knownness as the reason (Linga) the knowledge (of the pot) is inferred. Thus knowledge is only an object of inference for them. It is not perceived even mentally or cognised by another cognition like apperception. The Logician criticises this stand and holds that knownness is not different from being the object of knowledge (Jnanavisayatva) and not a separate category as the opponent holds. Both Atman and Manas are accepted for the production of knowledge. The former is eternal but the latter not so. There is a non changing element in the Atman.

The Mind's Role in the Field of Epistemology

The mind has an important role to play in the production of knowledge though the Buddhist does not accept one such for the purpose. All the other schools do have a mind. Even among the Buddhists the Vaibhāṣikas accept Ālaya Vijñāna which approximates to the 'mind' of the orthodox schools of philosophy. The Buddhists of other denominations on the other hand, admit a cognition itself for the understanding of the sensation of an object instead of mind. Thus for him mind is only a cognition following the immediately preceding sensation in the case of perception. But the difficulty in this view is that the earlier cognition already over-burdened with an object is to cognise another (object) and shed the previous one.

The Logician is obliged to admit mind (Manas) as the instrumental cause (Karaṇa) of the experience of pleasure, pain etc. which are purely internal and are objects of knowledge. Unlike to the Buddhist to whom mind is only a cognition (which grasps only the object and is self-revealed). Even when the soul sense organ – object contact is present sometimes cognition is not produced. This points to the fact that there is an agency called 'mind' which is also responsible for cognition. Further in deep sleep though the soul, sense organs and objects are present, there is no cognition of objects as the mind has no contact with the organ of touch (Tvak) when it is in a nerve (Nādi) called Purītat. Another reason 'why mind is accepted by him is that we don't find different cognitions arising simultaneously as taste, colour, smell and so on as the mind is subtle and concentrates on only one object. Whereas the sense organs may be responsible for cognition of external objects only 'the mind is capable of negotiating a cognition of internal objects like pleasure and pain. So it is maintained by the Logician that the mind plays an important part in the cognition of external objects too in collusion with the sense organs. According to the Logician the process of perception cognition is like this – the soul comes into contact with the mind, the mind with the sense-organ and the latter with the object concerned. It is only then that knowledge is produced in the soul. Mind like the sense organs is a sense organ but it is internal.

Further I think it is necessary to hold 'mind' also as the conveyor of all impressions of old. Otherwise how could the impressions emerge in a cognitive process. They have to emerge when mental constructions etc. are to be undertaken even for the Buddhist. I think this is a serious lapse if we don't accept mind as the efficient cause (Karaṇa) and its contact with the sense organ as its operative cause (Vyāpāra) in sense perception. Instead the Buddhist accepts the previous cognition (Samanantara pratyaya which is later followed by a moment in the same series) to serve the purpose of the mind which is questionable as it is itself a cognition and there is none to determine its series – the same or another.

Several definitions have been proposed for the mind by Epistemologists. The Logician defines it as the (internal) organ responsible for (as the instrumental cause of) the perception of pleasure etc. Some others defined it as one possessed of activity but without touch. The Mīmaṁsaka defines it as the seat of contact of the immaterial cause of cognition which (cause) is different from the soul. The mind is only a particular cognition for the Buddhist as stated earlier. If it is a mere cognition it will not be able to restrain the cognition of the individual to a particular object of perception.

To the Jaina mind (Manas) is the instrumental cause (Karaṇa) of the apprehension (Grahaṇa) of all objects. By the word Grahaṇa in the definition he excludes Ātman which is the agent of apprehension (and not its instrumental cause). It is also designated Anindriya or that which is not a sense (organ) or no Indriya (something different from a sense (organ). All knowledge that belongs to sense organs or otherwise is produced by the mind. Thus the knowledge of words also comes under its scope. Like the organs of sense, mind too has been divided into two – the Dravyamanaḥ (mind as a substance) and Bhāvamanaḥ (mind as an activity). The former is a substance consisting of items which have transformed themselves into the mind whereas the latter is the attainment (Labdhi) of the form of removing or destruction of the veil of past deeds (Karma) which (Labdhi) is no other than a particular operation (or activity) which makes the self prove to cognise the object (Upayoga). This mind is particularly seen active in producing the mental mode-cognition (Manaḥ paryayajñāna) which means the cognition of objects with the help of the different modifications of the mind substance in accordance with our thoughts (Cintana). It may be noted here that the sense organs and the mind play a collective or a destructive role in producing perception. If the sense organ plays a dominant part and the mind contributes to the production of the perception it is called sense-produced perception

(Indriyaja) but if it is produced only with the help of the mind depending upon its purity (viśuddhi) then it is called mano-nimitta or perception produced by the mind.

Thus unlike the Buddhist the Jaina holds mind (Manas) also as the instrumental cause of all kinds of cognition. It is material as it comprises of atoms and is also functional in inducing the self towards cognition. Thus the Jaina mind is material and has some properties like the mind of many schools of thinkers. But the Jaina does not stress on the necessity of accepting mind or its atomic size which are responsible for a particular cognition only at a particular time etc.

To the Buddhist knowledge only plays the role of the mind. To him either the immediately preceding knowledge (of any knowledge) (called Samanantara pratyaya) is the mind for some (Yogacara) as it is that which cognises the next cognition. To some others it is the Ālaya Vijñana (the Vaibhasikas) that constitutes the mind of the thinkers.

Here is may be observed that one cognition (the previous one) being loaded with its own object cannot overload itself with another object even in the same series. So it is better to accept both sense perception (Indriya Jñāna) and mental perception (Mano Vijñāna) as one single knowledge with the same object (cognised) as do the other Epistemologists since in both the cases the result is the Svalakṣaṇa the same thing.

To the Advaita Vedantin the mind is an internal organ (Antaḥkaraṇa) the seat of pleasure, pain etc. and its forms are desire, doubt etc. but it does not fall under the category of the sense organ (Indriya) as he contends that a definition of sense organ cannot be duly stated in case it is sense organ. Whatever the implication may be it must be admitted necessary to hold the mind as a sense organ as pleasure, pain etc. cannot be produced directly by the sense organs which are external. Hence mind should be sense organ though pleasure etc. at times are cognised by the Sākṣin.

The Ramanujite views mind as a sense-organ like the Logician and unlike the Śāṅkarite. It exists in the heart (Hṛdaya). This is the sense-organ which is the immediately preceding cause of recollection etc. When cognition is to be produced, the self comes into contact with the mind and soon and so forth as the Logician does.

The properties of the mind are also given by the Logician. It is one (in the case of each individual body, eternal, atomic in size and super sensuous (Atīndriya). As it is one in each body 'mind' is plural, in really of infinite number. It is considered atomic in size because we here to accept the non-material cause (Ātmamanaḥ Saṃyoga) relating to space as we have experiences like 'I have pleasure in my feet though I have pain in my head.' Another reason also is given. The self is considered ubiquitous by the Logician (and many others also) in which case the mind should be considered as atomic. Otherwise we have to establish a contact of the mind with the soul (two all-pervading substances) which is unwholesome. The reason is that if such a contact be allowed between two ubiquitous substances like the mind and the soul, then contact should be external and only cognitions should have to be produced incessantly and no sleep should be possible for any individual. But to the Mīmāṃsaka the mind is all-pervading. It is the seat of contact which is the non-material cause of cognition. Mind is eternal for the Logician. The mind is not a perceptual object. It is inferred on the grounds suggested earlier here. But the Jaina has a different view here. He considers mind as physical ultimate of atoms. The mind is possessed of activity and speed and as such it is a corporeal substance (Mūrtadravya).

Unless the mind also involved in the process of knowing impressions of old cannot play a useful role in cognising objects (unless the self itself is involved in it). It is the case with the Logician. The Sāṁkhya is of opinion that the internal organ has three constituents the intellect (Buddhi). When it doubts is called mind, Buddhi when it determines things, Citta when it thinks and egoism (Ahaṃkāra) when it displays ego. These three act at all times present and future and past and hold the objects (Dhāryant). The mind is responsible for accepting the object presented by the sense organ, the mind then presents it to the ego principle and produces it before the intellect (Buddhi), this intellect or Buddhi is the seat of the reflection of consciousness (Cit) as it is very clear. The property of the mind is observation (Samkalpa) and Cit, the ego principle is responsible for self-consciousness (Abhimāna). The reflection of the self in the modification of the insentient Buddhi gives it (the Buddhi) a semblance of sentience. Here cognition is only a semblance but not a property of the intellect as it is insentient. The Advaitin holds that the internal organ is responsible for the modification (Vṛtti) which is responsible for perception etc. Mind on the other hand, is considered as one of its modifications. When it is of the form of decision (Sankalpa) and doubt (Vikalpa) it is called mind. Mental modes like pride, fear, egoism, etc. its different forms are all those of (the mind or) the internal organ. It is possessed of the two properties of contraction (Saṁkoca) and expansion (Vikāsa) on account of which it gets velocity. It extends from one place to another while being in the body. It is non-eternal as all objects of the world are; consciousness is reflected in the pure internal organs mode and thus the internal organ becomes conscious as it were. But apperception, pleasure, pain etc. are perceived directly by the witness consciousness (the Sākṣin). It goes out and takes the form of the object etc. with which it comes into contact. In the case of perception the Vṛtti goes outside to the object but in the case of other means of knowledge i.e. inference etc. it would not i.e. when it doubts it is called mind, Buddhi when it determines things, Citta when it thinks and egoism (Ahankāra) when it displays the ego (e.g. I know the pot etc. having reference to I, mine etc.)

The Role of Atman (Self) in the Acquisition of Knowledge

According to the Buddhist there is nothing like a permanent source of knowledge. Knowledge is only momentary. Each knowledge (Citta) produces another knowledge (Cittāntara) and this process continues till the end of life, even at the time of death. Sometimes a knowledge of the same series is produced (as in the case of sense perception and its mental perception etc.). In certain cases it is one of a different series (Bhinna santāna) which presents an object different from the previous one. The Buddhist should account for this difference in the series, somehow.

He does not accept an entity which recollects (Smartā) but he posits that recollection (Smṛti) is the outcome of experience (Anubhava). Here the Buddhist is to be questioned as to who recalls the experience because recollection we notice in the same self that had the experience, but not in another (self). So also the Buddhist argues that enjoyment (Bhoga) is there but the enjoyer is not there.[25] He also declares that salvation is obtained by the cessation of desire (Triṣṇā). He argues that though the effect of bad action is still there since one of the causes of re-birth, desire, is destroyed no re-birth can ensue. But here we question to whom is salvation possible to all at once or to the particular one with that particular body actions.

The Buddhist also holds that if Atman were eternal and perception etc. were only temporary, then perception of different objects should occur simultaneously but not one after another (Kramika) for this reason that an eternal object does not depend on any other thing for its activity. But the reason given needs to be substantiated by illustrations and concomitance. We see that even time, an external entity, needs the help of some activity to cognise it. Another defect he points out is that if it be argued that the self is to wait for the activity of the sense organs etc., there is discrepancy in the argument that objects are perceived only one after another but actually we experience the dance of the dancing girl, her music and the fragrance there all at the same time. But this view is repugnant to others who hold that there are cognised one after another in quick succession only.

According to the Jaina Atman or self is one of the factors of attainment of knowledge. All the knowledge located in the Atman is covered by a veil consequent on the effects of destructive deeds. This overshrouded knowledge is unveiled when the necessary causes of Direct or Indirect knowledge are produced. This is a direct reply to the Buddhist who holds that if the Atman be the seat of all knowledge then all cognitions of small touch etc. should be produced simultaneously and not in an order as in practical experience. But the Jaina holds that even the sun's light is precluded by clouds etc. and when it is removed the sun shines again. In much the same way the unveiling of the particular part of the self reveals the particular object. The Buddhist criticises the Jaina holding that momentary cognition is enough to cognise objects not a self. It is true if Atman or mind is not accepted, the Buddhist will have to show a seat of the impressions of old necessary for the cognition of objects. The argument of the Buddhist is that the occasional cognitions are due only to an occasional causes (and not permanent ones). Hence an occasional knowledge like 'This is a pot' is engendered only by an occasional cause (ego which is not always present i.e. a momentary cognition) but not a permanent entity like the self (Atman). This view does not appear to be sound as the occasional nature of the knowledge of a particular object is due only to the occasional contact of the sense organ with the particular object (in perception) which also is one of the causes but not due to the non permanence of the self. The ego, even according to him may see another object at that time. To argue that a non permanent self needs no other cause like sense object contact does not hold good as its cannot be proved. When a particular object is perceived but not another particular one.

Further the Buddhist badly needs a store house of impressions (Vasanas) of previous lives etc. (as all others do). He cannot over burden the momentary knowledge produced at a particular time as their cause. Hence he has to admit a permanent self or the like for the purpose.

In the view of the Sāṃkhya, as the self (Atman) is immutable and does not undergo any change, it is only reflected in the very clear intellect (Buddhi) and brings about a semblance of sentience. The Buddhi directly serves the purpose of the self (Puruṣārtha) and makes him enjoy the pleasures and pains and finally it is the very same Buddhi that helps him in distinguishing between the primordial matter (Prakṛti) and the individual self (Puruṣa) as a consequence of which he attains salvation (Kaivalya). Here the doubt is whether a relationless Ātman can cast a shadow in the intellect and how the result is considered to be a semblance of sentience. The Buddhist objects to this view of the Sāṃkhya on the ground that, if the self is one and different from Buddhi (intellect), how is it possible that it experiences objects of several kinds in this world. Further if it is not the self that acts but the (Primordial matter Pradhana) how is it that the self is considered to be the enjoyer of its fruit? Verily the doer of the action should enjoy the fruit thereof.

In the view of the Mīmāmsaka, the self (Ātman) is an entity which has a form both distinguished (Vyāvṛtta) and common (Anugata). Though in its nature it is of one form it gets distinguished by its particular states of pleasure and pain. Its identity is there in spite of its different vicissitudes like serpenthood in a serpent even when its states-coiling and straight forms differ now and then. So also though the states of pleasure, pain etc. differ, sentience (Caitanya) is a continuing factor in the self. He argues that the recognition (Pratyabhijña) envisaged as in the statement 'I who cognised yesterday' am cognising now is proof of a continuing self in the body. The 'I' is the same in yesterday's and today's cognition as both the cognitions are never present together at any time. This recognition cannot be a 'series' as the Buddhist may argue, but it is not one as the 'I's are not present at one time. And also a series is not a real object (Vastu) as it is a mental construction. A non-real object, according to the Buddhist, cannot act. The Buddhist objects to such a self as advocated by the Mīmāṃsaka as he argues that, instead, the Mīmāṃsaka could hold that cognition (Buddhi) itself is permanent. But the latter holds that, if both the Buddhi and the self are eternal and one in number, difference in the objects cognised at intervals. This the Buddhist rejoins by asking the question 'what is the cause of a pertinent cognition like 'Here is a horse where there is no elephant etc.' (for details vide Tat. Sam

Atm. Par. 250 et. seqq). But I think the reply should be that the strong impression of old is responsible for such a cognition.

In the Śaṅkarite's opinion the self (Ātman) does not have any activity. Neither does it act nor is the enjoyer of the fruit of the action. On such a view he has to account for all kinds of activity, desire, impressions of old etc. These cannot be the functions of the mind as it is insentient. Being insentient it cannot undertake these above functions even in its proximity with the Atman. Further proximity of the self cannot be spoken of with the mind as the former is neither distant not far from it and does not attach itself with the mind. The Cit also is stated by him to get itself reflected in the mental mode which is against the nature of the self. Even if this reflection be held to be a mere appearance and hence false how could it produce an effect – a pot, a mat etc. real in his view in the pragmatic state. However the Śaṅkarite's view is that either the consciousness as determined by the mental mode (Vṛttyavacchinna caitanya) or the consciousness as reflected in the mental mode (Vṛtti pratibimbita caitanya) is the knower (Pramāta). Here a difficulty is that such a qualified mental mode is only temporary and hence as the knower is temporary he cannot have a later knowledge like 'I who knew the pot now know the mat.'

We have seen why the Logician accepts the self. It is proved by being necessary to accommodate consciousness (Jñāna) in it. No other Dravya else but the self is capable of holding it. Indeed consciousness is a property which has to reside somewhere and hence the self has to be accepted. Further according to him, it is the seat of desire, hatred etc. and also impressions of old (Bhāvanās) necessary in the cognition of objects. But it is not sentience itself but it is the locus of sentience (and hence probably decried as insentient). This is against the view of the Vedāntin who holds the opposite view that Ātman (self) is the sentient one of the form of consciousness itself. But the difference is that, according to the Vedantin it is the eternal consciousness that is called the self. Both the Advaitin and the Logician recognise the Ātman or self, while the Logician holds that cognition (Buddhi) stands for two minutes and is destroyed in the third, the former views that cognition (Buddhi) is a particular modification of the internal organ (Antaḥkaraṇa). It is of the form of determination (Niścaya). It is not really sentience or the sentient entity but it is necessary to be admitted as a modification (Vṛtti) of the internal organ either to remove the veil of ignorance (Ajñānabhibhavārtha) on one view on for painting of the object with, (Uparāga) in another view. The sentient self is reflected in the modification effected (Buddhi vṛtti) in the internal organ (Antaḥkaraṇa), an immaculate entity (which can reflect objects) and thus the insentient Buddhi appears to be sentient when cognition is produced. In the Logician's view, however, the contact of the self with the mind is the general cause of all cognition, while for perception the sense-organ-contact and object-sense-contact are also necessary. For inference etc. however the Logician holds that an additional knowledge of knowledge of concomitance (Vyāptyjñāna) etc. are particularly necessary.

Taking, this into consideration all aspects of knowing it is deemed necessary to accept a self the eternal seat of knowledge (or in other words, I think, the faculty of cognising objects etc. with the help of other particular causes) even though mind is separately accepted. To get all cognitional process performed with the help of cognition alone, as the Buddhist does, appears to be wrought with several difficulties as already observed. We know most of the schools of philosophy accept self except Buddhist and Cārvakism.

The Mīmāṃsaka View in More Detail

According to Kumārila, as in the other orthodox schools of philosophy, the self has a very important part to play in respect of its relation to cognition. The self (Ātman) to him is of the form of a potency of cognition and it plays a dual role when it produces cognitions etc. It is to him an entity which is a permanent (Anugata) while it undergoes changes too. This is described by an example of the snakes which being a snake all the while sometimes is like a rope, sometimes curled all the time not loosing its snakehood. In the same way the self also while undergoing successive vicissitudes like pleasure, pain continues to persevere as an entity with its being (Sattā) etc. His idea is that while the self, the potency of knowledge or cognition (Caitanya) continues the states of pleasure, pain etc. come and go. This stand of the Mīmāṃsaka neither leans to the side of the Buddhist who advocates constant change every minute (in the cognitions) nor to the side of the Logician who holds that knowledge inheres in it. On the Buddhist's stand the fruit of what is done by one self should be enjoyed by another self on his theory of momentariness of all objects. The Mīmāṃsaka holds that the result of what is done by one should be experienced by one oneself and not by another.

He infers the existence of the self with the help of recognition. There is the experience of people 'I know it earlier and I know it now.' Hence the theory of selflessness of the Buddhist does not stand to reason. In the above inference with the help of the mark, recognition (Pratyabhijñā) the cogniser is the same, be it the self or a momentary cognition. The former view is better, the Mīmāṃsaka holds.

Here a question arises in the Mīmāṃsaka view where the self is not different from cognition but is one faculty and eternal, how is it that differences arise in cognitions (like that of pot, mat etc.) whereas the self is one and the same. The reply of the Mīmāṃsaka is that the difference in cognitions is due to the difference in *the objects* of cognition. Due to some previous unknown causes (Adṛṣṭa) the sense organs come into contact with particular objects and they only are cognised and hence there is difference in cognitions. If the cognitions are not different due to objects (cognised) then there should be no recognition of objects, as the Mīmāṃsaka holds. Here the Buddhist raises an objection as to how some people are obliged to superimpose objects like elephants or goats where there are none in a spot. The objection is that the object is not a necessary precondition for cognition. The Jaina also contributes to this view. But the objection does not appear to be valid. We note in this world that only those objects which are cognised are generally perceived but where there is an intensive desire (Prabalecchā) to see another object then it is possible to see other objects. And again when everybody sees the object and cognises it as such and such there is no gain-saying it. If due to other reasons like inebriety, madness etc. in rare cases other objects not present are conceived it is an exceptional case which is accounted for in a different way e.g. as due to a defect of the mind or the sense-organ, desire for superimposition etc. Indeed[26] a few exceptions (of known or unknown reasons) cannot set aside the general rule. Further there is much brevity in holding that objects are responsible for their cognition as we experience in life.[27]

The self is considered eternal by the Mīmāṃsaka as it is the persevering entity in all cognitions like cognition of pot, cognition of mat etc. But to the Buddhist every cognition is produced and destroyed every minute and the next cognition should be admitted to be produced by the previous cognition which does not give the cognition of the required object.

Another question raised by the Buddhist against the Mīmāṃsaka is that if the cognition does not take the form of the object and the objects of particular places and times cannot be brought before the cogniser (as they are elsewhere) before it is presented to us he will have to admit that cognition or consciousness should be able to know all objects in which case the contingency is that all objects should be cognised at all moments.

It is an intriguing question whether it is the sense organ that assumes the form of the object or the mind or the self though the latter two alternatives alone are popular. The Logician does not speak of any assumption of form by any organ concerned though he advocates the contact of the object with the sense-organ and the sense organ with the mind and the mind with the self because probably he thinks such an assumption of form is open to dispute on many counts. The Śāṅkarite argues that the internal organ (Antaḥkaraṇa) assumes the form of the object. The Mīmāṃsaka and the Jaina appear to hold that the self itself is modified when the object is presented. The Sāṅkhya holds that the consciousness (Cit) is reflected in the intellect (Buddhi) when the object is presented to the cogniser.

The Śāṅkarite is of the view that the modification of the internal organ gets reflected in the eternal consciousness (Ātman) but the cognition though cognised along with the object is cognised by the witness consciousness (Sākṣin). This is probably because the consciousness as determined by the internal organ is busy with the process of knowing the object as it is involved in it but the witness consciousness is free and it is able to visualize the knowledge produced as it is not involved in the process at all.[28] But according to the Naiyāyika it is the immediately next mental cognition (Mānasapratyakṣa) that cognises the knowledge. This cognition is called apperception. It appears the Logician's stand is better in that it ensures even invalid cognitions to be cognised by the apperception itself while it is not the case with the Śāṅkarites Sākṣin. Though the Buddhist appreciates the view of the Śāṅkarite that consciousness is the cogniser he is perturbed over what they hold that the cogniser-consciousness is eternal. While every object is momentary even consciousness is one such as we experience in life and hence they had better advocate momentary knowledge as the cogniser. He contends that it knowledge were eternal the state of consciousness should even be of the same cognition (of colour or taste) and not in succession one after the other. There is no consciousness different from cognitions of colour, taste etc. and in such a case if there is difference between one knowledge and another what is it that is common to the self and the cognition, asks the Buddhist. An eternal self cannot experience different cognitions due to different modes of the mind etc. as an eternal substance cannot submit itself to change. He also changes that in the Śaṅkarite's view bondage and salvation (of the Jīva) are not possible since only one eternal knowledge either valid or invalid is present. It cannot be held that a knowledge of reality or Yogābhyāsa etc. are capable of giving salvation as the self is always eternal and static. In the Buddhist's view, however, due to difference in the series of the consciousness (Santānabheda) there is the possibility of liberation and bondage the Buddhist argues. But according to the Śāṅkarite as the consciousness is not directly connected with the objects etc. it is the mental modification (Vṛtti) that cognises when consciousness is reflected in it, as it is very pure and clear. Here also probably a question arises as to how the relationless Atman gets reflected in the mental mode.

The Logician's View in More Detail

The Logician is of the view that the individual self (Jīva) is an entity that is inferred as the seat of desire, detestation etc. Though it is of a nature different from consciousness (Cit) it becomes conscious with the help of consciousness (Caitanyayogāt cetanaḥ). This self is eternal and all-pervading (Vibhu). Though it is eternal it is the doer (Karta) because it is he who knows, desires and acts with the desire of getting the result. That is to say knowledge, desire etc. inhere in him and as such he is called the doer. He is also the enjoyer (of actions) as a knowledge of pleasure, pain etc. inhere in the self. Thus knowledge, pleasure, pain etc. inhere in it. But its contact (Samyoga) with the body, sense organs etc. is what is called its birth (Janma). Death is the separation from these entities. Virtue and Vice (Dharma and Adharma) due to the contact of the mind and the body are responsible for the migration of the self though it is eternal. The self is inferred like this: All the cognitions of taste, colour etc. involving different organs are considered as 'mine' by each individual separately, and hence there is a self which is responsible for the oneness in all these different cognitions.

The Buddhist however refutes this view. He is of opinion that there is no such thing as self but the notion of 'I' (Ahaṃkāra). It is only momentary consciousness that really exists and it is actually what knows things.

References

1. Jñā Avabodhane
2. Yuvoranakau – here the 'yu' in lyuṭ affix is replaced by 'ana' and the word jñā ana = jñāna is formed.
3. e.g. Vahnivyāpyadhūmavān parvataḥ.
4. Jñānādhikaraṇamātmā.
5. Jnatum yogyam (fit to be known i.e. all objects of knowledge).
6. But what this jñāna is and how it is defined is to be ascertained.
7. Nirviṣayajñāne pramāṇābhāvāt.
8. Arthaprakāsānukūla vyāpāraḥ – Here he has to explain what prakāśa is.
9. Neti Neti vākyāni.
10. For a criticism of this theory Vide Tar. Rak., p. 53. Also Ny. Kus.
11. Vijñātāramare kena vijānīyāt.
12. Knowledge for the Sāṃkhya is arthaprakāśa. Here prakāśa again implies knowledge to be defined. If it means 'illumination' it is only a similarity explained on the analogy of light but it cannot be the definition.
13. Vijñātaramare kena vijāniyāt.
14. Sarvavyāvahārajanakatāvacchadaka jātimattvaṃ.
15. Hereby phala is meant the identity of the object (by the delimited caitanya) with (the consciousness-delimited) internal organ (Antaḥkaraṇā vacchinna caitanya).
16. Atasmins tadbuddhiḥ.
17. Jñato ghaṭaḥ.
18. Pratitivyavahārābhyamartha siddhiḥ.
19. Vide Tar. Bh. PII-11 11-13.
20. Which he accepts under Svalakshana.
21. It is also called the Pramatṛ caitanya or Antaḥ-karanavacchinna caitanya.
22. The pot is also of the form of cit, and hence there is Abheda between the pramata and the object.

23. That is to say when the pramana caitanya (i.e. Antah karana vrttyavacchina caitanya) and the cit are in the same locus (this is their Abheda) the Jnana is called Pratyaksa.

24. Avisamvada jnanam pramanam.

25. Vide Pra. Var. Vr., p. 102.

26. Yatra phalaviṣayikecchā saiva prabata.

27. Pratītivyyavahārābhyām arthasiddhiḥ.

28. Antah karaṇāvacchinnam caitanyam, is the cogniser and Antaḥ karanopahitam caitanyam sākṣi (jīva sākṣi).

Chapter 2
The Theories of the Production of Knowledge

General

It is a very intriguing subtle and difficult aspect of the Theory of Knowledge as to 'how knowledge is produced.[1] The Sāṃkhya appears to have studied the production of knowledge for the first time with all its details which have been borrowed by the later school of theorists who accepted a store of Caitanya which makes the knowledge sentient. It is difficult to say whether knowledge is itself sentient or the one who is the locus of knowledge that is sentient. The rival theorists denigrate the Logician on the ground that he (the Logician) views the Locus of knowledge as the sentient being because the Locus without knowledge (the self) should be insentient. But the fact is that the Logician holds that knowledge always inheres in the self[1] though it may not be a manifest during deep sleep etc. The Vedāntin and the Buddhist believe that the locus of knowledge is no other than knowledge itself while the former of these argues it is only pure eternal knowledge that is sentient the latter holds that it is the momentary Sākāra (having a form or content) knowledge which is sentient. But I think we have to admit sentience (knowledge) as a property and it should be present in some locus as we experience in due life.

Now let us consider whether knowledge is produced or eternal. If it be eternal how is it that it is present only at times and in parts as knowledge of mat at one time and knowledge of pot at another. Here there appear to be two theories of production of knowledge – one that all knowledge is already there (as in the self) and only the removal of the veil covering it is effected by the mode of the internal organ (Vṛtti). The votaries of this particular theory are the Māyāvādin Śaṅkarite, the Jaina and the Sāṃkhya. There is also difference of opinion whether the mental mode (Vṛtti) is for the sake of removing the veil or painting (the knowledge with the object of the form etc.). Here a question also arises as to who understands or gets the knowledge when the veil is removed. The Mayavadin says it is the mind that knows,[2] in a secondary sense the Jaina says it is the soul, the Buddhist that the knowledge itself knows the object concerned and the knowledge too.

As to the question raised the Sāṃkhya as to how differes knowledges are called by the same name knowledge (knowledge of a pot, knowledge of mat etc.), probably the answer is that the knowledge common to all objects 'pot, mat etc.' is the faculty of knowing where the object is not specified but generalised.

Further if momentary knowledge were to know the object concerned and its cognition and infinitum how is it that the next knowledge is produced? To say that one cognition produces another cognition cannot be valid as the causes of a particular knowledge produce the knowledge concerned and there is no scope for them to produce another cognition. If it is said to be produced from its own causes, what are they? The earlier cognition cannot be one because in the Buddhist theory as it will have been already destroyed by that time (when the other is produced). Further the object is not a cause of knowledge according to him. If he argues that impression of the object or desire is responsible for the cognition of the object why is it that the particular impression alone is aroused in preference to another? He has then to admit that the mind (or self as you may choose to state) is the seat of impressions much against his own idealist theory. Further those impressions which would determine the object of cognition should be aroused. The impressions which determine the colour of the pot are different from those which determine its taste. What is the agency that arouses the particular impression in preference to others. Thus the mind or the self, apart from knowledge, has to be admitted which the idealist (Buddhist) would not. Again the Buddhist has to account for cognition either in its own series (Santāna) or of a different one in which case an agency which desires either of them (mind or self) has to be admitted. Again to argue that determinate cognition is produced from the indeterminate cognition though it is different in nature from it (just as the knowledge of the reason produces a knowledge of inference), does not hold good as a certain concomitance is cognised earlier between the reason and the object inferred but not in the case of the indeterminate the determinate cognitions). If this be not admitted any particular cognition would have to be produced from any other cognition quite against his view. He avers only some particular object are the cause of some particular objects just as sesame seeds are of oil (and not others).

Another difficulty for the Buddhist is that he should accept impressions, a category, which is different from (momentary) knowledge and is not momentary. Otherwise the impression (without an existence) cannot be aroused.

Again the cognition produced has to be admitted to form the impression later which cannot be properly accounted for with the theory of momentariness without which (impression) even false knowledge cannot be produced of objects. If an invalid cognition is to be its cause, the cause of knowledge of invalidity (like Jaundice etc.) themselves insentient, have to be considered the cause of cognition against his own theory. Thus the theory of momentary knowledge cannot produce one knowledge after another without the help of existing objects or their impressions.

In the case of some rival theorists the particular cognition is produced with the help of the mental modification (Manovṛtti) which unveils the particular cover on the seat of all cognitions (the self) and not the others. Thus the objection raised by the Buddhist against the Jaina etc. cannot be held valid. Even the Sāṃkhya holds that the self is reflected in mental mode. Though the self is immutable the mental modes which allow a particular order (Krama) of cognitions are rendered possible. Only the reflection gets the change according to particular cognitions one by one but not the self. Hence the objection of the Buddhist that the self involved in the process should itself be liable for a change is not valid.

If, on the other hand the faculty of knowing itself be admitted to be the cause of cognition – given the object, light etc. the faculty itself needs a locus to exist in and thus one will have to admit a self (or a mind) as the locus which again goes against the Buddhist stand.

Again if one mind (cognition) produces another the production of cognition should not stop even with the help of the four noble truths which generate a knowledge of those truths which should go on being produced in a series without break. There should be no evidence to the breakage of the chain of cognitions at any point of time.

Further on the Buddhist view recollection cannot be maintained intact as the cognition is destroyed in the next minute. Even if it be a case of invated cognition for the same reason no invalid knowledge too can be produced in regard to the object of recollection. Further if the cognition or the cogniser is stated to be destroyed does it mean that the entities are destroyed along with their causes in which case no other cognition or no other cogniser can be produced later. To argue that such a cognition is produced from its own causes does not rectify the difficulty in the stand unless the causes are specified. The question of the Buddhist as to why only a seed is capable of producing a sprout can be replied to by the rival theorists by stating that there are some unknown causes (Adṛṣṭakaraṇāni) also along with the known causes. And it should not be argued that the unknown cause alone is the cause when known causes also are definitely noted. That is why the Logician accepts Adṛṣta (the unknown) as one of the causes in general of every product and this stand too is not against experience.

In the case of recognition (Pratyabhijña) also it is difficult for the Buddhist to say the same object is not recognised by the person as in his point of view, there is neither the object nor the knowledge nor which can be recognised or the person who can recognise or which can be recognised.

The Buddhist is of opinion that there is no separate object external to the knowledge as, in the case of invalid knowledge there is no external object (to be perceived) but even then there is (invalid) knowledge. Hence he says objects are independent of knowledge. He holds that the desire of the percipient born of Avidya is responsible for the presentation of the object. A reply to this has already been given that simple desire cannot produce an object as we see in experience though it may be presented in the particular knowledge. The object in erroneous knowledge is possible to be presented even with the help of a wrong association of facts (the serpent in a rope etc.) because of some defect in the causes of perception. But in the case of valid knowledge he cannot hold that if the persons desire to know a mat is there, and actually a pot only is there, a knowledge of mat is not produced at all or even if it is produced it is negated when he says 'this is not a mat but a pot.' And again it is difficult for the Buddhists to establish a negative knowledge of the form 'this is not a pot' etc. In such cases the Buddhist has to maintain that 'the negation of pot' (absence of pot) is the form assumed by the knowledge concerned (this is not Sat). Here it may be noted that negation has no form though the pot has one. If negation be of the form of another object like mat then the knowledge would be of the form 'This is a mat' but not 'This is not a pot.'

Hence at least in the pragmatic view the Buddhist should hold that the objects – like matter, quality, action etc. are there and that they are not momentary in which case he cannot satisfactorily explain any point of a theory without using such words as the object, white, black etc. and eating; running etc. which he is obliged to use in the statement of his theory of knowledge. Further if the invalid cognition (Bhrānti) with regard to objects, as a cognition is destroyed in the next minute, how then does he account for the later action undertaken by a hallucinated person in the next minute and decide the invalidity of the cognition. That is why a Buddhist view is that a dependant existency (Pratitya samutpāde) has to be accepted for the pragmatic existence of this world of objects.

The Śāṅkarite Advaitin is of the view that while pure knowledge (Caitanya) is not produced but is eternal; what appears to be produced is the mental mode (Vṛtti) (the assumption of the form of the object by the mind) which has a beginning and an end. This Vṛtti is also called knowledge in a secondary sense as it is the determinate of knowledge (Jñānavacchedaka). This Vṛtti has a result (Phala) (in the form of the object and the consciousness determined by the internal organ becoming one (in other words, being in the same locus). Why Vṛtti is accepted is for the safe of removing the veil of ignorance or painting the internal organ with its own form. In the attainment of pure knowledge Phala is not necessary as there is no distinction of the cogniser, the cognised and cognition. The Śāṅkarite holds that the consciousness (Cit) is reflected in the mental mode (Vṛtti) which makes knowledge of objects possible. Here there seems to be a conflict that the pure consciousness (Cit) has the property of being reflected in the Vṛtti and being painted by it etc. which might go against his own stand that pure consciousness has no property at all. Even if the reflection be there actually who is the knower of this reflection? It should be the conscious self and thus knowledge would then be a property of the self (Jiva) to say that the mind may know the object is absurd as it is insentient along with the reflection produced.

Thus it appears plausible that as the Logician argues knowledge is the act of knowing (in circumstances favourable to it) whose effect is the knowing of the object concerned causes like the object light, sense organ - object contact etc. are the causes which form the activity form of knowing and the result part of it is the knowing (capacity of receiving the impression) of the object in the soul and reacting to the cognition of the object either by accepting its or renouncing it etc.). How the insentient object sense contact and the image produced become cognised (or produce desire for the object etc.) and kept in store in the form of an impression for future use, is to be admitted by positing that even insentient objects when they have a particular collocation of causes become sentient. Otherwise we cannot explain sentience as opposed to insentience or we have to suppose that sentience and insentience are two aspects of the reaction of objects. As to how the insentient self (of the Logician) is made sentient should be due to the cognition of the objects concerned. The physiological, the chemical, biological effects of the contact of the sense organ etc. and such other need not be estimated by him, nor is it his field to go deep into them. He is enough if he says the contact of the sense organ and to object etc. produce. Knowledge it is a mystery to actually point out what knowledge is from the points of view of any theory. I think in order to avoid this contingency, if we accept that a store of knowledge pieces is there and the Vṛtti or the assumption by the mind of the form of the object reveals that particular piece of knowledge is too combrous on the one hand and to ascertain why the Vṛtti calls forth only that part of the knowledge store alone is only any one's guess. That is why the Śaṅkarite maintains that pure consciousness or Brahman cannot be defined at all. The sages of old hence probably well understood the mystery of the theory of knowledge which is beyond the ken of human beings.

The Different Means of Valid Knowledge Criticised

In almost all the extant Darsanas only the means of valid knowledge (Pramānas) are discussed but not the means of knowledge in general (Jñāna karaṇa) and validity of knowledge separately, such a discussion would have simplified matters on epistemology and clarity assured for the readers.

The Buddhist also like all other Darsanakāras describes means of valid knowledge (Pramāṇa) as (knowledge that does not disagree (with the concerned object). That is to say that knowledge which gets for us the object (and that means only) which has the capacity of securing the object for us the object activity means valid knowledge. His idea is that such knowledge is the means and a knowledge of the object is the result (Pramāṇaphala) (Arthasamvitti). Of course this is the worthy case with the Sautrantika and the

Vaibhasika who accept external objects. In the case of the idealist (Yogacara) however, it is a knowledge of itself that is the result. Thus the idealist admits the same (valid) knowledge to be the means and the result, both. Generally speaking the means is what produces the knowledge or makes the object known and the result is its product (a knowledge of what is known) but the Buddhist does not admit this relation between the two – the knowledge as means and the (same) knowledge as a result. He does not admit the cause and effect relationship as that would entail the defect of the cause and the effect being present in one single knowledge at the same time which is absurd. He accepts, instead, in this case, the relation of the determinant and the determined (Vyavasthāpyavyasthāpakabhāva). His idea is that the same knowledge while it assumes the form of the object (blue etc.) or determines the object as so and so is deemed a determinant and the same knowledge when it is known (as e.g. this blue) is the determined or he holds a definite knowledge of the object (Adhyavasaya) as such and such is the means and the cognition of the object is its result. This is the Buddhist stand on Vyavastha. This is possible only when the Vikalpapratyaya comes into play.

Now here a question arises whether an individual knowledge is one or has parts. Because the Buddhist accepts knowledge also as momentary (like all other objects) he should not break the same knowledge into two distinct pieces with two different Sabdabodhas (import) which require two minutes at least to be produced. Even if it were two knowledge pieces combined into one yet the former one, the assumption of the form of knowledge by the object is not possible for the previous knowledge as it would have been destroyed as soon as the previous knowledge was produced. As per his maxim that one knowledge (Citta) produces another, he has to explain how the next knowledge can assume the form of the new object (say blue) as without this (content of) blue there can be no knowledge for, to the Buddhist knowledge is endowed with a form (content). If knowledge were there already it could assume a form but the former knowledge (say of mat) was destroyed and the new knowledge has not yet been formed, how could such a knowledge assume the blue colour? If, it be rejoined by the Buddhist that the knowledge was produced along with the object (blue) then it is not knowledge that can be regarded as having assumed the blue colour but it may be the mind or something else but not the whole knowledge that assumes the form of the object (blue). Even it knowledge becoming blue as a (Kriyā) is presumed (by him) as a knowledge that knowledge should be of the type 'This, my knowledge is blue' (the contingency here is that it takes two minutes for knowledge to assume the colour one minute and to cognise it in the next one). As the Buddhist holds the knowledge 'This, my knowledge is blue' should produce a knowledge 'This object is blue as my knowledge is blue.' Otherwise what relation can there be between the two knowledge pieces? Does he mean from any knowledge any other knowledge can be produced? Definitely not. Thus the latter knowledge should be an inference of the type 'This object is blue as it has given a blue colour to my knowledge.' This should be a case of cause and effect (and not identity) that is responsible for the inference as per his stand. Thus the contingency here is that the two above mentioned knowledge pieces come under cause and effect (Tadutpatti) relationship in inference but not as Vyavastapaka and Vyavasthapya.

Further what is presently required here is 'What is it that actually and directly produces valid knowledge (Pramana). The Buddhist replies 'it is' knowledge which does not fail to correspond with the object (on hand). This is only valid knowledge but not its means which is under our enquiry. The proper reply is how such a knowledge is produced. If the Buddhist stand is that the means and the result are one and the same (knowledge) the defects as mentioned above are sure to creep in. Even the Jaina who accepts the relation of the determinant to the determined between the activity of the subject (Bodha) and that with reference to the object undertaking of activity with the object should infer the same with the help of Karyakaranabhava (Kramabhāva) only and not otherwise.

In the view of the Mīmāmsaka the means of valid knowledge is the object sense organ contact along with the mind though for Prabhakara the mind is atomic in size and for Bhatta it is all-pervasive. Mind is also a sense organ for Bhatta as it is the direct cause of pain, pleasure etc.

Almost all the realist orthodox thinkers accept the sense-organ contacts along with the self-mind contact as the cause of perception. The self-mind contact is the cause of all types of knowledge.

Light also is needed as an auxiliary cause of visual perception though in the perception of darkness it is not needed but the sense organ-object contact of the eye with darkness (Tamo-bhava) should be Viśesaṇa Visesyabhava (as absence of light is perceived).

To the Sāṃkhya the means of valid knowledge is the material Buddhivṛtti (assumption of the form of the object by the intellect) that forms the means of knowledge with the help of the reflection of the Cit in it. As Buddhi is only material in its nature the reflection in it of the Cit is admitted by him to make it sentient or at least to have a semblance of sentience in it. The intellect is a very clear substance which is capable of assuming the form of the object to be cognised and of reflecting the Cit (consciousness) in it. The Vṛtti itself is clear and is capable of producing a reflection of the object and hence the particular object alone is known, not all. The sense organ also is to be associated with the Buddhi as otherwise the yellow hue in a conch (an invalid knowledge) cannot be explained. To the Logician the means of a piece of valid knowledge is only some other knowledge in the case of Inference, Analogy and Verbal Testimony but in the case of perception the means is the sense organ or the contact of the sense organ and the object concerned (new school). This is so because soon after the contact knowledge is produced, but for the validity of knowledge the means is the merit of the sense organ etc. for inference it is the correctness of a knowledge of concomitance etc. By valid knowledge he means the presence of that (property) in the locus of that (property).

Further the question stands, on the Buddhist view, how the latter Vikalpajñana (constructive knowledge) is produced from the earlier indeterminate knowledge or sense knowledge. The latter knowledge is of the type of Svalaksaṇa and the former is of the genus (Sāmānya) type. The latter knowledge is destroyed soon after it is produced. To this the Buddhist reply is that the perceiver does not make a distinction between the former and the latter knowledges (Ananyatādhyevāsaya). Here the contingency is that the Vikalpajñāna is not valid as it perceives the same object over again and this invalid knowledge is expected to induce one to action. But the Buddhist reply is that as both the knowledges belong to the same series (Santanaikya) Vikalpajñāna also may be taken as valid knowledge. But how can such a Santana be an existent?

Again the Buddhist idealist regards the (content or) form of the knowledge as (also designated Yogyata as the means (of knowledge) and knowledge of itself (knowledge) as its consequence or result (Phala). In such a case if the form of the knowledge is different from knowledge it cannot be a means, according to him, as it is insentient (and as knowledge alone is sentient). If form be the same as knowledge there should be total identity between the two knowledge pieces. Thus in spite of Vikalpa knowledge cannot be treated in one sense as the means and in another as the result. Further in any experience the means cannot be identical with the result as the one has to precede the other. Pramāna is the cause and Pramā is the result, the affix Lyut in the word Pramāna signifies only the immediately preceding cause (Karaṇa).

Further the Buddhist idealist defines Pratyakṣa (perception) as that (knowledge) which is devoid of mental (or verbal) constructions and which is not invalid (Abhrānta).[3] Here in the definition of the means of valid knowledge (Pramāṇa) there are two parts validity and the nature of its immediately preceding cause (Karanatā). The above definition does not speak of the validity part positively but shifts it to be detailed by the word (Abhrānta) (as that is not invalid). But validity has to be defined by the theorist as such and such. Validity cannot be definiteness of knowledge (Nirṇāyatva) as the Buddhist holds because it prompts one to action. If definite knowledge were identical with valid knowledge, even a definite knowledge that a pot is a mat (invalidly cognised) cannot achieve for us what a pot is desired to achieve for us though the perceiver undertakes activity. Thus the Buddhist will have to accept as real the object (Artha) and its activity (Kriya) served by it in order to establish the validity of knowledge.

Another doubt on the Buddhist standpoint is how the perception which is devoid of all mental construction (Kalpanā) is capable of cognising the object as different from all other genera of objects and from other objects of its own genus as the Buddhist has neither genus nor (even if it be accepted by him in some way) can it be cognised in the momentary knowledge along with the object itself in one moment.

The Jaina holds that the means of knowledge can only be knowledge even in the case of perception but not the sense contact as held by the Logician etc. for, even when the sense contact is there without knowledge there can be no (correct) understanding (valid knowledge). Here it may be noted that knowledge itself is the cognition and our effort now is to know from which immediate cause (valid) knowledge is produced. Thus this view appears to beg the question on hand. Not only does the knowledge know the object but itself also (Svaprakasa). Otherwise, the Jaina argues that knowledge cannot be known at all. He does not accept any knowledge which is not self-revealed. The Jaina also is of the view that what is already (previously) known cannot constitute a means of knowledge (Pramāṇa). For a criticism of this view the Logician's theory herein may be consulted. By the word 'Nirnaya' (definite knowledge) in his definition of Pramāṇa he intends to exclude doubt and invalid knowledge too. He defines what the above two cognitions are but not in such detail as the Logician does. To the Jaina the means of knowledge (perception) is removal of the veil and the result of it is the knowledge of the object. Between these two he holds there is the relation of the Vyavasthapaka and the Vyavasthapya and hence there is no discrepancy in the theory. The Śaṅkarite holds like the Mīmāṃsaka that by valid knowledge is meant knowledge of an object that has not been contradicted. This books better than definition given by the Buddhist inasmuch as it speaks of knowledge of an existent object (in the Vyāvahārika state) which is not disproved by any other practical means of valid knowledge such as perception, inference etc. Here the object, its qualities (though not genus) etc. are accepted by the Śaṅkarite and hence there is no difficulty in comprehending valid knowledge.

It may be noted here that if pure Cit is revealed all knowledge and not that of the individual (object only should be produced in the perceiver as pure Cit has no parts in it. If Vṛtti is responsible for the individual knowledge, pure Cit must be accepted to have parts in it or that it is affected by the Vṛtti changes. The objection on the Vedantist view is that the mind is stated to be the material cause of knowledge and the Pramānas etc. are efficient causes as they are all material in nature. According to Vedantins the Vṛtti is responsible for the removal of the ignorance, connected with the object (pot etc.) whereas the reflection (Abhāsā) makes it (the object) known. It may be noted here that the Vṛtti, the knowledge produced, pleasure, pain etc. are all cognised by the witness consciousness (Saksin). No separate apperception is required.

The Means of Valid Knowledge

The means of valid knowledge (Pramānas) accepted by different schools of Epistemologists are like this. (1) The Cārvaka perception (Pratyaksa) alone, (2) The Buddhist-perception and Inference (Anumana), The Jain two - (Pratyaksa and Paroksa), (3) The Sāṃkhya the Yogin (like Manu) three including verbal Testimony (Āgama). The Logician accepts four inclusive of Analogy (Upamana) - Prabhākara (Mīmāṃsaka) - five including (Arthāpatti), Bhatta (Mīmāṃsaka) and some Vedantins - six including non-perception (Anupalabdhi) - the Paurāṇikas - eight inclusive of possibility (Sambhava) and heresy (Aitihya); Prabhakara – also experience (Anubhuti).[4]

It may be noted here that the additional means of valid knowledge accepted by other theorists are to be included in the compact few accepted by the theorists as has been pointed out in the critique on the Means of Knowledge appended of this work.

Perception is the only means of valid knowledge that is accepted by all theorists (though in the final view the Śaṅkarite denies all objects except Brahman. The comparative validity of the means of knowledge is discussed elsewhere here which may be noted.

In the definition of perception the Buddhist includes the phrase (Abhrāntam) (not hallucinational or false). He should then define what is false (Bhrānta) knowledge first and then speak of its negation. What is this Bhrānti which you want to avert from the definition? Is it the presence of some other property in the locus of that (object)? In case it is not his stand as he has no object (Dravya) in his ontology, neither has no genus (Jati) as constituting a class of objects. How is one then expected to know what valid knowledge is and what its means is? Though the Vaibhāṣika and the Sautrāntika have objects in their ontology; the Yogacara (idealist) has none excepting the object in the knowledge.

Though the Śaṅkarite accepts objects in the pragmatic state he also is of opinion that the entire world of objects is falsehood (Mithya). Even the cognition of falsehood is false which is finally dispelled along with all other false conceptions at the time of salvation. This view is maintained by him on the testimony of the Holy Text as also by inference etc. as he holds. As soon as the final mental mode is destroyed the Cit alone shines forth. The perception of the absence or Negation (of objects) (Abhāva) is nothing else but its locus e.g. the absence of pot is identical with the ground as the Prābhakara or the Buddhist holds. Wrong cognitions are due to defects in the sense organs or external defects like being too distant, too near etc. Invalid knowledge and its production are discussed under the particular epistemological theories concerned.

The actual knower in the Śaṅkarite view is the consciousness as determined by the (mental) mode of the Internal organ. The knowledge is only pure Cit. The known is what is reflected in the mental mode.

To the Sāṃkhya the knower is pure conscious being (Cetaṇa) who witnesses the mental mode the known is the object (which modifies the internal organ) and knowledge is the manifestation of the object by the reflection of the mental mode (Buddhist Vṛtti) in the conscious agent (Cetana).

Perceptual valid knowledge is accepted by all epistemologists. Negation or Absence (Abhāva) for the Logician is capable of being cognised by perception where the absence of the object is only an auxiliary cause. To argue as the Mīmāmsaka does that non-perception is the cause of the perception of Abhava may not hold good as non-perception is itself a negation like the Negation of the object (under question). The Buddhist does not accept Negation as it is not an existent as it cannot carry out any activity. It is not known how he would explain the absence of medicine at the proper time killing a person or atleast aiding his death. If absence of the pot were floor itself, then a sentence like 'I could not get water as there is no pot here' means 'I could not get water as the floor was here.' Further if Negation were of the form of the ground (locus) then the contingency is that even when the pot is perceived on the floor, there should be the absence of the pot also as it (absence of the pot) is considered identical with the floor. The question of the opponent that negation (of object) cannot be perceived as there is no contact of the eye etc. with the object is answered by admitting the Viśeṣya Viśesaṇabhāva contact of the eye with the object. The ground is the Visesya and the absence of the pot its Viśeṣana. The actual fact here appears to be that the perceiver desires to see a pot in a place at a particular time but his desire continues to be a desire (as long as the object is absent). This is the nature of Negation (of objects).

The Jaina views perception as a means of knowledge which is not intervened by another means to produce the result. In other words it appears to be similar to the view held by the Logician that knowledge which has a means different from knowledge is (produced) perception.

The Jaina, unlike the Logician contends that recognition is valid knowledge and cannot be brought under perception as it has something more than mere perceptual knowledge, a memory of the previous object which can never come under in sense organs perceptive activity. Hence recognition is a case of non-direct (Parokṣa) knowledge for the Jaina embracing an admixture of perception and memory.

The Buddhist makes out a case for recognition also in his epistemology in spite of his theory of momentariness of objects. He holds that a momentary object while getting destroyed produces another moment of the same kind which does not very much differ from the previous one (which has not been destroyed completely) and thus recognition could be explained. He also contends that recognition cannot be an admixture of memory and perception as there is the additional identity component in it. This is a case of (wrong) inference for him as this is treated under inference. But inference cannot be wrong for him and similarity (Sādrsya) (Sadṛsa vastu) cannot be defined by him as he has no genus, qualities etc. in his ontology.

In a similar way recollection also is a piece of invalid knowledge as objects change every minute and the object recollected is not the one perceived earlier.

But in experience we find the same man recognised as so and so was charged with crime and given punishment, so also in the case of memory. Hence the Buddhist view is against experience. The Jaina does not accept the view that recollection is false in which case inference itself will not be possible as it depends upon recollection of concomitance.

The Sāṅkarite includes Recollection and Recognition under Perception (Pratyakṣa), Recollection is considered invalid.

Under Pratyakṣa the Sāṃkhya, the Logician and the Mīmāṃsaka accept Indeterminate cognition out of necessity. The Logician holds that without an earlier knowledge (of Pot and) pothood in an indeterminate cognition, there can be no knowledge of their relation (inherence) all of a sudden in the determinate cognition where the pothood is known as related to the pot by inherence. If this be not accepted even without a knowledge of staff a man with a staff will have to be cognised by a person. The Indeterminate knowledge of the Buddhist is of the form of Svalaksana (the thing in itself) and it with he help of a next minute object in its continuation. But this takes two minutes for its activity. Then the name, class etc. of the object are recalled and it then becomes Determinate.

The other epistemologists do not accept such a distinction as indeterminate knowledge. As inducement to action (Pravṛtti) is provided by the Determinate knowledge only there is no point in denying the status of valid knowledge to it (Determinate knowledge) by the Buddhist.

To the Śāṅkarite pure Cit (Sudda Brahma) was no attributes or qualities (Nirguna) and hence a knowledge of Brahman is Indeterminate knowledge (which is valid). There is no distinction of the knower, the known and knowledge.

It is an intriguing question whether any knowledge can be produced without the help of words because we understand everything only verbally. But a child, a dumb man etc. do not use words but feel that there is something before them devoid of all properties which the Mīmāṃsakas and other describe as knowledge which grasps only the real existent (Vastu). That is why the child tries to grasp an object with the hand when it is seen, we don't know any use for it in practical life. The Buddhists criticism that only indeterminate knowledge is valid is unacceptable to the Jaina too. It is not quite clear whether the Buddhist holds that the knowledge of pot (perceived in the indeterminate cognition) is valid. How could this validity be known without giving the object (pot) a name, without a recollection of its Arthakriya etc. and thus without some Vikalpas.

Inference

The Cārvāka is of the view that there is no means of valid knowledge other than perception. The arguments of these thinkers and their allies may be summarised thus: Inference is based on concomitance and concomitance is expected to be unconditioned by any external adjunct (Upādhi). The absence of such an external adjunct cannot be easily ascertained as concomitance is expected to relate to a class which includes the objects of all places and all times beyond our experience. The negative type of concomitance in particular in the case of every inference cannot be fully established. That is why he holds, that certain inferences become invalid. Hence he holds that concomitance is not possible.

But here it must be noticed that in the absence of a determined adjunct (Niscitopādhi) he holds there could be a doubted adjunct (Śankitopādhi). To this the reply given by Udayana in the Nyayakusumānjali may be referred to.[5]

He further argues that concomitance cannot be an object of perception and hence not also an object of Inference. This objection is refuted by the Logician by accepting the supramundane contact (Alaukikasamikarsa) between the sense organ and the object. It can neither be a mental perception as mind cannot negotiate with an external object.

The materialist (Cārvāka) further argues that concomitance cannot be ascertained between the sense organ and the object in all cases (in spite of the fact that many such cases have been observed). If it were observed in all the cases (with help of the said contact) there is no need for inference again as concomitance has been already cognised. This objection is met by the Logician and others who hold that though the concomitance in general is cognised the particular concomitance between the particular object on hand and the particular minor term has not been cognised.

Though the Cārvāka may raise such other similar objections he will not be in a position to vindicate his position that inference is not a means of valid knowledge without himself accepting inference as a valid means as the above observation is not a case of perception.

It goes without saying that the Cārvāka who does not accept Inference as a means does not accept the other means of knowledge as well.

Inference has been accepted as a means of valid knowledge by all the epistemologists except the Cārvāka. It has been shown how untenable a stand it is since he himself cannot establish any theory like 'Perception alone is valid or Inference is not valid' as he cannot give a reason for it as this involves inference itself.

The question whether Inference is capable of cognising anything particular newly as it comprehends concomitance (Vyāpti) of all the objects of the kind. But this doubt can be set aside by maintaining that though the concomitance of the Vyāpya with the Vyāpaka is only general, the particular object is also inferred newly as a result. That is why Inference is to. be considered as comprehending the Sāmānya as well as the Viśeṣya. The Buddhist also admits that the Sāmānya in inference is succeeded by a mental cognition of Viśeṣa. The indeterminate knowledge cannot be a means of valid knowledge (Pramāṇā) as the Buddhist holds as it cannot determine Arthakriya unaided by determinate knowledge itself (as Pramāṇa).

The Jaina argues that the object sense organ contact cannot be a means of knowledge as it is insentient. The above in view is held by the Logician, the Mīmāṃsaka etc.

As regards concomitance (Vyāpti) the Buddhist accepts Tādātmya (identity) and effect from a cause (Tadutpatti) only as contributing to inferential knowledge but the Jaina not conceiving it as comprehensive, holds that Avinabhava (invariable connection) as the cause of inferential knowledge. There he accepts both being together (of two things–Simsapa and Vṛksa) (Sahabhāva) and coming one after another (Kramabhāva) as between smoke and fire. This view gives sufficient scope for yellow colour to serve as a mark (Liṇga) for sweet taste in a mango etc. which objection was raised even by the Logician against the Buddhist.

The Jaina on the other hand accepts Avinābhava as determined by Ūha (Tarka) as the means of inference and this is of not two types as the Buddhist holds but includes Svabhāva, Kāraṇa, Karya, Ekarthasamavayi and Virodhi. A knowledge of concomitance is not produced only by perception as some view, but by Inference too.

According to the Buddhist how is concomitance rendered possible, as he has no generalizing agent (Sāmānya) in his ontology. The Buddhist replies that his view of Sāmānya is different from that of the Logician who latter defines it as 'what is eternal, one and inherent in many' for, the former views Sāmānya as Exclusion (Apoha). That is to say the generality of a cow is the exclusion of non-cows. In fact to exclude non-cows we must have a knowledge of non-cow. Unless we know positively what a cow (the positive counterpart) is, we cannot conceive a non-cow. Thus the defect here appears to be instead of knowing only one object 'cow' positively, on the Buddhist view, we are expected to know all non-cows which is not only impossible in practice but also too prolix to argue. Another objection in this connection is that he speaks of exclusion of a different genus (Vijatiyam). If thus genus be accepted why should he not accept the less prolix cow genus itself as Sāmānya instead of exclusion of the non-cow.

In general, the three requisites of concomitance are a property being present in the Homologue and its absence in the Antilogue and its presence in the minor term. The Buddhist on similar lines accepts three conditions positive concomitance, negative concomitance and presence of the mark (Liṇga) in the minor term. This scheme ensures the correct means of Inference. The two others 'Abadhita Viṣayatvam' (noncontradictedness) and 'Asat pratipakṣatvam' (not having a counterbalancing property as advocated by the Logician are unacceptable to the Buddhist. So also to the Jains.

Negation, Abhāva (Anupalabdhi) is a means of knowledge for the Mīmāṃsaka. The Sāṃkhya includes it under perception as any transformation of any object except sentience are cognised by the sense organs only. The Buddhist does not accept negation at all as it is a non-entity (Avastu) and thus it cannot produce or give rise to anything at all much less valid, knowledge. The Jaina includes Negation under Manasajñāna because an object is expected, its negative counterpart is recollected.

Verbal Testimony

The Buddhist holds that testimony is a valid means of knowledge if it does not disagree with the external object. As there is no other relation between word and its meaning except Tadatmya or Tadulpatti. Neither of them is the relation concerned here as one is not identical with the other or the one is not produced from the other (the pot is not produced from the word 'pot' but from clay etc.). If it is held that the relation of the expresser and the expressed exists between the word and its meaning, then even a man who does not know the relation should know the meaning of the word. This argument of the Buddhist appears queer as the relation of the word and its meaning as known is the cause of verbal knowledge not as unknown. It cannot be held that there is a natural relation between the word and its meaning in which case the Buddhist argues, the same word 'pot' etc. in different languages should give the same meaning which is absurd.

The Jaina refutes the Buddhist view that testimony could be brought under Inference. If it be brought under a more comprehensive head like Paroksa it might be admitted.

The Sāṃkhya includes Analogy under Testimony and Inference. Presumption is included under inference. It goes without saying that the other Pramāṇas are covered by inference. But non-perception (Anupalabdhi) is included under perception.

Arthapatti

The Buddhist does not accept Arthāpatti (presumption) as a means of valid knowledge. He contends that if a particular valid view is to be related to a non-perceptional view it should be so by the relation of Tādātmya or Tadutpatti which would automatically bring Arthāpatti under the scope of inference.

The Jaina includes Arthāpatti, the means, under Inference. He argues that Inference for another's sake is of two types, positive and negative. In the former 'there is the pervader where there is the concomitant' (positive aspect); where the pervader is absent the concomitant (also) is absent (negative aspect). Between these two statements though there appears to be a verbal difference, in essence there is no difference at all. In the same way in the stock example the two sentences 'The fat Devadatta does not eat by day' and the one 'The fat Devadatta eats at night' give the same meaning in essence according to the maxim[6] "The meaning of a sentence is that which is intended by it." Thus even Arthapatti is to be included under inferences.

Abhāva

The Buddhist does not accept validity because negation itself has no form at all. Negation has no capacity to produce knowledge at all nor can it be the cause of any activity. It is insentient and hence it cannot decide anything at all. He accepts Abhāva concept as valid knowledge if it is of the form of its locus which is only a difference in name (as negation). His idea is that Negation (absence of pot etc.) as well as its locus (the floor etc.) are both eligible to be perceived by the sense organ (eye etc.) but as even then the pot is not perceived, it is inferred that the negation of pot is there. Here we see the fault of self-dependence (Atmāsraya) as the fact that the pot is not perceived, the reason, itself is a negation which has to be cognised. Hence it is only Abhāva concept which is a sense perception.

The Śaṅkarite admits Arthāpatti as a separate means of knowledge as the Mīmāṃsaka does. This he does because he does not accept inference of a negative type. The Logician includes it under inference.

The Jaina is of opinion that Abhāva (negation) is not a means of valid knowledge and he includes a knowledge of it under perception. He contends that a non-knowledge (negation) cannot be a means. Thus perception, in his view covers (the cognition of) Abhāva as well as the recollection of the opposite as it is invariably connected with the latter.

Analogy

The Buddhist finds fault with the Mīmāṃsaka who speaks of an object as qualified by similarity (Sādrśya) with another object. He does not accept similarity as different from the two similar objects. He questions whether it is a perceivable object or not. In the former case as it is not practically perceived it is not there. In the latter alternative how can an object not cognised at all serve as a mark in inference. Here a question appears pertinent as to how things are observed to be similar without similarity. Otherwise a sentient and unsentient object may be taken to be similar (which even the Buddhist does not accept). He holds that a nonsentient contact of the object and sense organ cannot be a means.

The Jaina includes Analogy the means, under recognition an indirect (Parokṣa) Pramāṇa. But the Logician hold that Analogy is of the type of a relation between an object and its designation, though the Mīmāṃsaka and the Śaṅkarite hold a different view about it. It may be noted here that Analogy does not comprehend identity between the past and the present objects but it comprehends only the similarity between the two different objects and consequently the name of the unknown object also.

Other Means of Valid Knowledge

The Jaina includes Memory, Recognition, Uha (responsible for Inference) and Verbal Testimony, under the means of valid knowledge called Paroksa. The Buddhist includes Testimony also under Inference. Memory for the Logician is the means of valid knowledge if it relates to a previous valid experience. Recognition for him (the Logician) is perception, while testimony is a separate means the word of a reliable person. Many theorists include Sambhava and Aitihya, under Inference.

Objects–Are They Real Existents

It is a very interesting and illuminative exercise to the intellect to go into the truth of the existence of objects and much of the philosophical and epistemological talent of theorists has since early times has been spent on this primary issue. It is true we find objects really existing around us and all the realists like the Logician, the Mīmāmsaka and a host of other thinkers aver that objects are really existent (and some of them are destroyed after a time). But the idealist especially the Buddhist (Vijñānavadin specially) holds that it is only knowledge that takes the form of the object (which is its own form) that is really existent. Apart from it there is no separate object. The Śaṅkarite is of opinion that the objects are mere fictitious entities which have no actual reality in them. They are not found, truly speaking, in their own locus. No relation can be established between the object and the knowledge which is not related to anything. The relation cannot be contact or Inherence. The relation of the object to the cognition (Viṣaya Visayibhāva) is not a relation inasmuch as it cannot be present in both the object and the cognition. Thus the Śāṅkarite speaks of pure knowledge without any content in it (Nirviṣaya) which is real. Others hold that there is no knowledge but has a content but knowledge has no form (Ākara) of its own. Let us try to go to some depth in assessing the value of these disputations.

To the Buddhist (idealist) there are no objects at all in this world. It is only knowledge (Citta) that takes the form of the object and appears to be external (to knowledge). Though the Sautrāntika and the Yogācara believe in the existence of objects (either as percepts or objects of inference) it is the idealist Buddhist (Vijñānavādin) that refutes the actual reality of (the existence of) objects. He holds that an object exists only as it is cognised. Thus the object is only a form of knowledge as it is cognised alongwith the cognition but not-something external to it. How, otherwise, could objects of the dream state and objects of the past and future cognised be explained? Even if objects were there, no relation could be established between the sentient knowledge and the insentient object. Neither of the two identity (Tādātmya) and the production (Tadutpatti) can be obviously stated to exist between the object and the knowledge concerned. The Śāṅkarite also, of course, takes a very active part in refuting objects and tows almost the same line of argument according to his own theory. Neither can inference (Samavāya) nor contact (Samyoga) be established between the knowledge and objects (as in future and past objects there is no contact), he holds. Further the Buddhist (idealist) argues that there is no possibility to admit objects as properties and then existence has been refuted by him, hence much less does its substantiate object exists.

The Buddhist's contention that there are no objects but knowledge alone as in the dream state there are no objects but only knowledge (of them) is not tenable for, the objects in the dream state could as well be accounted for by treating them as those recollected from the waking state experience due to some defect. But why should he deny the object which is practically experienced in life by one and all. Further says he the object did not exist (for us) as we had not cognised it does this mean that it is, therefore, the person or his knowledge that has cognised it on his or its own. Thus the same object should be existent for one and non-existent for another which stand is inconsistent with experience. It is a better stand to accept existence of the object. Further if knowledge cognises heat in a (hot) touch it must be admitted the knowledge is not (identical with knowledge) and the knowledge of heat or of hot water should give us a hot bath and not the external object which is contrary to experience. A Buddhist goes to tank to quench his thirst but the tank (a par of a knowledge itself) does not quench his thirst even if he has a knowledge 'I quenched my thirst' in the tank. Thus objects have to be physically admitted. A knowledge of medicine does not cure the Buddhist but the medicine as a physical entity. Then an object like a stone lying on the way of a passerby uncognised should not hurt his leg as it is really non-existent, as it is not known. Again if objects were not existent how could impressions (Vāsanās) which are quite essential to his theory formed? An impression needs the contact of the object with the knowledge concerned somehow. If impressions are held to be beginningless how is it that new impressions are formed only after new objects are invented? For example the non-existent impression of a Television set cannot be beginningless as it was not experienced as such previously. If it be admitted that some impressions are formed later the Anāditva of impressions held by him is at stake. Then again, in perception, we find the object of the knowledge in contact with light is cognised. If impressions are formed due to our innate desires (Icchaḥ) then desire would be another reality (existant) and a seat of desires and a cause for their arousal would be embarrassing to the Buddhists. No light is necessary for past or future objects or dream state as they are recollected objects. When such a perceived (Dṛṣṭa) cause is present for perception it is injudicious to believe that an unseen impression (Adṛuṣṭavāsana) is the cause. It has also been shown how the impression also cannot be formed without a previous experience of the object concerned. Again when he sees a broken pot does the Buddhist posit that the pot (object) is broken or the knowledge (or pot) is broken? What does breaking of knowledge mean? Knowledge cannot have a form as without a corresponding object he holds. If it has a form after the distribution of the knowledge in the second minute, according to him, there should be a knowledge which has no form; or he has to admit that an impression of its own accord without any cause has been aroused. Further if one pot is destroyed and consequently the knowledge is destroyed the knowledge of another pot should not be produced as the second object is not there at all and the previous knowledge is destroyed. Even if it be argued that the previous impression is responsible for cognising the second pot, then the impression should be held to be different from a knowledge and his theory that every object is of the form of knowledge or is identical with knowledge is at stake.

Further there is the cognition 'I know the pot (object)' etc. but not 'I know the knowledge' or 'I know the knowledge or the knowledge, pot, and the pot.' Further there is no identity (Abheda) spoken of between pot and knowledge ('this knowledge is pot'); on the other hand there is the differential relation (Bheda Sambandha) of the form 'this is a knowledge of pot and not that of a mat.' Further without objects there is no criterion to establish difference in objects as pot, mat etc. as knowledge is one and the same persisting in all objects alike. If objects be not there even according to him how can casual efficiency (Arthakriyā Kāritva) be cognised? Again why should the Buddhist wait for a minute to cognise Arthakriyā Kāritva to establish the validity or otherwise of knowledge. If the knowledge were of the form of the objects, the same knowledge could have cognised causal efficiency also. If the difference in cognition like pot, mat could not be due to objects, it should a much be due to light, contact of the sense organ etc. which are also the causes of the production of knowledge which is absurd.

Further the contention of the Buddhist that unless knowledge (also) is known Pramā (validity of knowledge) and Apramā (invalidity) will not be known, is far from truth as it is only the object (as known) that is responsible for validity or invalidity of knowledge and not the knowledge known. Knowledge, by its very existence (Swarūpa Satī) is responsible for Pramā or Apramā but not a knowledge of it. The object only should be known (Jñātaḥ).

The Jaina is of the view that there are objects and that they stand for some time. How otherwise can a momentary object serve causal efficiency if its ceases to exist the next moment it is produced. It is an existent entity that has an order in time and place without this order how can a series (Santana) be produced even from the Buddhists points of view. It should not be urged that moments (Ksaṅas) are responsible for the series as the series itself is an non-entity (Avastu). Even if it be an existent moments by themselves cannot produce any speciality (Viśesa) in the objects concerned they all serve momentary and hence objects exist and are not momentary.

In the Jaina's opinion an object (Dravya) is the object of a means of knowledge which is produced, continues to exist and is destroyed (Dravya paryaya). That is the real existent as it is what is responsible for Arthakriyā. Acceptance etc. of objects (Artha) is possible only if the object has the capacity to do some work.

To the Sāṃkhya all objects except purusa are constituted by the three elements of Sattva, Rajas and Tamas. To the Logician those are objects which are possessed of qualities or action. Even the self and the mind are much objective in nature as their other counterparts. They are made of atoms (except those that are eternal).

The Śaṅkarite is of opinion that in the real sense (Pāramārthika Satta) there is no object at all, much less qualities etc., the one and only one Brahman of the form of pure consciousness is real. All the three forms of Sat (existence), Cit (consciousness) and bliss (Ānanda) are one and the same and that one is Brahman. Knowledge is existence and it is bliss. There is no distinction among these which may be doubted to be different attributes, even if objects were there no relation could be established between the object and the knower (Dṛṣya and Dṛk)[7], even Visaya-Viśayibhava relation is decried.

As we have seen above it is only Brahman of the form of pure consciousness (Suddha Cit) without a second that exists in the real sense all else – this entire universe with all the Gods, men and materials (all objects) is a mere figment of our imagination due to Māya. Even though Māya is beginningless (Anādi) it is finally liable for destruction and every one after final release is one with Brahman or is Brahman itself.

But Māya in his view cannot be said to be real in its true sense. It cannot be defined like the highest self Brahman or pure consciousness, cannot be defined. All our knowledge of the objective world – this is a mat, this is a pot etc. is what is called Jñāna in its secondary sense. They are all cognitions having mental modes (Vṛtti). These Vṛttis with their objective contents are also designated Jñāna because they determine knowledge (Jñānavacchedaka).

Quite in consistence with the theory of their inexplicable Māya they contend that there is a three tier reality in this world. In the Vyāvaharika (verbal usage) stage of existence all the objects appear to be there though in essence they do not exist (i.e. though they are not either true or permanent); unless this stand was accepted by the Śaṅkarite there was no scope for him to come to the pragmatic level of cognition of objects. He has his own peculiar theories of pure consciousness, pragmatic existence and illusional existence. Due to a beginningless hallucination (Bhrānti) or (Adhyāsa) the entire world of objects is projected before the mind and the relation between objects and knowledge is false (Ādhyāsika)[8] and once the illusion is dispelled shines forth pure consciousness which is no other than ones' ownself. The objects of the dream state are created, he posits, and are latter destroyed. The entire world of objects is sublated by the dawn of Brahman-Knowledge. This is all in accordance with the Vedic dictum 'Ekamevādvitīyam Brahma.' Though most of the arguments countering the Buddhist stand on objects as given above apply to the Śāṅkarite, their acceptance of the Vyāvahārika reality (Pragmatic reality) has saved the theory from becoming too idealist and unpragmatic.

Further, if knowledge, as the Mayavadin holds, is eternal and without content then there should be no difference in knowledge pieces. If different Vṛttis, on the other hand, are held to be responsible for the differences in knowledge, Vrtti should be another reality (at least temporarily) along with pure knowledge. Even if this position is accepted at the pragmatic level how could it be that the relationless pure knowledge gets related to the Vṛtti by reflecting itself in the Vṛtti?[9] If it is all due to hallucination (Adhayāsa) the theorist has to reply whether Adhyāsa itself is one other real along with Brahman. If it is held to be (somehow) a second reality along with Brahman how could it be that one of such beginningless positive entities is considered eternal and not the other? If it is due to testimony of the Holy text of course there can be no rational answer. Further if the objects of the world and Nescience (Avidya), both be without a beginning then the Śāṅkarite cannot argue that the latter one is the cause of the former. Further in case Jivacaitanya is not covered (Anavṛtti) then the Śāṅkarite admits that Vṛtti is for the sake of giving such and such form (of the object) to the knowledge in which case separated objects will have to be accepted by him.

If the Buddhist holds, knowledge is endowed with some form (Sākāra) (which only is called the object), knowledge and form (of the object) cannot be simultaneous entities as knowledge is expected to take the form of the object which is thus a cause of taking the form. If knowledge is produced later than its form than the form (of the object) becomes another existent. Even the relation of the determined to the determinant is not possible as the determinant is a cause of the determined and hence is earlier and the momentariness of his knowledge is jeopardised. Again the Buddhist maintains that one knowledge produces another. How could this be? For, the knowledge of pot cannot produce a knowledge of mat in a different series. We have to account for the difference in the knowledge as due to objects (either perceived or remembered).[10] If knowledge alone were responsible for cognition why not light also be considered as knowledge.

Many arguments of a high calibre of disputation have been carried out on this theory of reality of objects as on many others. The Advaitasiddhi and the Laghuchandrika have bombarded the rival theories of the dualists (object realists) in the face of unapproachably subtle disputations. The theories and their disputations vehemently vie with each other in scholaisticity, sincerity of purpose and are very interesting but brain fagging. Thus it is with much diligent study that even a great scholar should venture to criticise the Śāṅkarite views as set forth in those works. Hence the author proposes to leave the discussion on the matter to the aspirants themselves.[11]

In the Sautrāntika view which accepts the momentariness of objects, an existent object of a momentary nature cannot get related with knowledge of the momentary nature as they cannot co-exist.

Thus it appears it cannot be denied that objects are different from knowledge and that some of them exist for some time at least and are grasped with the help of knowledge. It is better to hold with the Logician that when all the causes of knowledge (including the object or its impression) are present the knowledge of the object is produced.

The Properties of Knowledge

According to the Śāṅkarite, knowledge is the only real existent in the universe. All other objects are figments of our mind – an illusion. It has no properties as there is no second to it. Even existence (Sat) and bliss (Ānanda) are one and the same with knowledge or Cit. The distinction shown in the definition of Brahman as Sat, Cit and Ānanda is simply to assert by implication that the Brahman is not different from any one of these three. In the pragmatic reality of (Vyāvaharika sattā) the different properties of knowledge are accepted by him. It is only after the final mental mode (Carama akhaṇḍā kāravṛtti) that knowledge remains in its own pure form.

The Logician thinks that it is necessary to hold that a substratum is needed for knowledge and by judicious exclusion the soul is the seat of knowledge. The soul is of two kinds – The Supreme soul (Paramātma) and the individual soul (Jīvātma). All knowledge is eternal, valid and immediate (Aparoksa) for the supreme soul while the knowledge of the individual soul stands (generally) for two minutes and is destroyed in the third. The knowledge of the Jīvātman is not eternal but is produced (Janya) and also false at times. It is a particular property of the soul which has eight specific properties (Guṇas) in addition to its general properties. Knowledge does not completely pervade its object (Avyāpyavṛtti). It is produced in one minute, stays in the second and get destroyed in the third (generally) unless it is a case of knowledge in succession (Dhārāvāhikajñāna). It has invariably an object as its content (Ṣaviṣayaka). Knowledge has no form. The object alone has a form.[12] This is quite against the Buddhist stand. It also becomes an object of apperception (in a knowledge). It is one of the possessors of object (Viṣayins) along with desire, activity and impression (Bhāvanā). It is present as long as the soul-mind contact is present. An ascertainment of the absence of an object in a certain locus obstructs a knowledge of the object as also the absence of its pervading object. It is finally the true knowledge of objects that is responsible for final salvation (Apavarga).

To the Sāṃkhya also knowledge is one of the products of premordial matter, rather the first product without which no usage of words (Vyavahārā) probably is possible. It is finally the knowledge called (Viveka) that leads him to salvation (Kaivalya). The self as distinct from nature (Prakṛti) is the intelligent one (Cetana).

To the Mīmāṃsaka a knowledge of the Vedic ritual and the corresponding performance is responsible for emancipation and not knowledge direct. Knowledge derived from Vedic sentences induces us to activity and the performance activities (Karma) results in the final goal (be it heaven or any other thing). This is the only theorist who gives prominence to action (Karma) rather than to knowledge as he is an authority on Vedic sentences and their meanings and purport. Even to the Buddhists it is a knowledge of the four noble truths that brings the final salvation (Nirvāna) by dispelling all innate Vāsanas. To the Mādhyamika nothing can be established though knowledge is considered to lead to Nirvana finally. To the Yogācāra there is only knowledge in this world and no object. For the others knowledge as well as objects exist either externally for some or inferentially for some others. However it is with the help of a knowledge of the four truths liberation is attained. But who is it that attains salvation. But they hold void remains as there is no permanent self.

To the Jaina also knowledge is of great importance. Pure knowledge (Kevala jñāna) gained by the removal of the veil of all cruel actions (Ghātikarma) with the help of the three jewels (as they are called) leaves the Ātman of the nature of luminousness, gets a knowledge of entire universe without the help of any other sense organ and the like. How such a soul could be obscured by Karma is on the analogy of knowledge being vitiated by drinking wine etc. How such a soul could undertake action is because it is eternal and can transform itself (Parināṃinitya).

To the Buddhist (Vaibhaṣika) object is an existent (Sat) though knowledge is expected to assume its form and present itself. To the Sautrantika objects are inferred and then it must be different category in a way but to them also objects are known through knowledge. To the Yogācāra knowledge is the only existent. It cannot be stated to be a Dravya, a Guna or any other category as they have been refuted by him. Then the Paramartha sat (the true existent) is only knowledge. Of these thinkers (Yogācāra's) some are of opinion that knowledge itself appears as pot, mat etc. due to difference in impressions (Vasanā vaicitiya). While some others of them hold that Avidya (ignorance) is responsible though by itself knowledge has no form (Ākāra) of its own. It is a dependent reality (Sanvṛttisatya). Thus some of them are Sakāravadins. At any rate both of them agree that there is neither the known nor the knower but the knowledge is at ways self-revealed. Thus the knower and the known are due to mental construction for some and for the others true knowledge is like a spotless pearl (Suddhasphatika) and objects are false forms imposed on them.

The Nihilist (Mādhyamika) however refutes the reality even of knowledge as it cannot be established as a Sat. A Sat (existent) is expected to have either a particular nature or different natures.

It should not however be urged that knowledge has no corporeal body whereas an object has, as the Buddhist holds that knowledge endowed with a form (Sākārajñāna) is to be called a corporeal one. The only difference as the idealist views is that he holds objects are internal but his opponents hold that they are external. But it is this that makes all the difference.

Self-revelation of Knowledge

The Śaṅkarite, the Jaina and the Buddhist hold that knowledge is self-revealed (Svaprakāśa). The word Svaprakāśa (revealed by the knowledge itself. 'On the very face of it appears to be self-contradictory'[13] as the same knowledge activity has to reveal the object in addition to itself (the knowledge itself). In fact two different objects (classes) cannot be revealed in one and the same moment. Again if the same knowledge is the cause of its own revelation there is the absurdity of holding that knowledge is not only the subject (revealer) of the activity of knowing but also its object (by revealing itself).[14] Further unless the knowledge activity be completed there can be no knowing of it. Hence knowledge is not known alongwith the knowing of the object. If the knowledge is held to be known after the knowledge activity is completed on the Buddhist view as the knowledge has already been destroyed by the next minute it cannot be known at all. If the knowledge persists for more than a moment there may be a case for knowing the knowledge but we need some other causes for it separately a desire to know the knowledge, a contact, a recollection of the object of knowledge etc. It cannot be argued that the same Samyoga contact with the eye is enough to produce knowledge of knowledge also. Further the Anuvyavasaya should be of the form 'I know the object and the knowledge too which is not experienced in life. Further the knowledge were self-revealed we should know other knowledge also.

The argument that knowledge is self-revealed by its own like light (as the nature of light is such) does not satisfy us as light is only a helping cause (Sahakāri karana) of knowledge production only helping the eye to be in contact with the object so that the object may be revealed, but when light itself is desired to be the object of knowing as it directly contacts with the eye only the space there is seen but the light which covers it shines forth but not the space which it covers completely. In fact a Sahakarin does not require the help of another Sahakarin for its own cognition.

But Buddhist view that Svaprakāsita or self-revelation is of the form of not being an insentient object[15] has the fault of self-dependence (Ātmāsraya) as unless insentience is known Svaprakasita is non known and vice versa. He takes recourse to the above argument as the defect of one and the same object (knowledge) being the subject and object of the activity of knowing which he admits is in cognition. Hence he advocates that between the above stated two aspects of being the subject and object of the same activity of knowing there is no cause and effect relationship but only the determinant-determined relationship (Vyavasthāpya vyavesthāpakabhāva). But it has been shown how this relation informed by him cannot but be a cause and effect relationship only which is absolutely necessary to infer the relation as Tadātmya is ruled out between the two. Further the Buddhist points out that a particular cause (Hetuviseṣa) responsible for the nature of the object is the determinant of what is determined by it is Vyavasthapya (the determined). But unless particular cause is identified he cannot maintain it.

Actually when we say light reveals itself, it does not mean the light is the actual revealer (but only the self according to the Logician or knowledge according to the Buddhist) but is only an accessory for revelation. Light is not the knower but the helper of the eye and the consequent knowledge. It is only a helping cause. Hence actually in this case there is no subject-object relation at all. Indeed light does not reveal itself to itself. So also knowledge does not reveal itself to itself. Several other definitions of self-revelation have been attempted. Some of them are refuted by the authors themselves[16] and the final views established. One such accepted definition is that the self-revelation of knowledge is what is the cause of the usage of words (Vyavahāra kāranatvam or more precisely Vyavahareyogyatvam) while not itself being the object of knowledge. But there is a difficulty here for the Śaṅkarite (and for the Buddhists and others too) as he thinks that knowledge should be known before it is used for practical purposes and that hence it should be self-revealed. But this knowledge of knowledge is not necessary for the usage of words or practical purposes for it is enough if the knowledge is there (i.e. if it exists, Svarupasat) but may not itself be known (Jñāta). It is enough if the object is known for us (not the knowledge). That is to say e.g. This is a pot (i.e. a knowledge of pot, the object) is enough for the purpose but not a knowledge of the knowledge 'I have a knowledge of the pot' or 'I know the object pot' we say only the object is[17] known but not 'I have known the knowledge of pot in me) which latter is only an apperception.

To the other epistemologists knowledge becomes an object of knowledge and is either cognised by apperception (to the Logician) or by inference (to the Bhāṭṭa).

Varieties of Knowledge

The common varieties of knowledge are valid knowledge (Pramā) and invalid knowledge (Apramā). Apramā is again of three types doubt (Saṃśaya), false knowledge (Viparyaya) and Tarka (Reductio ad absurdum). There is again the division into doubt

(Saṃśaya) and ascertainment (Niścaya)... etc. Under perceptional knowledge, determinate and indeterminate knowledge have already been discussed herein. Another division as practical or normal (Laukika) and supernatural (Alaukika) are accepted by some schools under Pratyakṣa. The distinction between experience (Anubhava) and recollection (Smṛti) has been drawn by the Logician in detail. As there is not much of controversy about these divisions they need not be expatiated further here.

The knowledge of the three states – waking, dream and deep sleep states the forte of the Vedantins is another division. Herein the Logician argues that the dream state knowledge is all false (Ayathārtha) and is of the form of recollection (Smṛti). Such a knowledge is due to a particular vitiation of the soul-mind contact – the contact between the mind and the Nadi (tube) called the Medhyā. This contact is effected when the mind is situated in the region connecting the Puritat (wherein situated the mind induces sleep) and its outer area. Why dreams are produced may be accounted for by a reference to one's own unseen (Adṛṣṭa), the vitiation of the three humours and constant thinking of particular objects. In the dream knowledge too the individual soul is the inherent cause, the Doṣa etc. the instrumental (Nimitta) and dream, the non-inherent cause. The Vaiśeṣika agrees that it is a mental perception occasioned by the supernormal contact Jñāna lakṣaṇa. The Sāmkhya holds that dream is only a modification of the intellect (Buddhi). The Māyāvādin Vedāntin also holds the same view but the accepts this is all false knowledge though he accepts that dream objects are produced and are false as the Veda declares. To him even the waking state knowledge is as false as the dream state knowledge, the only existent being Brahman. Other Vedantins also entertain a different view regarding dream state knowledge.

Knowledge is considered by the Buddhist as having form (Sākarā). The form is that of the object but the fact is that object itself is of the form of knowledge. Every determinate knowledge has also some content. The indeterminate knowledge also has for its content Svalakṣaṇa. It is the form of blue assumed by the knowledge that decides the knowledge of blue. All knowledge is self-revealed. No other need to reveal it.

To the Logician, the Mīmāṃsaka etc., knowledge is formless (Nirākāra). The object is real and it has a form. This form of the object is cognised by knowledge. Every cognition also has a content (Saviṣaya). There is no knowledge which is contentless (Nirviṣaya).

Knowledge is revealed by another knowledge (apperception or inference).

To the Vedantin (Advaitin) knowledge in the pragmatic reality has a content, but in reality pure knowledge is contentless. Pure knowledge gets reflected in the mental mode (Vṛtti) and the result (Phala) of it is the knowledge empirically gained and this knowledge is cognised by the witness consciousness (Sākṣi) pure knowledge has neither content nor form. Nor can it be defined as it is the knower. The knowing agent (Dṛk) can never be defined.

To Prabhākāra knowledge has a content but it is self-revealed. Even the ego(s) is cognised along with the object. Rāmānuja also thinks all knowledge has content in it.

There is another kind of division Vṛttijñāna and Svarūpajñāna as enunciated by the Śāṅkarite. He thinks that the former one is called knowledge because it happens to determine knowledge though it is not actual knowledge. The Viśiṣtadvaita speaks of knowledge as a property (Dharma) and a substrate of properties (Dharmin).

Knowledge and Its Sub-Divisions

Knowledge is of different kinds or classes. Let us note some of them as classified by the Logician.

Valid and Invalid Knowledge: Valid, true or correct knowledge may be defined as one having that (a particular property), as the attribute (Prakara) in the locus of that (Tadvati). Hence validity (of knowledge) has been defined by the Logician as given below (See F.N.).[18] If you see a pot and cognise pothood in it it is valid knowledge. This kind of knowledge is called Pramā and it has Pramātva or Prāmāṇya in it. Invalid knowledge or false or incorrect knowledge may be defined as one wherein an attribute is noticed in the locus of its absence[19] e.g. If you see a pot and notice mathood in it (which property is not there at all) it is invalid knowledge. It is called Bhrama or Viparyayajñāna.

Definite Knowledge – (Niścayajñāna): This is knowledge which has a particular property as attribute (Prakāra) but which has not the absence of it (i.e. the property). This may be valid or invalid. Still it is of the type of (definite) knowledge.

Doubt: This is knowledge which cognises more than one mutually opposed properties in one and the same substrate (Dharmin). In the same object one apprehends two mutually opposed properties e.g. Is this a serpent or a rope? Hence in the same rope (not cognised as such) both ropehood and snakehood are perceived as attributes. Though ropehood and snakehood are not mutually opposed to each other, it must be admitted that there are two alternatives here opposing each other. Is this the locus of snakehood or is it not? And also 'Is it the locus of ropehood or its absence?' A doubt is generally produced by not noticing the uncommon property (Asādhāranadharma), noting the object (Dharmin) and by an alternative arising in the mind due to the knowledge of a controversial statement 'Is it a serpent or a rope etc.[22] In the case of doubt the two forms of the doubt are equally strong so much so they don't permit a definite knowledge to arise. A doubt is a sense-perception (and a definite knowledge) as it arises from a proximity (Sannikarṣa).

Viparyayajñāna: It is another name for one kind of invalid knowledge called Bhrama. This is a case of definite knowledge which cognises a property not present in the substrate as present in it. e.g. 'This is a snake' where there is really a rope present.

Āhāryajñāna: This is a type of knowledge which is produced in an individual due to his desire even when there is a knowledge of its stultification (Bādha)[23] e.g. 'This is Moon'[24] with reference to the face of the beloved. The lover, it may be noted here, knows that it is the face of the beloved and not the Moon. But he is inclined to cognise that it is the face of his beloved. This is sense perception according to the Tarkika but to the Rhetorician it may also be verbal testimony.

Tarka (Reductio ad absurdum): This is the third type of invalid knowledge after Viparyaya (Bhrama) and Doubt (Saṃśaya). This is called reductio ad absurdum. Gautama defines 'Tarka' as critically examining the true nature (of a thing) with the help of reason when it (the true nature) is not known.[25] It has been defined in the Tarkasamgraha much briefly and precisely.[26] The idea is this – Say there is an inference like 'The hill has fire as it has smoke.' Here a contender may argue 'Let there be smoke on the hill there may be no fire.'[27] This can be counteracted by an argument of the type 'If there were no fire on the hill there would be no smoke (at all).' This latter is the form of the Tarka. That is why it has also been defined as the occasion (Prasaṇga) of an undesired consequence.[28] This Tarka is called invalid knowledge as it presupposes and accepts the case that there is no fire on the hill as the opponent states (which is invalid knowledge) and in that case the undesired eventuality of there being no smoke is raised. Thus Tarka predicts an undesired event in case the contender's stand is admitted. Though Tarka is not actually a Pramāṇa or means of knowledge, it helps the means of knowledge to establish the truth of the concerned knowledge (Pramāṇānugrāhaka).

This 'Tarka' has been divided under five heads – Ātmāśraya (self-dependence), Anyonyāśraya (mutual dependence), Cakraka (dependence on one another in a cycle), Anavasthā (Regressum ad absurdum) and Tādātmya bādhitārtha prasaṅga.

Sambhāvana: 'Probably this is Caitra' is the form of this type of knowledge. This is a type of inclination to think of one thing as one in all probability. The difference between doubt and Sambhāvana is that in the latter though there are alternatives they are not of equal strength but there is a tendency to lean towards one of the alternatives possible. In such a knowledge the person may be Caitra or Maitra or Devadatta but the cogniser is inclined to believe (due to some reason) that he is probably Caitra. Further reason Sambhāvana has been defined as 'doubt where one is inclined to swing to the side of one of the alternatives present.[29]

Recollection (Smṛti): is knowledge which is produced only from an impression (Saṃskāra).[30] The word 'Saṃskāramātra' has been included in the definition so that it may not over apply in the case of Recognition (Pratyabhijña) which is produced from not only an impression (Saṃskāra) but also from sense-perception (Pratyakṣa) both. The latter knowledge is like this 'This is that Devadatta' – a knowledge of one earlier seen and now recognised as such after a lapse of time when he comes into contact with the eye of a person. An example of recollection is 'That is the pot' (which I saw yesterday). Such a knowledge is invalid in the Buddhist view as the same Devadatta is not there now nor the pot. Whatever is existent has only one minute's life.[31] The Logician believes that recollection is valid if its corresponding experience (Anubhava) of old is valid, otherwise not. This is possible in the case of Epistemologists who hold that objects exist for more than a minute.

Recollection when engendered destroys the impression and a new impression is formed again – some Logicians hold (the new school). Others however hold that the impression is destroyed only after the last recollection. What property is actually responsible for an impression (Saṃskāra) is according to the old school only experiencehood (Anubhavatva) but the new school holds it is knowledgehood (Jñānatva).

Recognition (Pratyabhijñā): This type of knowledge is of form 'This is that Devadatta.' Here we recollect the individual object of the past time in a different place by sense contact with the concerned object in the present time. Thus we ignore the time and place difference in the individual's cognition. Unless we accept this stand Recognition cannot be valid. To the Buddhist of course this is invalid knowledge but not to the Logician. Thus the sentence 'This is that Devadatta' produces an import like 'Devadatta as qualified by the present time and this place is non-different from the Devadatta as implied (Upalakṣita) by the past time and a different place.[33] Thus the time and place content of the past is ignored and non-difference is established between the two Devadattas. This type of knowledge is classified under the category of experience (Anubhava) by the Logician though in one of its parts, the time past and the place past it is only a recollection. He does not include this under recollection (Smṛti) as the latter is defined by him to be produced only from an impression.[35]

The Buddhist argues that though objects are only momentary yet they are falsely apprehended as the same even after a time since they are produced again and again in succession having similarity with the previous one and due to ignorance (Avidya). Hence recognition he holds is a false knowledge of non-distinction among things which are momentary. This view of the Buddhist appears too prolix as every minute all objects are held to be created and destroyed. Hence it may be admitted that objects are non-permanent and stand for sometime and are destroyed in circumstances favourable to their destruction. It may be noted that the Buddhist has no eternal objects like the self (Atman), Ether etc.

The Śāṅkarite however, is of opinion that sentences like 'This is that Devadatta' and 'Thou art that' (Tattva masi) produce an impartite meaning (Akhaṇḍārtha) as the 'One Ātman' with the help of implication called (Jahadajahallakṣaṇā) (where the incompatible parts of the knowledge are abandoned). In the sentence – meaning of 'Thou art that' the Sarvajñatva and Sarvasāktitva of 'that' and the Kiñcijjnatva and Kincitśaktimatva of the 'thou' are left off and the one Atman alone is signified by the sentence by implication. Thus it is only the Prātipadikārtha that is signified by implication. In their view there is no scope for relation (Samsarga) here as it is only one object that is referred to.[36] But as Vṛthjñāna the sentence has to mean identity between the two selves.

In the Logician's view since cognition is considered as only perception there is no need for verbal import (Śābdabodha). If, however it be urged, that such a sentence signifies meaning in actual experience, then it may be explained as stated earlier in the Logician's view. It is also explained that the attribute parts (Viśesaṇas) may not be taken into account but only the substantive part (self etc.) for, in experience we find sentences like 'the pot in non-eternal' though the pothood part of its meaning is eternal.[37] This view is accepted by the Advaita Vedanta Paribhasa.

Anubhava (Experience): This is a kind of knowledge which is different from recollection (Smṛti)[38] e.g. A knowledge produced by a sentence like 'This is a pot' (Ayam ghaṭaḥ) when your eye is in contact with it etc. This experience to the Logician is of four kinds – sense perception (Pratyakṣa), inferential knowledge (Anumiti), Analogical knowledge (Upamiti) and verbal knowledge (Sabda).

This experience is the cause of Impression (Saṃskāra) some thinkers like Prabhākara argue that all experience is valid (probably because it induces one to action). This experience[30] may be valid or invalid as the case may be. It is the invalid experience that is divided into doubt (Saṃśaya), mistaken knowledge (Viparyaya) and Tarka.

Experience has been divided under the above stated four heads–perception etc. which may either be valid or invalid for their own reasons.

Perception: This is knowledge produced by the contact of the sense-organ with the object (concerned) e.g. 'This is a pot' where the pot is related with the eye (sense organ) by the relation of contact (Samyoga). Six kinds of such relations (Sannikarṣas) with the different sense organs have been identified by the Logician. Others modify them to suit their theories of knowledge.[40]

In addition to these six relations which are called supernormal proximities (Alaukika sannikarṣas) have been identified. One is responsible for a knowledge of genus (Jāti) when an individual object is perceived. The second is responsible for certain sense-perceptions (Pratyakṣa) like smell in the sandal when the particular sense organ is in contact (only) with the eye and the third is Yogajapratyaksa (perception of saints) which is responsible for all kinds of knowledge by perception.

This Pratyakṣajñāna also is termed Aparokṣa jñāna by the Śaṅkarites etc. The Jain also accepts Aparokṣajñāna with some modifications in it.

This like other knowledge pieces is produced with the help of the object concerned, contact, light etc.

Determinate and Indeterminate Knowledge

We have noticed that perception has been divided under two heads - indeterminate (Nirvikalpaka) and determinate (Savikalpaka). The Logician's stand that all qualified knowledge presupposes a qualified knowledge without which the former cannot be produced. In his opinion a knowledge like ('pot' and 'pothood' are perceived in the Nirvikalpa stage where there is no cognizance of pothood as an attribute in pot as the substantive. This knowledge of the necessary attribute and the substantive (not as such) are a must for a qualified knowledge this is a pot.

The Buddhists Indeterminate knowledge does not provide for this as I think since all Vikalpas (all mental constructions of name, class etc.) are totally barred in his view. What then is the attribute part of this that goes to make Manovijñāna, its later counterpart, a knowledge fit for usage of words in that connection. So Buddhist has to come to the point of view of the Logician. Further the Buddhist Nirvikalpaka cannot be considered a knowledge at all since nothing is cognised in it (at the Indriyajñāna stage).

Even the Advaitin will have to admit such a stand as the Logician does.

In the Savikalpaka stage the Logician holds that relation is established between the attribute of the substantive already perceived (though not as such).

Anumiti (Inferential Knowledge): This is a type of knowledge produced from a knowledge of concomitance (Vyāptijñāna) of an object say smoke e.g. 'where there is smoke there is fire.' From these two knowledge pieces that there is smoke on the hill and smoke is the concomitant of fire a knowledge of the type 'The hill is possessed of smoke pervaded by fire.' This is called consideration (Parāmarśa) and from it inferential knowledge of the form 'The hill is fiery' is produced.

Here the means is the concomitance (Vyaptijñāna) or according to the new school of Logicians (Parāmarsa). This inference and inferential knowledge have been studied in great depth by the Logician. Verily it is his forte. Very few can argue with him in a controversy on inference.

Upamiti (Analogical Knowledge): This is knowledge produced from a knowledge of resemblance or similarity as its instrumental cause

(Karaṇa). e.g. From a statement made by a forester as 'The Gavaya is like the cow' a person (who does not know the Gavaya animal) goes to the forest, sees a being like a cow (Gosadrśapiṇḍadarśanam) and recalls the statement of the forester 'The Gavaya is like the cow' (Atideśavākyārtha smaraṇa and ascertains that the word 'Gavaya' signifies the animal (called) Gavaya. Thus with the help of an analogical statement heard at first, later recalled when such a being is seen the signification of the word in the particular meaning is ascertained. This knowledge is analogical knowledge.

This knowledge is accepted as a separate category of knowledge by the Logician but may others don't accept this but include it either under inference or verbal testimony (Śābdajñāna) or both.

Verbal Knowledge (Śābdajñāna): This is knowledge derived from a sentence used by a person. This becomes valid when the person utters an authentic word but not otherwise. First we hear the words of the sentence, get at their meanings with the help of either convention (Sankata) or implication (Lakṣanā) and due to the combined utterance of these words we understand their mutual relations (Samsarga) and arrive at the final verbal import. This is verbal knowledge.

The accessories of this knowledge are mutual relation of the words (Ākānkṣā), their reconcilability (Yogyatā) and their necessary proximity to one another.

The Vedantin holds that verbal import also produces a knowledge of Aparokṣajñāna as in the case of a sentence like 'You are the tenth man' where one does not count himself as the tenth one. Though most thinkers accept 'Śabda' as a means of valid knowledge, others reject it, but bring it under inference.

Presumption (Arthāpatti): It is a knowledge of what is presumed (Upapadya) which later cannot otherwise be satisfactorily proved. e.g. 'The fat Devadatta does not eat at day time.'[41] Here the fatness of Devadatta cannot be proved otherwise than by presuming that he eats at night.

This type of knowledge as produced by Arthapatti as a means, is not accepted by many thinkers even of the non-sceptical schools. Instead it is included under inference (especially negative inference). But the Mīmāṃsaka and the Vedantin are inclined to believe that a negative inferential means (Vyatirekyanumāna) cannot establish the positive aspect of it and hence they accept it.

Abhāvajñāna: This is knowledge of negation. e.g. 'There is no pot, (on the ground). (This is a case of Atyantābhāva). 'This is not a pot' this is a case of mutual negation (Anyonyābhāva). 'There will be a pot here'[42] (Prāgabhāva); 'The pot is destroyed[43] (Pradhvamsābhava). A knowledge of negation sets aside a knowledge of the presence (of the particular object) e.g. 'This is not a pot' bars a knowledge of the sentence 'This is a pot.' One point to be noted is that in the knowledge of absence (of a particular thing) a knowledge of the counterpositive (Pratiyogi) is necessary. A knowledge of Abhāva is produced by the means (Pramāṇa) called Abhāva (negation) or Anupalabdhi. This is the view of Mīmāmsakas, Vedantins etc. But to the Logician Abhava is not a means of knowledge. It is known through Viśeṣaṇaviśeṣyabhāva contact etc. e.g. 'There is no pot on the ground.' This is known with the help of the eye where the ground only is the Viśeṣya and the negation of pot is its Viśeṣana (property). The Bhāṭṭas believe that negation (of pot etc.) cannot be a case of Pratyakṣa (with the sense organ as the Karana) as there is no normal contact with the object concerned. In the opinion of the Logician the nonapprehension of the knowable object[44] is an ancillary cause. The Prābhākaras believe that Abhāva is not different from its locus.[45]

It is an intriguing question how a knowledge of negation is produced.

Sambhava: This is knowledge wherein there is the possibility of including a certain object which is invariably included in another object[46] e.g. 'fifty is in hundred.' That is to say if one has one hundred rupees it goes without saying that he has fifty rupees. This is a separate Pramāṇa for Pauranikas. But the Logician includes it under inference as it is based on concomitance. Fifty is a concomitant of one hundred.

Aitihya: Is heresy the original source of which is not known[47] e.g. 'There are five Yakṣas on the Banyan tree.' This is considered as a separate Pramāṇa by Paurāṇikas etc. but the Logician brings it under verbal testimony (Śābdajñāna). If it is invalid Aitihya is not a Prāmaṇa at all.

This also is not accepted by many but brought under verbal knowledge.

Apekṣābuddhi (Mental Faculty of Adding Up Individuals): Knowledge wherein there is the conception of 'This is one, these are two' etc., thus causing a knowledge of twohood (Dvitva) etc. upto infinity (Parārtha). It is with this type of knowledge that army (a number of soldiers) and forest (a number of trees) etc. are made possible. Thus a knowledge of two, three etc. are formed. Though twohood (Dvitva) etc. reside in the two objects separately by inherence (Samavāya), it has to be stated that it is present in both the objects together by a different relation (which is called Paryāpti by the Logician). This is due to the fact of our comprehension 'one is not two' and a non-comprehension of the type 'one is two.'[48, 49, 50]

This Apekṣābuddhi stands for three minutes as against ordinary cognitions which stand only for two minutes and get destroyed in the third.[51]

Sometimes it appears that the Logician is an Advaitin while accepting this Apeksabuddhi for he treats all this world as one (in the true sense) and it is due to Apeksabuddhi that you see several things. Once this Apeksabuddhi is destroyed, 'oneness' along remains.

Samucayajñāna is knowledge wherein one and the same object more than one attributehoods are noted e.g. the hill has fire and smoke, or even the tree has contact of the monkey and its negation. It is defined as knowledge which comprehends two alternatives in the same locus but does not comprehend opposition.

Vikalpajñāna: This is a knowledge of two objects which are equally competent in performing a particular activity which can be performed by either one of the two e.g. 'one should sacrifice with either rice or barely.'

This is defined otherwise by others like Sāṃkhyas.

A Knowledge of the Qualified (Visistabuddhih): This is one wherein there is an attribute e.g. 'This is a pot' where pothood is the attribute in the pot.[52] It may be noted here that the knowledge of the attribute (Visesana) is a condition precedent for a knowledge of the qualified one (Visiṣta).

Knowledge Wherein One and the Same Locus There are Two (Ekatra Dvaymiti Rītyā Jāyamanam Jñānam) : e.g. the man who has a stick.[53] In this knowledge the one substantive (Viśeṣya) has two attributes – manhood (Puruṣatva) and stick Daṇḍa. This is different from doubt wherein, in the latter the attributes are only mutually opposed to each other. This is also different from Samuhalambanajñāna in that in the former there is only one primary substantive with two or more attributes while in the latter there are two or more primary substantives.

A Knowledge of Relation with What is Related (Viśiṣta Vaiśiṣṭyavagahijñānam) : e.g. In a knowledge like 'The man who has the stick.' Here it may be noted that stickhood is the determinant of the attribute 'stick' (Viśeṣaṇatavacchedaka)[54] which attribute as such is cognised in the man.[55]

It may be noted here that between the attributehood (Prakāratā) and the substantivehood (present, in one and the same object) some like Jagadīsa hold that there is the relation of non-difference (Abedha), while Gadādhara and his followers refute it and hold that it is the relation of the determinant to the determined (Avacchedyāvacchedakabhava between the two). Thus e.g. knowledge produced by the meaning of a sentence like Daṇḍavān puruṣaḥ is (according to Jagadisa) like this: Dandatvaniṣṭha prakāratānirupita ya daṇḍaniṣthā prakāratā tannirupatā yā puruṣaṇisthā viśesyatā tacchalijñānam.

A Knowledge of a Substantive Having an Attribute and that Latter Again Having an Attribute etc. (Viśesya Viśesaṇam Tatrapi ca Viśeṣaṇam) : e.g. In a knowledge like the man who has a stick' – the man has an attribute (stick) and the stick has its own attribute (stickhood). Stickhood here it may be noted, is not directly an attribute of Puruṣa (the person). This is the difference from Viśiṣṭavaiśiṣṭyavagāhijñāna.

Dandatvaniṣṭhaprakaratānirupita ya dandaniṣṭhā viśeṣyatā tadavacchinnā yā daṇḍaniṣṭhā prakarata tannirupitā yā puruṣanisthā viśeṣyatatacchati jñānam.

Samuhalambanajñāna (Collective Knowledge)

This is a knowledge wherein there are more than one primary substantives (Mukhya viśeṣyas)[56] and as many attributes also e.g. This is silver, this is nacre. Here we find the primary substantives silver and nacre and two attributes silverhood and nacrehood. This is a collective knowledge of two sentence meanings (combined into one). This knowledge is different from Samuccaya jñāna wherein the latter there is only one primary substantivehood and two or more attributehoods e.g. The floor has a pot and a mat.

Dhārāvāhikajñāna: Knowledge in a series – It is knowledge which continues in the same form one after another for more than two minutes. e.g. This is a pot, This is a pot etc. The Śāṅkarite thinks that as long as the mental mode (Vṛtti stands) the cognition is produced.

Controversy (Vipratipatti): This is (the knowledge of) a set of two sentence which signifies two mutually opposed meanings e.g. Does knowledge derive its validity from the very causes of knowledge or does it not? The 'yes' reply is Vidhikoṭi and the 'no' reply to it is Niśedhakoti. Due to a knowledge of controversy a doubt is produced in a person. But controversy itself is not a doubt.

Ignorance (Ajñāna): This is absence of knowledge to the Logician. This comes under Abhāva padārtha for him. But to the Śāṅkarite etc. and other Vedantins it is of a positive form (Bhāvarūpa). His idea is that Ajñāna like a veil covers Jñāna and that is why we say 'I don't know that' etc. When once this veil of Ajñāna is removed, Jñāna dawns. This is possible for him as what is existent is Jñāna only and it is covered by Ajñāna or Avidyā and hence one has to try to remove the positive veil to attain Jñāna. He speaks of Tūlājñāna and Mūlājñāna. When one gets rid of Mūlājñāna one gets Salvation. Some Vedantins hold Māyā and Avidyā are the same and some other hold the opposite view. Avidyā has no beginning but surely has an end as the Holy Text testifies.

The Means of Knowledge

The first question is whether there is that is called the means (Karaṇa) of knowledge different from knowledge or not. The Nihilist denies its existence[57] on the ground that, if the means of knowledge could be established from some other means, there would be the fault of infinite regress. The Nyāyabhāṣya puts it prima facie that perceptual knowledge etc. are not valid means (of knowledge) as they are not established in all the three times present, past and future (with reference to their objects of knowledge).[58] According to the Buddhist 'Knowledge' is the means and as a result of its application the objects are ascertained. If the knowledge of smell etc. (Pratyakṣa) be considered to have existed earlier (i.e. in the past) before the object (smell) was ascertained then we will have to accept that it (the knowledge of smell etc.) is not produced from the contact of smell etc. (which is said to be the means). If, on the other hand, the means is to be later (i.e. in the future, after the object is ascertained) then it cannot be a means. If, otherwise they both are considered to exist simultaneously, knowledge pieces do not occur in a particular order (in accordance with the particular object with which the sense organ is in contact) and the aphorism of Gautama "The non-production of simultaneous pieces of knowledge is the sign of (the existence of) the mind"[59] will be at stake.

The question is whether the means of knowledge is a knowledge as the Buddhist and the Jaina are inclined to think or whether it is the sense organ (Indriya) etc. in the case of Pratyakṣa as most other schools hold. The Buddhist holds that the same knowledge is both the means and the end (Pramāna and Pramiti)[60] for it is the similarity with the blue that is responsible for a knowledge of blue. Thus both the means as well as the result are of the form of knowledge as similarity also is of the form of knowledge for him. The Yogācāra view is that there is nothing else but knowledge in this world in the actual sense and as such knowledge alone should be the cause as well as its result. The relation between them is not one of the producer and the produced (Janyajanakabhāva) (as it is a contradiction to state that the same knowledge is the producer and also the produced) but only one of the establisher and the established (Vyavasthāpya-vyavasthāpakā-bhāva). This view is opposed to the established cause and effect theory (Kāryakaraṇa-bhāva). Again if the former knowledge be the cause of the Second knowledge, there would arise the question "What is the means of the former knowledge itself." You have to seek another former knowledge and so on ad infinitum. If knowledge is to be beginningless such a knowledge should have to be admitted against the Asat Khyati theory of the Buddhist. Further the same knowledge cannot be considered to be the establisher and the established as there is no criterion to hold them exclusively as such as one as the establisher should precede the established. The Nihilist's opinion that nothing can be established does not serve any purpose as his view is not conducive to explain any theory of knowledge.

The Sāṃkhya View of the Means of Knowledge

The Sāṃkhya view of the means of knowledge also is that the reflection of consciousness (Citpratibimba) is responsible for the production of knowledge. This is in pursuance of his effect-in-cause theory (Satkāryāvāda). According to him a sentient cognition cannot be produced from an insentient internal organ. That is why pure consciousness (Cit) has to be reflected in the mirror-like mental modification (Vṛtti). It is thus the reflection of consciousness that should produce knowledge and not the sense organ (Indriya) or Buddhi (intellect) both of which are only evolutes of the inert primordial matter (Prakṛti). The Sāṃkhya also admits that the sense organ (Indriya) is the means when the Vṛtti jñāna is concerned– that is when we cognise 'a pot' etc. When the sense organ goes and assumes the form of the pot etc., the sense organ is considered the efficient cause. But when a cognition like "I know the pot" is effected in the self (Pauruṣeyabodha), the Vṛttijñāna transformation of the intellect (along with the sense-organ) is considered to be the efficient cause. An almost similar opinion is held by the Māyāvādin (Śāṅkarite) who states, on the one hand, that knowledge alone can produce knowledge (by the theory of Satkāryavāda) and on the other, that there is nothing other than knowledge that exists in the final view, though he accepts a pragmatic existence (Vyāvahārikasattā) also for the empirical world of objects. It is because he accepts this kind of practical reality that he can admit the sense-organ or the reflection consciousness as the Pramāṇa. It is doubtful whether the mere reflection of the self in the transformation of the intellect (Vṛttijñāna) is capable of producing knowledge with its sentient character–in which case there is no difficulty in accepting the inert sense organ itself as the means of producing knowledge. To argue that the reflection is not inert may not be quite sound. If the reflection also be considered sentient or produces a notion of sentence there will be two separate sentient entities admitted. Further it is difficult to prove in clear terms the reflection of the self in the Vṛtti but a mere contact (Saṃyoga) of the self with the mind (Internal organ), as the Logician holds, appears to be enough for the purpose. It is also very much doubtful whether the cognitions "This is a pot" and "I know this is a pot" are cognised separately, though, of course, there is the possibility for the latter knowledge to be separately produced from the relevant causes. Further according to the Sāṃkhya theory, in the case of invalid knowledge also, we will be obliged to accept the reflection of the self in Vṛtti as producing false cognition which position is very unhappy.

Satkāryavāda

While considering this theory we have to undertake a criticism of the 'effect-in cause theory (Satkāryavāda) and decide whether knowledge alone can produce knowledge or inert objects could produce them. We here attempt only a few important arguments against the theory. If the effect be present in the cause itself why should it (the cause) not serve as an effect (e.g. the seed does not serve the purpose of a tree). If it be held the cause awaits manifestation (Abhivyakti) as the effect then state whether this manifestation itself is something already existing. If it (Abhivyakti) previously existed why should the cause wait to be manifested as the effect; if, on the other hand, the manifestation did not previously exist, such a non-existent (Asat) could not come into existence according to (you who hold) the effect in cause theory. If it be objected, then, that anything may be the cause of any other thing (on the opponents' view) we reply it is not so. Only certain things are the causes of certain other things e.g. the seed is the cause of the tree etc. If, as the Votary of Satkāryavāda thinks, the seed is the tree why does it need the help of other causes like water, earth etc.? Thus we have to admit that, though a (previously) non-existent effect is produced, the inherent cause (Samavāyikāraṇa) is found to exist in the effect but it is really a number of other causes too that bring the effect (Kāya) into being.

Thus there is the possibility of the sense-organ producing knowledge in the case of perception and of a particular knowledge producing another knowledge in the case of inference etc., thus the two means of knowledge in general may be said to be the sense-organ and knowledge itself (which produces another knowledge).

To the Buddhist (Sarvastivadin) the result of the means of knowledge is a knowledge of the object (Arthāvagati) (or Svasamvedana for others). The means is similarity with (or the assuming the form of) the object (which (similarity) is also a knowledge for him in the real sense as he has no object at all). Hence he appears to hold knowledge alone as the means and the result both. If the means of knowledge is only knowledge itself as it only is sentient then that means knowledge also should have another knowledge for its means and that another and so on ad infinitum. If an insentient object is the means as the Logicians hold there is no difficulty. Even if it is held by the Buddhist that one knowledge (Citta) produces another and as such there is no difficulty in his view; it will have to be accepted that the result knowledge also produces another in the same series (Eke santana) and no other knowledge in a different series would be possible. The Buddhist holds that only because the knowledge takes the form of the blue colour it establishes a knowledge of blue; but it cannot be stated that the eye is responsible for the knowledge of blue as others hold. The blue form is followed by a mental perception in the same series. How could it be then that the same activity of knowledge is the cause and the effect both? To this the Buddhist replies, here there is no cause and effect relationship between the two, but it is one of the determinant and the determined. As the sense perception (assumption of the form of the object) it is the means and as the (mental) perception it is the result both (by Vyavasthāpyavyavasthāpakabhāva). Hence in one part of it the knowledge is a determinant (similarity with the blue) and in another it is the determined. Hence there is no controversy according to him. It is to be noted here that the knowledge of similarity with the blue is held to be the means (Grāhaka) and with the aid of determination the knowledge of blue is determined (Grāhya).

Here a question arises as to how the knowledge which is a non-material substance becomes blue. In our experience we don't find it so. If it is, however, to be accepted as there is no other way to explain it even then it must be admitted two knowledge pieces are combined together into one, one being the determinant and the other the determined (as there is nothing but knowledge to the idealist). They cannot be simultaneous as one is the determinant without which the other cannot be produced. As a matter of fact the two cannot be held to be separate pieces of knowledge as in the former of them there is no attribute and substantive as required by the nature of knowledge as similarity with the blue a simple sense perception of the Buddhist cannot be knowledge as there is only the assumption of the form of the object which is insentient and it cannot be knowledge. If it be experienced as 'My knowledge is similar to blue' it cannot beget a knowledge of (i.e. I have a knowledge of) blue as there is no relation between the two knowledge pieces. One's knowledge may be blue but there is no criterion to hold that one has a knowledge of blue. If it is held that it is an inference like 'I have a knowledge of blue as my knowledge is blue.' It should be a case of inference with the concomitance 'whosoever's knowledge is blue, he has a knowledge of blue.' This cannot be denied to be a case of inference with such a concomitance as it is a case out of the purview of perception. The Buddhist cannot however deny that it cannot be a case of inference as it is a case neither of identity (Tadātmya) nor production from something (Tadutpatti). If he accepts inference in this case he would be forced to accept it in some other cases like 'This mango is sweet as it is yellow.' Here the taste is the concomitant of the particular colour which is neither of the two cases, Tādātmya or Tadutpatti. Further the knowledge fully gained is not a knowledge of blue as the Buddhist holds but it is the knowledge 'This (object) is blue' as in our daily experience. If he has no object at all in his view then the perception should be of the type 'My knowledge is blue' or 'My mind is blue' (or 'I am blue') as the knowledge for him is not different from the other theorists' mind or soul or their contact. Further, assumption of the form by the cognition is not possible in the case of genus (Jāti), qualities etc. which are not existent for him.

Again the Buddhist argues, that determinate knowledge is produced from the indeterminate one due to Vikalpa. How could it be when all objects including knowledge are momentary for him? The previous knowledge is not present when the latter is produced. If it be accepted it is possible due to sameness of the series even then what is destroyed already and recollected and is somehow related with the latter knowledge cannot be a valid means (as it is only a case of recollection of the object previously perceived).

Hence the Buddhist may not have any objection, I think, to accept that though it is the Svalaksana that is cognised in perception Vikalpa provides if its name, class etc. as per the words of their meanings in vogue. Thus determinate knowledge is only an expression in words of the indeterminate knowledge already experienced to which is only for communication with others.

Another objection to his theory is that only the knowledge which corresponds with the object is the means (of valid knowledge). Hence the knower is to wait for the knowledge of the validity of his knowledge till he cognises whether it corresponds with the object. Till such time as he ascertains its validity in this way his knowledge can be neither valid or invalid. Surely it cannot be neither as it should be either of the two.

Another point is what does he mean by the statement 'correspondence of knowledge with the object.' How can knowledge agree with an object as the latter itself is another particular knowledge. How can either the general and the particular or the particulars agree with each other.

Another defect in the theory is that there is no evidence to prove that the knowledge is of the form of blue or similar to blue, as knowledge is not corporeal (Mūrta) but blue is. Thus it is against experience if this be a case of perception as knowledge is not an object of perception (by the eye). In case it is held that it is (a case of perception) of knowledge the resulting knowledge should be of the form 'This is blue and also knowledge' or 'This is blue knowledge.' To prove this by inference you cannot take recourse to Tarka (Reductio ad absurdum) as it can be said that even without knowledge being blue blue may be perceived by holding that blue is only an object of the knowledge with which the eye is in contact.

There is no direct contact of the eye with knowledge as we know. Hence the above is not even a case of inference.

Further even if the knowledge were blue you cannot conclude from it 'I know blue' or 'This is blue.' With any amount of perceptional causal aggregate you can at the most conclude 'this my knowledge is blue' as it has the colour blue. So you need another means for the cognition of blue. As a matter of fact knowledge cannot be revealed there as it has no contact with the sense organ.

Further in each individual experience the Buddhist will have to admit, blue colour, yellow colour, black colour etc. to different knowledge pieces. How does he account for them without a different external object in each case at different times (with regard to the same class, knowledge)? Thus he will have to admit external objects also in addition to knowledge objects against his own stand.

Another objection is that the eye is in contact with blue and not the knowledge and hence the eye may assume blue colour but knowledge cannot assume the blue colour. To argue that knowledge was blue even before the object sense organ contact then why should not knowledge be yellow or white. What is the criterion? A reply becomes due from him. If reply is it is the blue colour or the knowledge that makes it blue then to the external object blue is established (as red and yellow objects) also have a claim as they are present in the impressions.

It cannot be stated by the Śāṅkarite or the Buddhist that empirical knowledge has only an empirical reality or a dependent reality and real or pure knowledge has a permanent reality. For, reality or unreality is one and only one and not a graded one. If it is definitely called hallucination on the other hand, it has to be treated as unreal.

If every object be identical with knowledge how could the different knowledges like perception, inference etc. be established by him (as he does) as everything is knowledge itself (in general). Further it is not possible to state what the idealist means by 'knowledge' which is present even before it assumes the form of blue. It should have been without a form which is against his view.

Another difficulty is that the sentient knowledge cannot be identical with the insentient or material object.

Further the main theme of disputation is how is (valid) knowledge (Pramā) produced. If the Buddhist contends that knowledge is not a product at all (and is the only existent) he has to account fcr all knowledges at all times. If knowledge, on the otherhand, is produced (as it is momentary) what is the immediately preceding cause of it (Pramāṇa). If it cannot be held by him that the knowledge of pot is produced from a previous knowledge of mat. He has to find out an immediately preceding cause (Karaṇa) for knowledge. In fact it cannot be an impression because an impression needs to be manifested for some reason or other. If it is by some unseen cause it is unjustifiable when there is a seen causes like the object pot sense organ and their contact. If it be impression in general that is the cause of the present knowledge all kinds of knowledge of colour, taste etc. should be produced at one and the same time.

Again since the Buddhist does not accept sense organ etc. as the cause of knowledge, as it is insentient then he has to admit that knowledge is not produced at all. If he holds that the previous knowledge is responsible for the succeeding knowledge, we object that knowledge of pot cannot produce a knowledge of mat even if there is change in time moments. That is why probably he is of the view that the same knowledge is the cause and the effect. But he should admit this in the case of production of knowledge also. Otherwise knowledge cannot be a product and momentary. But he holds that this is not a case of being produced (Utpādyotpādakabhāva) as it would be ridiculous to hold that the same knowledge is produced from itself against all logical conception. So he takes recourse to the different argument that the relation between them is the determinate and the determined relation between the two aspects of the same knowledge (Pramāṇa and Phala). Even here the determined is produced from determinate knowledge. Otherwise why should one produce the other? Further as already stated, the inference of Vyavasthāpaka Vyavasthapya-bhāva made by the Buddhist (in this case) must be due to the relation of Tadātmya (identity) or Tadutpatti (being produced from it). In the former case a cause has to be found as why it has become the determinant for which another knowledge should intervene. In the later view the Buddhist will have to admit that the same knowledge is produced from the same knowledge which stand is absurd. If on another view the former knowledge (Vyavasthapaka) is only of the form of assumption of the form of the object, then it cannot be case of identity and the contingency of producedness (Tadutpatti) is obvious.

The Śāṅkarite's View on the Means of Knowledge and Allied Theories

Who is Saksi and Why is He Accepted?

The Śāṅkarite unlike all other non-Vedantin Epistemologists accepts an entity designated witness-consciousness (Saksin) different from the individual self (Jīva) which is the meaning of the word 'ego' (Aham). By witness consciousness is meant that consciousness which without itself undergoing any change does not partake in any actual activity but witnesses activities directly. There are various views regarding the definition of Saksin. Some hold that Saksin is the consciousness as conditioned by Antahkarana or the internal organ whereas Jiva is consciousness as qualified by (or defined by) the internal organ. The difference between the Upādhi (condition) and a Viseśaṇa (qualification) is that the former does not actually take part in the activity (predicated) concerned whereas in the latter it does e.g. In fact a 'witness' even in law is one who knows the facts but is not affected by them in any way. Saksi had to be admitted, as Vidyaranya states, in order to cognise the not-very-vivid bodies (the Sthula and the Sūkṣma one) between one modification and another. As, when there is no Vṛtti (modification) there should be no cognition of the two bodies, Saksi had to be admitted as a permanent agent always cognising the two bodies without mental modifications. Though probably this could otherwise be secured, the Saksin has been admitted as an Epistemological entity on the authority of the Holy Text.[63] Thus it is this Saksin that cognises all the states of the ego, vital forces etc. as it always cognises all the states and Vṛttis, their rise and destruction, their differences etc. It cannot be urged that the individual self itself might do all these things as it (the self) cannot be expected to be a simple witness when it actively undertakes all kinds of activities, enjoys, feels pleasure and pain.[64] Nor can it be urged that the aggregate of individual selves itself be the agency concerned as one individual self cannot cognise the pleasures, pain etc. of other selves.

How Does the Mental Mode Remove the Veil of Nescience

The Śāṅkarite holds that during perception what happens is that the nescience (Ajñāna) relating to the object (pot etc.) only is removed but not all Nescience in which case Mukti is to be attained by the self and the Brahman-consciousness reveals the object. Here a question arises at the time of the perception of an object (say pot) what Ajñāna is destroyed by the mental mode (Vṛtti). If he replies it is the nescience of pot (Ghaṭajñāna) how is it that when a number of Ajñānas are present at that place why should only the pot-Ajñāna come into play and get destroyed. A mat Ajñāna may be destroyed instead. In reply to this the Śaṅkarite should maintain that, as the pot is related to the sense organ the pot Ajñāna is removed. This stand leads to a discrepancy. To know the pot Ajñāna the pot (the object) itself should be known first. This means even before the pot Ajñāna is destroyed the pot is perceived. If the pot Ajñāna, on the other hand, is stated not necessary to be cognised but only as existing in the place uncognised (Svarupasat) then it is not cognised as different from a mat Ajñāna and hence a mat also may be perceived in its place. There is yet another question what object the Ajñāna covers when the object has not come into being and again when the object has been destroyed. Again unless the object pot is accepted its Ajñāna cannot be spoken of. A number of such questions arise in the wake of the stand on Ajñāna. The replies given to these questions are found in treatises on Vedanta.[65] They may be assessed by the interested readers themselves. A point that may be noted here is that on the view that the individual self though all-pervading is delimited by the internal organ and hence it has to take the help of the mental modification. It is also alternatively suggested that the individual self delimited by the internal organ cannot make objects known but with the help of Vṛtti it makes the object known by being one with the Brahman consciousness as limited by the particular object. Certain others are of the view that the individual self, though all-pervading and in contact with all objects, does not cognise it as it is enveloped by Ajñāna and hence the Vṛtti serves to paint the object for it and thus dispel the covering veil.

Are These Sentences Which Consist of Meanings of Words Not Syntactically Connected?

According to the Śaṅkarite Vedantin there are such sentences e.g. 'Brahman is knowledge, Bliss' (Vijñānam manandam Brahma), 'Thou art that' (Tattvam asi). His idea is that, though other sentences like 'Bring the cow' (Gamanaya) consist of words which are syntactically connected (Samsrsta)[66] in the Mahavakyas of the Holy text as cited above and in sentences like 'This is that Devadatta' Syntax has finally no role to play as the entire sentence gives one whole or impartite meaning (Akhandartha). I think the Śaṅkarite is the only one theorist holding this view of sentence meaning. He defines Impartite meaning (Akhandārtha) as that meaning in denoting which words are not connected syntactically are either as subject, object etc. e.g. In the meaning of a sentence like 'Thou art that,' at the outset, there is syntax the relation of non-difference between the meaning of the word 'thou' (Individual self as qualified by knowing only some objects etc.) and the meaning of 'that' (The Brahman or the Higher self which knows all objects etc.). But the syntactical connection (non-difference) is vitiated here is the one cannot be non-different from the other for obvious reasons (where the attributes are opposed to each other). Hence the Vedantin takes recourse to implication (Laksana). In a strange way he proposes, partial implication in each of the words 'Thou and that.' Hence 'Thou' by implication means only mere consciousness or self and 'that' means only the same (mere consciousness) and hence there is no contradiction in the relation of non-difference in the implied meanings between the mere consciousness (Suddha Caitanya) as the fact is only that only one mere consciousness exists[67] on the authority of the Veda.[68] Hence the Śāṅkarite argues that the entire sentence 'Thou art that' by implication means '*mere consciousness*' unrelated to any other word meaning. That is why it is called 'one that has no syntactical relation.' Sureware alternatively defines Akhandārtha as the meaning given by the nominal base (Prātipadikārtha) which is mere consciousness.[69] In both the views syntactical relation is rendered useless as it relates consciousness with the same consciousness. That is his stand.

Citsukḥa alternatively suggests that by Akhaṇḍārtha is meant[70] 'the culmination in the meaning of only '*one Nominal base*' of different words which are not synonymous. The author of the Advaita Paribhasa proposes, that partial implication for each of the words is not necessary (it is prolix and is not accepted by many theorists); instead it could be said that in a sentence like 'Thou art that' since there is no difference in the substantive forms of both the words (which is self or mere consciousness) the contradiction in the attributive forms of the words may not be taken into account. He argues that such a practice is in vogue even in the Logician's view e.g. he says 'the pot is non-eternal.' But 'pot' means for him the individual pot as qualified by pothood. Here though pothood (the genus) is eternal it does not matter in its identity with the non-eternal (individual pot) as the former is only an attributive part. Here it may be noted that though implication is not found necessary, to explain the above sentence, a knowledge of the non-existence of the limitations of the individual self in the higher self based the knowledge of the identity between the two selves. Hence I am obliged to think that implication should be resorted to. Though the actual truth is that both the selves are non-different, the Holy Text proposes to let us understand that the 'Thou' appears different from 'That' as long as the invalid knowedge exists, the non-difference is experienced only when the invalid knowledge (Bhrānti) is dispelled. That is to say though the truth may be one and eternal a knowledge of that truth when experienced in the Vyavaharika state takes into account the pragmatic difference into account and refutes it though there is no word in the sentence to express refutation; simple Pratipadikārtha as the meaning (of the sentence) is not warranted, in the sentence as it is secured by other Vedic texts.[71] The latter meaning may be admitted as a later meaning derived from the implicational meaning. The subject-predicate relation (Uddisyavidheya bhāva) has to be admitted in every sentence.

Akhandartha

The view that the meaning of the nominal crude base is Akhaṇḍārtha may not be quite plausible as two words are actually used in a sentence like 'Thou art that.' In fact the meaning can as well be arrived at by using only one word. But this criticism appears unjust as a sentence and not a word is required to take recourse to implication and the final meaning disposed of as an identity in spite of the fact that there is only one existent for the Śaṅkarite.

Even Citsukha's view that the culmination into one nominal base meaning of two non-synonymous words constitutes Akhandartha justifies the use of more than one word as (both) the words are used to distinguish one from the other. Otherwise the answer 'thou art that' to an enquiry like 'Who am I' is not justified. But it should not be urged that as a distinction is made between two objects syntactical relation sets in for, even though the distinction there only the form of the objects is intended to be stated.[72 & 73]

The view of Citsukha that in a definition sentence like (Prakṛṣṭaprakāśascandrah) 'the Moon is the great light' the word 'great light' is used in its own form (Svarūpamātrapara) may not be quite sound as, among the heavenly bodies present there 'great light' clearly distinguishes between the light of the stars and the light of the Moon. In fact the word Prakrsṭa itself in the context of the sentence must be a distinguishing attribute.

What is Knowledge and How is It Produced?

Though the philosophers of old have explained in detail how knowledge of so many varieties is engendered, they don't appear to have said in definite terms what knowledge actually is. The Logician states that when the self and the mind come together, the mind contacts the sense organ (Indriya) and the sense organ the object, there is perceptual knowledge. But what actually knowledge is or what actually is meant by the process of 'knowing' appears not to have been dealt with by the theorists clearly. Of course, we cannot expect them, as philosophers to explain the physiological process of knowing which requires a study of the body and the mind, the nerves, the centres of understanding and so on which is not their field but at least they (except the Logicians) could have stated in general terms what knowledge actually is. The Sāṃkhyas and the Śaṅkarites require the reflection of consciousness in the mental modification (Vṛtti) for the production of knowledge. But it is not explained what this reflection is, how this reflection is carried back to the individual and consciousness effected.

It is stated by some that knowledge is the (impression of/or) the reflection[74] of the object (on the mind). This reflection of the object is carried back to the mind through the sense organ (eye etc.). It carries with it all the details (size, colour etc.) desired to be cognised which it is capable of cognising, to the individual and it is this formation of this reflection that we call knowledge. The theory of perception applies mutatis mutandis to the other kinds of perceptual knowledge also (auditory perception, gustatory perception and so on). Even with regard to the other types of knowledge (inference etc.) it is obligatory that (an impression of/or) the reflection of the object inferred also is effected though the Vṛtti may not go out.

Apperception

In the Buddhist view there is no need for apperception as knowledge is self-revealed (Svasaṁvedya) like pleasure, pain etc. He fears regressus ad infinitum if knowledge were to be cognised by another knowledge and that by another and so on. Further as the original knowledge is destroyed in the second minute of its production according to him, it cannot be validly cognised at all. In the case of perception the sense-organ cognises the object that is to say it assumes the form of the object and in the next minute with the aid of this assumption the object is ascertained (in the mind) in the second minute. Thus perception is considered to contain a twofold cognition (Dvairūpya) wherein the latter is the determined and the former the determinant and a mental construction (Vikalpa) is the cause of this mental construction.

The Buddhist contends, if knowledge were not self-cognised how a statement like 'This object is known to me' after the production of knowledge could be maintained, for, the knowledge of a qualified entity cannot be produced without a knowledge of the qualification itself.[75] Here the object is the qualified and 'knownness' is its property. If the knowledge is itself not known how can the object be qualified with this notion of knownness. Hence knowledge, he argues, is self-revealed. For a criticism of this theory the Jaina theory immediately following may be looked up in.

The Jaina too does not believe in a separate apperceptional process. In his view cognition of an object arises along with the apperception part e.g. This is a pot; I know this is a pot. Thus knowledge is not only an object revealer but also a revealer of itself. Otherwise there would be infinite regress. The objection here is that the pot alone is cognised by the percipient as the cognition pertains only to the object pot but not to the cognition too in which case the congition also should get the objective case along with the pot e.g. I see the pot and the knowledge. Further the perceiver interested only in the object part of the knowledge but not in the knowledge part. We also known how, if knowledge is to be known, a separate effort is needed. A knowledge of knowledge is not necessary for Arthakriyā unless there is a doubt about it. Another defect in the theory is that if every knowledge were followed by another knowledge of it (apperception) there would be no end to the series of apperceptions as each knowledge should have an apperceptional knowledge after it. Again the Buddhist may hold that unless the specific knowledge of the object is known previously the knowledge of knowledge cannot arise. Pot this does not stand for apperception only knowledge of the object is enough. It need not be known too. The object is a sense-percept but its knowledge is a separate mental percept as no sense contact is possible in its case, to the objection that, in the knowledge of knowledge the latter knowledge becomes 'what is revealed' according to the Jaina, (the Jain) he replies that it is not so, as it is simply expected to remove the veil on the object. To another objection as to how the experiencer (knowledge) becomes the experience (Anubhāvya) he rejoins that is known only as an experience only. This argument is to be carefully examined.

The Antagonists objection that the Logician's apperception cannot be maintained as, according to him (the Logician) the Vyavasāya is destroyed in the third minute. But the Logicians reply to this is that the Vyavasāya is revival again before the apperception is produced.

Miśra on the other hand holds that apperception is a mental perception soon after a cognition without any further effort. It is not a case of sense-perception but a mental perception.

Bhaṭṭa the Mīmāṃsaka holds that knowledge is not perceived but inferred from objects when they are cognised. Thus knowlede is inferred with the help of the knownness pertaining to the object (Jñātatā) (as the reason in the inference) and thus he accepts all knowledge by inference.

In the Śaṅkarite's opinion knowledge like pleasure and pain is cognised by the witness – consciousness (Sākṣin). It is difficult to know the knower (of an object). It is not the mere soul (Ātman) as it is unrelated to all. Neither is it the internal organ that cognises as it can only produce the mental mode (Vṛtti), which is inert. Hence the Śaṅkarite holds that consciousness is reflected in the mental mode and cognition is produced. He does say in clear terms that what actually cognises the object is the mind. The mind itself is insentient, the self is unattached and hence no combination of these is possible; reflection too is insentient.

In the case of all those theorists who hold that Vṛtti (mental mode) or the assumption of knowledge of the form of the object, though psychologically sound appears to suffer from some drawbacks. One such is that all objects (of perception) like heat, touch, absence (of objects like the pot, mat) dream, strength etc. cannot be reflected nor are they experienced to be reflected in practical life, though sometimes an image of the object comes into the mind on seeing an object etc. That is why its appears more sound to hold that a contact of the object with the sense organ or mind is accepted or better with the sense organ coupled with the mind so that if necessary pleasure, pain etc. might all be included under perception. Further it is too profix to hold the Vṛtti transformation in hundreds of cases of perception and then destruction. What we perceive is only contact of the object and sense organ and hence the view is accepted by the Logician. There is no necessity, on this view, to accept a Sākṣin as the Vedantin does.

In the Logicians view knowledge is not self-revealed but is revealed by another knowledge. Apperception is different from memory (Smṛti) as the former reveals not only the object concerned but also the knowledge, whereas the latter reveals only the object. It is not also different from inference. Apperception through following knowledge is not necessary to induce activity as it does not serve any purpose in the ordinary course. But when there is a doubt about the knowledge acquired it comes into play. Soon after a knowledge is produced in an individual (e.g. This is a pot) a mental perception of the type 'I know this is a pot' is produced through this does not account for the validity of the former knowledge, or inducement to action. It is called the first apperception which only denotes the acquiring of knowledge e.g. I know this to be a pot, since pothood is seen by me as a property of the object in front of me. The fact that pothood has been seen in the substratum of pothood is known only later in the second apperception when found necessary (as both pot and pothood are known in the first apperception) and their relation is cognised in the next minute. Sometimes (i.e. on subsequent occasions), of course, validity is inferred from an inference. This is a pot since it gets water just as a previous pot seen. Whereas apperception is of the Sākṣin according to the Śaṅkarite, to the Logician it is a mental perception but validity is known by the second apperception or an inference. The Buddhist objection that knowledge cannot be perceived by another knowledge produced later as the earlier momentary knowledge will have been destroyed by that time, is untenable as knowledge stands for two minutes and is destroyed only in the third minute.

He holds that apperception is not necessary for inducement to action (Pravṛtti) and thus he avoids infinite regress even without self-revelation of knowledge. If it be objected that the apperception again may require another apperception when desired or required, he admits that as long there is a doubt about the object or its validity another apperception must follow it but it never goes on endlessly as, in the course of the series, a doubt may not arise about the previous knowledge or due to brain fag the individual may cease to think about it.

The inference that knowledge can be known like any other object is like this 'knowledge is an object (of a knowledge) as it is an entity (Vastu) just like a pot' surely there are statements like ('I know that I know only that level Sanskrit' which go to prove that knowledge is a knowable entity.

This theory of apperception appears to be sound inasmuch as it solves most of the difficulties in the theory.

Self-revelation of Knowledge

If knowledge were to invariably reveal itself as some phiosophers (like the Śaṅkarite, the Buddhist, the Jaina, and the Prābhākara) think, we will have to admit that two cognitions like 'This is a pot' and 'I know that this is a pot' are simultaneously apprehended which we don't experience in life. That is a wrong conclusion according to the Logician's view as, when a knowledge is produced at one time knowledge of this knowledge is produced in the next minute only as the one the knowledge is the object of the other. It should be urged that knowledge which experiences cannot be the experienced for, as the Jaina says, knowledge is experience with regard to the object only but with regard to itself it is the experienced. If apperception be produced after the cognition according to the self-revelation theorist it cannot be said to self-revealed as the cognition requires some other causes to produce the apperceptive knowledge as it is not of the form of the earlier cognition.

If it be urged as done by Venkatanatha 'that it is necessary' to accept self-revelation for all knowledge as, otherwise the omniscients (God's) knowledge itself will not be self-revealed.[76] But this argument may not stand as God as an omniscient is expected to know all objects at all times and without sense organs etc. He is an exception to our general rule as his knowledge is eternal but ours is timed. The second argument in favour of self-revelation of knowledge as advanced by Venkatanatha is that if knowledge has to be cognised at all it should be only self-revealed.[77] As stated above it is not necessary to cognise the cognition for all practical purposes. However, if it is needed in the case of a doubt by the cogniser it is known by a mental cognition. As already stated one experience is that knowledge cognises only the object. If that knowledge also is to be known there would be infinite regress (Anavastha) and on the other hand no other knowledge can be produced at all. Further if, in the mental perception as the arousal of the impression (Samskarodbodha) is required, it may not be urged that both the Viśaya Samskāra and the Jñāna Samskara are simultaneously produced as in practical life there is no demand for the Jñāna Samskara and hence Udbodhaka Samāgri is not there for it. Nor is it produced after the original cognition as it is not required. Another reason why self-revelation of knowledge cannot be accepted is that the cognition of cognition is not necessarily desired by the cogniser nor is there any use of it in inducement to action. A knowledge of the object alone is necessary for it. Another defect is that the Śāṅkarite should admit that (consciousness or) Ātman should also be known along with the object. If he contends it is only the Vṛttijñāna that is cognised and not the Svarūpajñāna it may hold good as the Vṛttijñāna is insentient and cannot by itself cognise even the object. Further the cognition of cognition is unnecessary for activity except when there is a doubt about the validity of knowledge. Even if knowledge is revealed by itself the revealed knowledge again is to be revealed by another and so on ad infinitum. The Advaitins objection that the knowledge piece destroyed in the third minute cannot be apprehended by an apperception (Anu Vyavasāya) may not be correct as the apperception is not a desideratum for a knowledge of the object unless a doubt about the object is engendered in the individual. Thus that the necessary juncture knowledge with the object is recollected at the time apperception and a mental cognition ensues and knowledge is known.

When once this experience (of an object) is completed, an impression (a Samskara) of the same object is formed in the mind (or the soul) which lasts for a length of time the strength of which is in proportion to the strength of the reflection formed.

Recollection

Recollection is the mental cognition of the particular object once previously experienced. The way in which recollection is effected may be stated thus: you must have experienced say, a particular pot previously when an impression of the pot is produced in your mind. If on a different occasion later, there is a stimulus (Udbodhaka) in the form of your friend referring to the particular pot etc., this stimulus brings before your mind an image of the previously experienced object (pot) which is already there in the form of an impression. Thus recollection, as the Logician says, is knowledge generated with the help of an impression only. 'Only' in the above sentence, as has been already stated, is intended to preclude recognition from its range wherein the actual perception of the object also is necessary. Stimuli are of the form of deliberation, similarity etc.

Here there is a controversy. The older Logicians think that the particular impression (Saṃskāra) and the particular recollection are caused by that particular experience (Anubhava) viewed as experience only, but not viewed as knowledge (Jñāna) as the Modern Logicians think. The view of the former is that it is too cumbrous to view experience as knowledge when it is found enough to view it as experience (since experiencehood is less pervasive than knowledgehood). But the latter hold that since impression (Saṃskāra) is destroyed by producing its effect (recollection) there is the contingency of any experienced object to be remembered only once and not a second time. Hence the latter hold that experience as Jñāna is the cause and not experience as experience. But the former view appears to be more reasonable as the impression persists even after producing recollection.

Recognition

By recognition (Pratyabhijña) is meant the knowledge of an object determined by its former state,[78] as e.g. This is that Devadatta (whom I saw sometime back). Here what happens is that the person Devadatta experienced on a previous occasion (as a young boy etc.) is brought to our mind by Upanītabhāna (that which is secured by the Jñānalakṣaṇā contact) when Devadatta (as a man now) is actually perceived. Here it may be noted that the object also should be currently perceived. In recollection this is not the case.

Though most philosophers accept recognition as valid the Māyāvādin Advaitin gives a marginally separate status to it and holds the view that such sentences as this is that Devadatta. Thou art that (Tattvam asi) etc. speak of one unified object (Akhanpadārtha) as there are actually no two objects there but one and one alone. Here it may be seen that the definition of a statement (sentence) that it should remove a doubt (of some kind) is violated, since here the doubt is whether the man infront is Devadatta or not but not whether he is one or two.

Knowledge and Its Self-effulgence

Knowledge, according to Śaṅkara is self-effulgent. No other agent is required to reveal knowledge. Buddhi, however, to him is a form of mental mode (Antaḥkaraṇa Vṛtti) and the reflection of consciousness in the Vṛtti is also called Jñāna (but in a secondary sense) and it is this reflection that makes the insentient Vṛtti a sentient one. In a secondary sense the mental mode is also called Jñāna as it is the determinant of Jñāna.

The Sāṃkhya is of opinion that Buddhi is determination where the mental mode is made sentient by the proximity of consciousness (Citsannidhāna). He also makes a distinction between Buddhi and Jñāna. The latter is defined as the knowledge of distinction of consciousness (Puruṣa) from the primordial matter (Prakṛti). To the Yogin by Jñāna is meant only cessation of mental activity.

Guru of the Mīmāṃsaka school is of opinion that along with the subject (the knower) the object and the knowledge are revealed in the knowledge itself (Tripuṭīpratyakṣatāvāda).

The Buddhist and the Jaina both agree that knowledge is revealed by itself along with the object. Some of them hold that the object is nothing else but knowledge.

The Naiyāyika holds that knowledge is cognised with the help of apperception (Anuvyavasāya) which is a mental activity. It is the second apperception which reveals it in the very first cognition of an object.

Misra, the Mīmāṃsaka also is of opinion that right after a knowledge of pot a mental cognition of the type 'I know the pot' is produced and here comes in the revelation of knowledge.

The Bhāṭṭa of the Mīmāṃsaka school, however, believes that knowledge is cognised with the help of a mark (reason) designated Jñātatā (knownness) or Prākatya by means of an inference. Thus knowledge is transcendental (Atīndriya) for him.

Prabhākara thinks that knowledge is produced by an activity of the self. The self is the subject of the activity and a momentary activity later than the self-mind contact is responsible for revelation of knowledge. This is a transcendental activity.

Thus there is a wide range of difference of views on the self-revelation of knowledge. The difficulty in this matter is that, if knowledge is self-cognised there is the contingency of the knowledge itself becoming the subject as well as the object of cognition. How can the same entity be the subject and the object of the activity of knowing as the object is the locus of the result of the activity part of any action (Vyāpāra); the subject is the locus of action and the result of action is produced only later than the activity part of it. The Jainas hold that like a lamp and its light it is possible to have them at the same time. But even in the illustration given we have to accept that the lamp is lit and then the light emerges however small the interval between them be. Further the philosophers of self-revelation of knowledge hold that if knowledge were to depend on another knowledge (like apperception) for its revelation and that again on another and so on there would be infinite regress.

But the Logician is of the view that sense-object contact etc. produces knowledge and it is the efficient cause of knowledge because right after it the knowledge is produced. But he does not state in definite terms how the insentient sense object contact produces the sentient knowledge. But probably his stand is that the soul-mind contact is capable of making the self involved in the process by comprehending the object where soul is the seat of knowledge.

Further it is not necessary that the knowledge should also be revealed in order to undertake activity (Pravṛtti) as a person is induced to activity if the object is ascertained, there is no need for the knowledge to be revealed.

Further if knowledge where to be revealed by another knowledge the question arises (How is the latter knowledge revealed? It requires another knowledge for the purpose and so on ad infinitum.

The Logician holds that the soul is possessed of eight special properties and thus it is responsible for desire, activity etc. It is only the individual soul that is responsible for volition, perception etc., of objects, undertaking activity and so on. The impressions also are located in the soul. Thus in his view the merit is that there is a directing agent, the individual soul which cognises particular objects. It is difficult, on some other theorists points of view to ascertain who the director of all these activities is inasmuch as the mind or the internal organ is insentient for them all (though some hold that its immaculate nature allows it to reflect the pure consciousness in it). Even to the Advaitin (Śāṅkarite) the individual soul is a composite body (in the pragmatic view) wherein the internal organ determines the Cit part of it neither of which can undertake activity (Vṛtti) as the former is unattached to anything and the latter is insentient even according to him.

To avoid this difficult if it is held as the Sāṃkhya and the Śāṅkarite do, that either the proximity of consciousness (Cit sannidhāna) or the reflection in the consciousness (Cit pratibimba) is admitted to make cognition sentient there also arises a question as to how the proximity or the reflection, itself insentient is capable of making it sentient. Another question also is how the contact less (Asaṅga) knowledge (Cit) reflects the Vṛtti.

But in the Advaitin's opinion as knowledge is ubiquitous and the only real existent. When with the help of Vṛtti the veil of Nescience (Ajñāna) is destroyed with reference to a particular adjunct (Upādhi) the knowledge of the object shines forth. The Jaina also speaks of the removal of veil and he holds that the self realises the object. These two views appear to be sound in establishing the sentient nature of knowledge as compared with the other theories of Epistemology. To the Śaṅkarite Nescience (Ajñāna) is a positive object in the form of a veil which conceals (Āvṛnote) the consciousness (Cit) and it is the removal of this veil which presents the Cit to us; with the help of the Vṛtti however it tends to produce a knowledge of objects by dint of its (veils) Vikṣepaśakti (projecting capacity).

Buddhist's Knowledge

The Buddhist argues that knowledge alone is capable of cognising (objects). The sense organ etc. which are insentient cannot be the cause of cognition. This argument needs a critical approach. Since all things in the world are momentary for him what is the way in which the first cognition (a produced one) is produced. Cognition is not eternal since he does not accept any eternal cognition like the Vedāntin. If he is of the view that cognition has been there without a break it would be beginningless (or in a sense eternal). Further he speaks of impressions without a beginning (Anādivāsanas), while maintaining non-existent (Asat) as the cause of the existent (Sat). How are these (impressions) maintained intact according to his theory of momentariness of all objects? If a series of moments (Kṣhaṇikasantāna) is responsible for holding them together even as one cognition they become non-momentary and the Vāsanās should be stated to be held by the series of momenta (an insentient object). It is also well-known that sentient ones like the scorpion are produced from dung etc. as the Sāṃkhya argues. Unlike in the Advaitin's view, how is this possible in the case of the Buddhist who does not accept an eternal (soul or) cognition which enters the individual at birth? Hence cognition should be accepted on his stand as produced from even insentient objects like sense-organs as even a permanent entity (which latter is against his own theory).

Further the Buddhists' objection that the insentient sense organ cannot be the means of cognition does not hold good. The Logicians' view is that the insentient organ and its contact (its activity) immediately precede the cognition but the cognition is actually the souls. The soul is in contact with the mind. Hence the actual seat of knowledge according to the Logician is the sentient soul and not the sense-organ. In the view of the Śaṅkarite, however, what actually exists is consciousness. It is veiled by a positive substance called Nescience (Ajñāna) and with the help of the sense organ the mind assuming the form of the object gets the paintry (Upraga) or gets the veil of Nescience removed (Avaraṇābhibhāva) and then the eternal consciousness is reflected (Pratibhimbta) in the mind and thus the mind appears to be sentient cognising the particular object. Hence in both the Logicians' and the Vedantins' views there should be no objection regarding the insentient sense-organ being the means of cognition. Even the Buddhist cannot escape the contingency raised by him against the Logician as he too has to identify the necessity for the contact of the sense-organ for perception.

In the case of Pratyaksa all the contacts enumerated by the Logician cannot be admitted by the Buddhist. He refutes most of the categories of the Logician. He first rejects the composite whole (Avayavin). He says only the parts (forepart, hindpart etc.) are seen and not the whole. But what does he mean by saying so whose part is it? Without accepting an object how could you say it is the forepart or the hindpart? Further without an object and its name how can recollection of Vyāpti be effected in inference for the concomitance is of the form 'where there is smoke, there is fire.' In addition to this even though one individual smoke and fire are known by perception and 'concomitance' only between those individual smoke and fire is cognised how can the concomitance between another smoke and another fire be cognised without the help of genus – the genus (smoke) and the genus 'fire'? existing in objects. Hence genus also cannot refuted by him. Even in his definition of Svalakṣaṇa the Buddhist includes the form (Ākāra). If the object is only a mass of atoms, where is the form? If the form of the mass of atoms, also is cognised, does it mean that the atoms are in a particular shape, attached to each other and have a name in which case he accepts the constituent whole. Again with regard to properties if properties themselves are regarded as 'object,' how can change of particular properties and the endurance of other qualities be established? Hence qualities have to be accepted as inhering in individuals as also actions. Further it is against common experience that statements like 'This pot is black' etc. are invalid according to his view as the pot (the object, Avayavin) does not exist. It is also surprising that refuting all these categories the Buddhist uses them in plenty in his statements made and arguments advanced as they are essential requirements for a knowledge of all things (e.g. words like Sārūpya, Paricchedakatvaṃ etc.).

Objects – The Buddhist's Theory

To the Nihilist there is no object at all nor even knowledge. The Yogacara admits no external object. It is only the cognition that assumes the form of an external object. The cognition of object is due to the beginningless impression of old or the existence of objects is even due to invalid knowledge. If objects were really needed for knowledge how is it that we cognise objects in a dream without any external object? Says the Buddhist 'on the same principle we could accept that there is no need to postulate objects even in the waking state in order to cognise them. This is the Buddhists stand.

An objection here is if it is knowledge alone that shines forth as the object how is it that one object appears as a pot to all people and another as a mat. If the Buddhist replies that it is due to impressions of old why is it not that the pot appears as a mat and the mat as a pot to all alike since all these impressions are already there. If the Buddhist holds that it is due to some unseen cause (Adṛṣṭa) (which he should not of course admit) why should the unseen cause be common to all those that perceive alike. Further how were the impressions of those objects first formed without the objects concerned not in existence? How can the form of the object (concerned) be assumed by the cognition without the object itself. In such a case when a pot is actually perceived, it may take the form of a mat and not that of a pot. He further argues that an object (as stated to exist by the opponent) is cognised only with the aid of cognition. It is there when the cognition is present and not there when it is not present. Hence the object is not different from the form of the cognition.[79] To the objection as to how that there are differences in cognition (pot, mat) he holds that they should be stated to be due either to the object or the impressions of old – either of them. But the former alternative cannot be accepted because he holds, the necessary cause, cognition as an attribute is necessary for cognising blue etc. and hence the form of the cognition itself should be the cause and not the object (necessarily).

The Buddhist also refutes that the individual object is not there but only the forepart, the hindpart etc. But here he is to be questioned whose forepart and whose hindpart it is that is seen. If all the group of atoms are a single heap how can there be a forepart. If then be no individual (particular) object why not some of the atoms (of that particular object) be considered as a part of the second (object) heap of objects present contiguiously in the same area.

Further how is Artha Kriyā itself produced if only knowledge were there. A mere knowledge of the pot, an internal entity, cannot bring water but the actual object pot which is external.[80] If, according to his stand the cognition itself assumes the form (Ākāra) of the pot why is it that it would not hold water in it disturbing his own theory of Arthakriyā Karitva and why is it that he has to wait for the validity of knowledge till the correspondence of it with the object is ascertained.

Further even in the case of inference knowledge assumes the form of the object but Artha Kriyā is not possible there. So he accepts Artha Kriya is possible only in the case of an object of perception where something other than the form of the knowledge (i.e. the object) is necessary to be accepted. Another point that occurs to our mind is whether knowledge (the object) itself becomes hot and with a mere hot thought could we take a hot water bath? One need not approach an object for the sake of hot or cold things as the Buddhist Yogācara views. Does the cognition of a pot hit our foot on the way or the actual pot? Further if knowledge (as the self) also is cognised along with the blue colour (of pot etc.) the resulting cognition would be of the form 'The knowledge is blue' or 'I am blue' and not 'This is blue.' In order to admit distinction in cognitions like blue, red, pot, mat etc. it is quite necessary to hold that the object blue etc. separately exist which stand is more judicious than holding that some unseen cause or impressions of old are responsibile for it. Further we perceive that a pot is broken, not the thought. We also speak of the absence of objects (Ghaṭabhāva etc.) which is (an object of) cognition. Does it mean that cognition has ceased if the object is not perceived or that the cognition itself is broken? If, on the other hand, it be held by the Buddhist that broken pots etc. are also cognitions produced by the previous impressions, all world activity comes to an end as there is no particular object for cognition and causal efficiency and his theory of perception and inference would be at stake. Of course Advaita Vedānta has its reinforcements against this which concedes an empirical reality also just as Buddhists hold a similar category Samvṛtesatya. Further what is meant by Validity of knowledge according to the Buddhist? If it is Arthāvisaṃvādakatva the object (Artha) has to be accepted. Otherwise in the Yogācāra view the cognition itself should agree with the cognition (which is also the object as he holds). Further the Grāhyagrāhaka bhāva of the knowledge is adversely affected in the Yogācara view. Since the same knowledge is the Grāhya (object) and the Grahaka (knowledge). No Vyavasthā can operate in this case as there is no Grāhya (object) separately from the Grāhaka. He has to give a precise definition of knowledge. According to him this knowledge that cognises itself. The objection of the Yogācāra that if the object exists, when its colour is perceived by the eye taste also should be perceived does not stand to reason as the necessary contact with taste is not present at that time.

Seeing the obvious difficulties involved here, the Vaibhāṣika objects to this view held by the Yogācārin and holds that objects do exist. To this class of thinkers the perceptual object only is the existent (Sat) but not the inferred one. Thus they divide objects into two types – perceived (indeterminate) and the others determined by inference which is not valid. It is held that the intelligent persons were preached Sūnyavāda by the Buddhist, the less competent the thought-object Vada (Yogācāra) and the Vaibhasikas, Sautrantikas and others that objects exist but in the earlier view the object is perceptual and causally efficient but in the latter it is only inferred. Though in the Buddha's opinion everything is really void (Sūnya) still he had to express these different views regarding objects in deference to the level of understanding of particular classes of people.

The Sautrāntika also contends the position held by the Yogācarin and states that objects like blue are seen only once a while while cognition is always present and hence objects do exist; but they are to be inferred. The idea is that though the Ālayavijñāna (the Ego) is always present blue etc. (the objects of knowledge) are apprehended by the cognition (Pravṛṭṭivijñāna) only once a while. Hence in order to justify such knowledge of non-eternal things, objects have to be admitted.

The main objection of the Yogacāra is that even without objects there are cognitions in the dream state and on similar grounds we can admit only cognitions without objects in the waking state also is not quite sound as in the dream state either a defect or an impression of a previous experience as the cause, but in actual life when there is a perceived object his stand cannot be admitted. Another point that he raises is that objects cannot be held to exist as none of the objects of the world as proposed by the opponents stand to reason, matter does not exist, hence properties and action don't; nor even Samavāya; no space, no time, no ether too. To this the reply should that he mentions all these objects by name and discusses that non-existence and hence objects cannot be discarded.

That is why while rejecting the view of the Buddhist's object negation theory, the Logician defines earth as one possessed of earthhood etc. Further as Bhaṭṭa holds the object is the enduring one where the qualities may change e.g. A Jamun may be red in colour. The same changes its colour in course of time. But it is still the same Jamun with all its medicinal and chemical properties. Hence it is safe to admit that cbjects do exist and they are different from knowledge (Jñāna).

The Object – The Jaina View

According to the Jaina the object of valid knowledge is a thing which is subject to production and destruction because it is only that is capable of carrying out activity (Arthakriyā), it is not the simple thing which is not a Paryāya.[81] Such a thing is the actual existent according to the Jaina unlike for the Buddhist to whom it is only that which is capable of activity (Arthakriyāsamartham). He argues that the simple thing (Dravya) cannot be the cause of activity either mediately or immediately.[82] He criticises the Buddhist view that even a series (Santāna) of the previous and the succeeding moments can bring about order (Krama) because a series is not an object (Vastu). Even if the series be held to be a real object (Vastu) there would be no difference between the series and the moments. If the series, on the other hand is considered not momentary then his theory of momentariness is at stake. He also defends his theory against possible attacks by his rivals.[83]

The result of Pramāṇa (a knowledge itself), to the Jaina, is a knowledge of the object (Arthaprakāśa). But he observes the obvious difficulty in this stand like the Bauddha and takes a stand akin to his and states that one knowledge is the determinant of the other. Thus the same knowledge like 'this is a pot' is the determinant and the other part of it 'I know the pot' is the determined. Of course this view expressed by both the unorthodox philosophers Buddhist and Jaina needs to be suitably illustrated. Then only it can be accepted.

In order to avoid all this difficulty it would be better to hold the sentient self (Ātman) as the revealer of knowledge as it is in contact with all knowledge in the Logician's view.

Buddhist's Theory of Momentariness

The Buddhist philosophy holds that whatever (really) exists is momentary.[84] All objects which are considered existent by the other schools are considered by them to be momentary. That is to say an object exists for a minute and is destroyed in the second. An object is produced either as one destructible or indestructible as the Buddhist views. If it is destructible then it should destroyed soon after its production. If on the other hand it is said naturally to exist for some time why does it not continue to exist even if it is hit with a staff? Though this stand is true to some extent, we have to admit that we don't equate a pot broken (destroyed) with a pot in the second minute after its production (when not destroyed finally). Further it the cogniser himself too is destroyed in the second minute after his production is a different cogniser can never cognise not only the sense percept but even the next minute object with which to effect mental construction (Vikalpa) and the minute itself will not be the next one as he did not experience the percept earlier. To the Logician, on the other hand objects like word, cognition and action are produced in the first minute, in the next they exist and are destroyed in the third minute. Thus these objects survive for two minutes and get destroyed in the third minute. Other objects are enduring and they have a real objecthood (Padārthatva) in them. As against the Buddhist view the Logician maintains that earth is what has earthhood in it and so on. If all existent objects are momentary as the Buddhist holds, there is no scope for recognition. We say 'this is that Caitra' wherein identity is established between the Caitra of the present moment and the Caitra of the past. This is not valid knowledge for the Buddhist as the Caitra of the present time is different from the Caitra of the past and hence there could be no identity. But in experience we find identity established between them. If this be not admitted how can a man be punished for his crime after some time as he is quite a different man in the next minute? Or how could a pot seen now be expected to carry water as a pot did in the past as it is something different now? Hence we have to accept that there is a genus called 'potness' which is responsible for designating another object also as 'pot' on the lines of the previous pot experienced. Thus the Buddhist is obliged to accept the contact 'Sāmānyalakṣaṇa also and as a consequence genus (Sāmānya) also. How otherwise can he defend concomitance (Vyāpti) too?

The Buddhist's argue that if the pot has the same individuality (Svarūpa) at the very time of its production as when it is destroyed with a club then it should be stated to be destroyed with a club then it should be stated to be destroyed only the next minute after it is produced. But the opponent's position is that the pot is produced from its own causes and exists for sometime and then gets destroyed due to particular causes. The Buddhist objection that what naturally exists after production cannot be destroyed later by anything what so ever; but the opponent may hold that even a naturally existent object is liable to be destroyed by causes like the blow with a club etc. (or even by constant wearing away).

Further if an object is momentary how can it be the cause of another object as it is already destroyed? If cognition also is momentary how can the sense organ which takes a minute to assume the form of the object be cognised again by the mind (Citta) in the next minute and who is the actual cogniser that cognise the sense perception as the cogniser himself is destroyed and another has taken its place. If it be urged the series (Santana) of the same cognition (after the Samānantarapratyaya) that cognises the object of sense perception (Svalakṣaṇa), how could the series a non-real (Avastu) cognise it?

Hence it is judicious, as I think, to admit that though there is a minute change in objects in a state of flux the short-timed change of properties etc. in the object does not affect its practical utility like carrying water which is not altered and hence with an eye to the result produced by the object we may have to admit that the object exists, as it is, for some time. If this position be not accepted we will have to go on admitting in innumerable objects and their properties, changes in activities of the objects and so on giving them a name every minute of their existence e.g. A chain is a chain which provides accommodation for a person to sit on. It would be a chair even though its colour may change or a part of it is broken till it allows a man to sit on. After a few months or years it may be broken, the form (Akṛti) may also change and then it becomes gradually a broken chair, pieces of wood and so on and finally it becomes one with the earth.

The Self-Cognition Theory of Knowledge of the Buddhist

The Buddhist holds that knowledge is self-cognised (Svasamvedya). The Advaita Vedāntin holds that knowledge reveals itself i.e. not revealed by another. The idea of both is that knowledge needs no other agency to reveal it. The Buddhists' idea is that an insentient object like a pot cannot cognise another object and, therefore, it is knowledge alone that can cognise objects. If that knowledge also were to be cognised by another knowledge and that again by another there would be infinite regress. Hence his contention that knowledge is self-cognised. Here a question arises as to how knowledge cognises itself. In order that (a particular) knowledge may be cognised it is necessary that the original knowledge itself (along with the object if it is separate) should be produced formerly and then a cognition of it can ensue. It cannot be argued that the same knowledge is cognised piecemeal as it is the entire knowledge 'This is a pot' 'I know this to be a pot' etc., that is cognised as in a cognition like 'I know that this is a pot.'

Further what is the purpose served by admitting a cognition of knowledge? We see that no purpose is served by such a cognition. If it be urged that the Validity of knowledge is known by such a cognition even then it is not necessary to be accepted as it is not useful for undertaking activity (except when there is a doubt about its validity or about the object concerned). This doubt etc. arise only when a knowledge (after it is produced) is doubted and not earlier. Again we have to admit that knowledge is a cause of its (own) cognition which should precede the effect – its cognition. Another point to be objected to is that not all knowledge but a variety of it (Svasamvedya is considered to be self-cognised by some Buddhists. Is it only objects like pleasure, pain etc. that are cognised by their own selves? In such a case it is to be admitted that one knowledge cognises another knowledge as pleasure, pain etc. are only pieces of knowledge for a Buddhist, in which case a knowledge also becomes an object that is revealed by another (Paravedya). Another defect in the theory is that two objects are cognised – one the object (pot etc.) and the other the knowledge. Here a confusion arises whether the object serves to prompt one to action or the knowledge (as 'I know the pot' etc.) cognised gives him satisfaction and nothing else. Further the objection raised by the Buddhist that there is infinite regress in assuming that another cognition cognises the former cognition etc. ad infinitum i.e. applicable to him also – for a knowledge of (the self-cognition of) the knowledge would also be cognised by itself and this would be cognised again by itself and so on endlessly. Thus self-cognition of knowledge stands on loose ground. It is better to admit knowledge is cognised by another knowledge when necessary.

Buddhist Determinate and Indeterminate Knowledge

Almost all philosophers accept Indeterminate knowledge except a few like Rāmānuja. The need for accepting such a knowledge has already been discussed. But there is much difference between the view of Indeterminate knowledge as held by the Buddhists and by the others. All philosophers hold that it is a knowledge which does not apprehend any distinction (Vīkalpa) name, class etc. like the knowledge gained by a child, dumb person etc. Though it is produced by sense contact it does not comprehend any particular thing. What is its content then? It is only the 'mere object' (Vastumātra) (pot and pothood not connected). In the next moments after this knowledge is produced the determinate knowledge of it is produced. Some say it is not necessary to have any other cause, some hold that it is produced along with the Indeterminate knowledge (Guru). Some say that the determinate knowledge is a mental perception (Mānasajñāna) (Miśra). The Logician also accepts a consequent determinate knowledge derived from indeterminate knowledge. According to Bhaṭṭa however all knowledge is inferred with the help of knownness (Jñātatā). This indeterminate knowledge is not purposeful in experience. The need for it justifies its existence. It is only the determinate knowledge that is helpful in actual life. Indeterminate knowledge, according to the Logician is neither valid nor invalid. Some of them hold a different view also. The form of an indeterminate knowledge is like this 'This is something (Yatkiñcit).[85] Unless this basic knowledge exists no name, class etc. can be spoken about it as the qualification is to be known earlier than the qualified. That is their view. Some of them hold that there is objecthood in this knowledge too but it is of a fourth type.

To the Buddhist of course, indeterminate knowledge is almost the same as to the other philosophers being devoid of class, name etc. But he maintains that that alone is the actual perception. The determinate knowledge is not included under perception as it is something produced with the help of other factors like memory, association of name, class etc. which are not included under perceptual aids. Determinate knowledge is invalid (knowledge) for him. This is so because existent objects get destroyed every minute and a new object is produced again. If it is so what is the purpose served by the penal code. In this minute a criminal commits offence and in the next minute punishment is given to an entirely different person as the previous one is destroyed. Thus there is the contingency in his opinion, of a person securing a result for what is not done by him and not securing the result of action that is done.'[87] This is a very awkward position. Further the Buddhist admits that inference is derived from perception. How could it be that concomitance is perceived between two objects which, according to his 'Indeterminate perception,' have neither name or class? It is the simple thing in itself (Svalakṣana) that is perceived according to him, and it is only invalid knowledge that is gained later. Further we have to question him how the cognition of name, class etc. (Vikalpajñāna) arises as the name, class etc. are not present in the object on the one hand and are destroyed in the second minute on the other by the time the next knowledge is produced. If the class, action etc. are not previously perceived in the indeterminate knowledge how can they be cognised and given names? So he too has to accept that they are all perceived later on in the same knowledge. But this cannot be due to perception as the eye function ceases or to inference as there is no concomitance present between the object and the class etc. not cognised.

It is only the object and its genus that are perceived earlier in indeterminate knowledge which are later connected (Saṃsṛṣṭa) and verbally expressed and further action is taken on them after the production of determinate knowledge.

If a series (of the perceptual knowledges), on the other hand, is stated to perceive the name, class etc. it is to be definitely stated whether the series is insentient or sentient. If it be insentient it cannot perceive the object of determinate knowledge and if it be sentient it will not be different from the knowledge previous to it and hence no new knowledge can be produced.

Further to argue that indeterminate knowledge is valid does not stand as class, name, properties etc. are not cognised by the percipient at that stage and action cannot be induced by such perception.

Further the statement of the Buddhist that valid knowledge should correspond with the object is not intelligible since knowledge cannot correspond with an object as they are mutually different. He has only to say that the object of knowledge should be known to be possessed of its property or genus.

In the Yogācāra view since the cognition is of the form of the object the cognition should agree with itself. The truth of this determinate knowledge theory appears to be that as soon as the indeterminate knowledge is produced laterly all the Vikalpas name, class etc. are recollected; even the Buddhist has to accept this. In such a case it is wise to accept that the concerned objects name, class, which actually exist in the opinion of the other philosophers are apprehended and then name, class etc. (Vikalpas) are recalled with the aid of impressions of the past. If the object is not seen at the time of perception how can name, class etc. be recalled which depend upon a previous knowledge of the object of its name, class etc. and hence objects of necessity have to be accepted by all philosophers. Hence it is probable that the Advaitin accepts a different being (Sattā) for all pragmatic objects which are in reality an illusion in the ultimate truth.

Further no object entirely changes itself as it serves the same purpose for at least some time, has pratically the same name and is also recognised later as the same object and has mostly the same properties. Properties may change but not the object. After all that is an object which serves a purpose and that purpose is not generally obstructed in a minute. The properties also are not obstructed. They stand for sometime. Further we don't give a name to the object and a specific purpose to it in each moment of the existence of the object. The Keśondruka before the eye etc. are due to some defect in the eye and the object we see there is not actually present; hence it is a case of illusion.

Thus many philosophers accept the existence of objects though some don't, some others hold that they are momentary, some others that they exist only till they are repudiated by the dawn of knowledge.

Varieties of Valid Knowledge – Perception Etc.

Some hold that there are only two varieties of valid knowledge 'perceptual and inferential' (Pratyakṣa and Anumita). Others hold that there are three including testimony (Śabda). The Logician holds there are four varieties of valid knowledge, where he includes 'Analogy' (Upamita) also in addition. The Prābhakara adds presumption (Arthāpatti) and makes then five. Kumārila includes negation (Abhāva or Anupalabdhi) as a sixth one. The Śāṅkarite follows suit. Others again are there who variously include possibility (Saṃbhava), tradition (Aitihya), action (Ceṣṭā) etc. Now it is for us to examine whether all these are exclusive varieties which deserve to be retained or whether they could be simplified and conveniently brought under a lesser number without jeopardising the theories of knowledge. As the first step in deciding the varieties of valid knowledge we have to define validity. If by validity is meant 'the presence of thatness in that' (Tadvati tatprakārakatvam) by valid knowledge is meant a knowledge of thatness in that.

Now let us try to subdivide this knowledge of thatness in that from the point of view of the source from which it is produced (i.e.

from the standpoint of the means of knowledge). There has ever been a large amount of divergence of opinion in not only the production of knowledge, the object of knowledge, the varieties of knowledge and the nature of the means of knowledge (i.e. Pramāṇatattva) but also in the number of the means of knowledge (Pramāṇasaṃkhyā). There are according to each school of philosophy as many means of knowledge as there are varieties of knowledge. And each one of them believes it is an exclusive means, whereas the opponent who believes in a lesser number of these holds that some of the means enumerated could be brought under one or two of the fewer means accepted by him. We have already seen how the Buddhist tries to include analogy etc. in the two kinds of means accepted by him (perception and inference). Presumption is included by the Logician in inference and so on and so forth. But how is this dispute about the number of Pramāṇas to be settled? No attempt at arriving at a solution acceptable at all appears to have been made though very subtle dialectics have been undertaken to establish each one's own view by each philosopher separately. Let us try to examine these subjects by comparison and contrast.

The Common Varieties of Knowledge

Perception is the only means of knowledge admitted by all classes of philosophers including the Cārvāka. Nobody dared to deny it as the entire world of objects and of knowledge would go blind if it is not accepted as a Pramāṇa. Further all the other Pramāṇas depend upon perception directly or indirectly for their existence.

The definitions of Pratyakṣa as given by the Logician, the Mīmaṃsaka etc. cover almost all the requirements that are needed to bring both the determinate and the indeterminate knowledges under them. It may not be possible to agree with the Buddhist that determinate knowledge is different from sense-perception as name, class etc. are not ocular perceptions, for it is only the objects perceived by the eye etc. that are given names for communication with others and for inducement to action. Simple Svalakṣaṇa cannot be so.

Further the Vṛtti of the mind as admitted by the Advaita Vedāntin or the Sārupya (assuming the form of the object by the cognition) cannot be accepted as perception as in that case the mind or the thought itself should be stated to assume hot and cold touches etc. which are not experienced in life. It is enough if only contact is established between the sense organ and the object as the Logician thinks.

The view of the Buddhist that only momentary Vijñāna can cognise objects is not true for obvious defects. Instead the self (Ātman) which is possessed of the capacity to know and which is the seat of knowledge, may be accepted as cognising objects. If the minute changes are accepted every minute no corresponding Anthakriyā is possible to be proved.

It may also be noted that the Buddhist stand that the same knowledge which experiences similarity with the blue (object) etc. also produces a cognition of the blue (object) cannot be admitted because, if knowledge is to assume the form of blue (without cognising blue already) an object blue different from knowledge has to be accepted even by the Yogācārin. If the knowledge has assumed the form even before the blue is cognised, there is no case for assuming similarity with the blue. Further the knowledge which starts functioning to perceive blue etc. which is already overloaded with its previous object cannot cognise blue etc. If the former knowledge is already destroyed and there is no separate object what form does the knowledge take?

Mental cognition (perception) cannot be included under perception without admitting mind (Manas) as a sense organ as it cannot be included under inference.

Unless the normal contacts of the sense organ with the object are conceded the differences in perception like colour, colourhood etc. cannot be distinguished; and without the supernormal contacts it is not possible to have a knowledge of class, erroneous knowledge, Yogijñāna etc.

Even to recall particular objects from among the impressions of old, as in a dream, in the working state, there is no store-house of knowledge (except probably in the case of those who accept Ālayavijñāna like the mind which is permanent). The question is who stimulates and who recalls the impressions? Even admitting that an impression is recalled why is the particular impression recalled when there are hundreds of impressions of old. Assuming that an unseen cause is responsible for it presumes that Adṛṣṭa is another category for the Buddhist. Further it has to be admitted by him that the same Adṛṣṭa (unseen cause) strangely affects all percipients alike (when a blue object is seen). Hence it appears to be better to accept objects which too are not momentary but existent for a time and then get destroyed sooner or later.

The objection of the Buddhist that an insentient sense organ cannot cognise an object does not stand as it is only the Sentient Atman (self) that cognises the object and in the case of the Sāmkhya and the Advaitin it is the Vṛtti (mental mode) in which Self (Atman) gets reflected and thus there is the touch of sentience. The Jaina also is of the view that the veil on the object is removed as the Advaitin thinks. The sense organ or the mind (along with its contact or the mind along with the Vṛtti) is only the efficient cause (Karaṇa) congenial to the production of perceptual knowledge. Thus it is not the sense organ, in any theory, that actually cognises.

Mind (Manas) also has to be accepted as a means of cognising external objects with the help of sense organs and also internal objects like pleasure and pain without their help. If mind be not accepted there is no restriction of one particular knowledge being produced in the self at a time, according to the Logician. In the Advaitin's opinion an explanation is needed why only one object is cognised at a time, the Vṛtti being admitted for the sake of removing the veil etc. It is also a question as to who directs the mind to have a mental mode in the form of a particular object. If it is the composite self (Jīvātman) consciousness with mind as an adjunct that desires the mode, then the mind an insentient object should be responsible for the desire. If it is argued that the consciousness desires in the presence of the mind as the adjunct, then it should be held that the consciousness should be the seat of desire. In the Buddhist's view which does not accept a separate sentient self there is no way in which perception etc. are produced. It cannot be said momentary knowledge is produced of its own accord as we find in experience that an object as desired is perceived or inferred only occasionally. Further the agent of desire should be stated by him. It is not cognition itself that can desire. If desire is of the form of cognition we cannot have the experience of pleasure, pain etc. as objects as we normally have.

'Is the Mind a sense organ or not' is a debated question. The Logician holds mind as a sense organ with the help of an inference. His definition of a sense organ includes not only the five sense organs but also mind.[88] But the Advaitin rejects this view on the ground that the mind itself a sense organ (Manas) cannot be the substratum of soul-mind contact itself. It appears that this objection may be counteracted by defining a sense organ in a different way.[89] By this definition not only Ātman is excluded from its scope but artha (object) too. By including the phrase Asādhāraṇa . . .

Samyoga, only the mind-sense organ contact and the Ātman-mind contact alone are included, thus permitting mind and Indriya both to be included. The distinction between the mind and the Indriya is that the one is an internal Indriya and the other an external one. Further unless the mind is accepted as an Indriya (sense-organ) how can pleasure, pain etc. be cognised even when the external sense organs ceases to operate? To hold that the witness consciousness (Sākṣi) cognises pleasure etc. as held by the Śaṅkarite, may not be possible as the objects, pleasure etc. and a connection is established unless they are objects.

The Śaṅkarite also objects to the existence of objects in the truly real (Pāramārthika) state but accepts them in the Vyāvahārika or the pragmatic state of reality. But his contention that there are no objects must be true only in the Pāramārthika state.[90] To denounce the reality of objects on the analogy of the dream state objects may not be accepted as we know the unknown impressions of the waking state are responsible for them; but in the waking state there is an obvious manifest contact established between an object and the concerned sense organ which alone is responsible for the perception. It is not wise to accept an unseen cause in preference to a seen cause in such cases.[91] Otherwise one may be stated to approach a mountain for water to quench ones thirst (as the Adṛṣṭa may be there) but one goes to a water-tank for the purpose (a seen cause). To argue that no contact is possible between the object and the sense organ is unreasonable as we know it for certain and we achieve the result thereof. Further impressions (of objects) also cannot be established for nominating them as the cause of perception. Unless you accept another Herculean myth that the impressions have no beginning. Further here it may be questioned why impressions alone should be admitted without a beginning and not objects themselves, which stand solves the whole question satisfactorily. Further to one and all validity of perception is arrived at with the help of the actual object only. Further if Avidyā (Nescience) and Bhrama (hallucination) are both beginningless then the Śaṅkarite cannot argue that the former is the cause of latter.

Supernormal Contacts

Sāmānya Lakṣana Contact

The Śaṅkarite and the Mīmāṃsaka do not admit the supernormal contact called Sāmānya Lakṣana. They hold that it is ridiculous to comprehend all fires from all smokes mentally presented on seeing one smoke in the kitchen. Their contention is that the eye is in contact only with the mountain smoke and not with all other smokes and hence all smokes past and future cannot be perceived even by the said contact. The Logician does not admit this stand of theirs. His argument is that if all smokes are not (mentally) cognised with the help of Sāmānyalakṣanā contact when one smoke is perceived, then there should be no doubt about the concomitance of smoke with the fire on the mountain as there is no knowledge about it. Of course the concomitance is decided in the case of kitchen smoke and kitchen fire and hence in the case of past and future smokes and smokes in other places concomitance is not established and hence cannot be doubted. Without a doubt inference cannot arise.[92]

According to the Advaita Siddhi the Advantin's opinion is that in the kitchen itself the smoke perceived along with (more) smokehood and hence from all smokes all fires could be inferred. But in his view the kitchen smoke can only be the concomitance of kitchen fire, not all fires (as in the kitchen smoke there is no mountain fire). If, for the sake of concomitance all smokes are admitted with the help of Samyukta tādātmya contact of the eye with the kitchen smoke, it should be admitted by him that mountain smoke also is a concomitant of mountain fire. With the help of this reason that the mountain smoke and fire also are of the same genus (Sājātya) as the kitchen fire and smoke but this militates against his own theory accepting a genus (Jāti) which present in many and is eternal according to the Logician. Hence a doubt about the fire on the unperceived smokes of past and future smokes etc. is not possible in the Śaṅkarites and Mīmāṃsaka's views. The other objection that if all fires are inferred from any smoke then one would become an omniscient is ruled out as per the arguments advanced in the Nyāya Siddhānta Muktāvali. Though they are all perceived in general they are not cognised in particular in the Logician's view. That is why in the Logician's view a doubt about fire on the mountain *in particular* is rendered possible as the mountain smoke *in particular* has not been previously perceived.

Another point, as I think, in favour of the Sāmānyalakṣaṇā contact is that a child which perceives a cow in the first instance is able to cognise a different individual cow in a different time or place. How is this rendered possible? It has seen only the particular cow. But this individual cow gets connected with the cowhood known earlier in the indeterminate knowledge and in the determinate perception this general cowhood cognised serves as a contact (Sāmānya lakṣaṇa contact) and with its help all cows are cognised later. This is seen in experience. But the Śāṅkarite does not accept this.

The point here is that the Śāṅkarite owes an argument as to how the kitchen smoke (*a particular*) perceived is a concomitant of fire (*in general*), when all other smokes are not presented to the mind. If, he thinks that mere (general) smokehood is perceived even in the kitchen smoke then even a mountain smoke (with smokehood in it) must have been perceived automatically and the mountain fire too must be cognised then and there with its help. Thus there will be no scope for a doubt about mountain fire for him on seeing mountain smoke subsequently.

This contact is a strong tool in the Logician's kit to explain the concomitance of all smokes etc. with all fires.

The Śāṅkarite thinks that though with the help of kitchen smokehood itself cognised concomitance is determined, his contention is that a doubt about concomitance is rendered possible with the help of mere smokehood (smokehood in general) but actually it is not known and the Advaita Siddhi cites the author of the Cintāmaṇi in his own favour. But this cannot hold good as the case cited is one of the Kevalavyatireki type. But in the present case the concomitance is of a particular type which cannot be applied to all types in general (in its positive aspect). Further when the object of perception is a particular how can general concomitance be arrived at to help the inferential process needed?[93]

The Jñānalakṣaṇa Contact

The second type of supernormal contact called Jñānalakṣaṇa (one that is of the form of recollection of Smṛti) and it is to be admitted at least for the sake of establishing erroneous or invalid cognition (Bhrama) of objects e.g. the serpent in a rope. The rope is mistaken for a serpent in certain conditions of twilight etc. and the large amount of similarity of the rope with the smoke in its length, coils etc. It may be noted here that it is not the genus (serpenthood present in the serpent) that is perceived but only some properties mentioned above. Thus, according to the Logician, as there is no doubt about the snake (as the details are not perceived in the twilight time) the man mistakes the rope for a snake by recalling into his mind the snake seen previously. This recollection (Smṛti) *of the snake* acts as a supernormal contact and produces a transcendental mental *perception* of the same object (recollected i.e. of the snake itself).

The objection raised by the Śāṅkarite to this theory of invalid knowledge is that since the object (serpent) is not in contact with the eye the serpent in the rope illusion cannot be an instance of perceptual knowledge for in such a knowledge the Śāṅkarite accepts the Anirvacaniyakhyāti theory (of a mistaken cognition) where he points that the object (serpent) and the knower should be in the same locus (Samāna satva). As they are not like that in this case this is not a perception, the Śāṅkarite would argue. Now is this a case of inference as the necessary causal aggregate to infer that it is a serpent is not there? Even if it be argued by the opponent that the causes present themselves produce an erroneous inference of snake in the rope, (even then) the Logician is obliged to state that recollection and the consequent perception of the snake gets precedence over the inferential causal aggregate. The Śāṅkarite may argue that in regard to the knowledge of the same (i.e. only one) object (serpent) when aggregates of perception and of inference are both available, though perceptive causal aggregate is more powerful still as this is not a case of normal but supernormal contact, the latter is less powerful and hence Jñānalakṣaṇa contact cannot work. But this should not be accepted as in the case of this perception the supernormal contact, here the casual mental perceptual aggregate takes precedence over the inferential aggregate as recollection is more immediate and less prolix. As soon as the length, coils etc. are seen in the defect of twilight etc. without any knowledge of reason or mark the impression of the serpent experienced (before in life) in his mind is aroused and the serpent comes into his knowledge (the inferential knowledge is more prolix and requires more time). Hence Jñānalakṣaṇa has to be admitted for fear of prolixity.

The mistaken notion of the serpent in the rope can be further elucidated thus. It cannot be a case of inference of the snake from the coils, its length etc. as it is less prolix to hold that it is case of recollection from the few reminding factors (Udbodhakas) like length, coils etc. The snake formerly known is recollected earlier than inferred from insufficient data like coils and length as the process of inference needs all these items of contact of the object (rope) with the eye, taking into account only the length, coils etc. of the object, falsely to deliberate generalising them without sufficient data (where there are coils, length etc.) that, there must be a snake, and finally considering (Parāmarśa) it (as possessed of the insufficient

Linga) as a snake. In the case of recollection, however, from the two or three powerful reminding factors (Udbodhakas) the length and coils, the quick mind jumps to the conclusion (by recollection of a snake seen earlier) more easily. Here it may be noted that the supernormal mental perception of snake is engendered in the mind with the help of the recollection (Smaraṇa) itself[94] which acts as a contact of the sense organ with the object in front.

Another point that may be noted here is that if the snake in the rope be a case of inference on the basis of the Advaitin's contention, their perception may be completely done away with (as a means of knowledge), for, when the sense organ contacts a pot its form (Kambugrīvādimattvam) may serve as a (Liṅga) mark to infer a pot as (This is a pot inasmuch as it has the form like the pot already seen by me). Of course there is not much harm in calling it a process of inference but there is prolixity in it. When it is possible to recall that a pot seen earlier with the help of the form etc. (or strictly the Jati in it) it is not judicious to bring the cognition under inference.

It cannot be urged against the Logician that as the serpent is not actually present before the eye, inference is the only way to cognise the snake in the rope because when there is possibility for a mental perception possible with the help of recollection (of the snake) as a proximity (Jñānalakṣaṇa) it is better to accept supernormal perception in such cases.[95]

Further, the Advaitin's theory of error is more cumbrous, admitting the production of (not a cognition of) a snake from the rope materials (which are not a cause) and establishing contact of the sense organ with them and finally when the error is cognised admitting that the snake materials are destroyed is all too prolix and too far from experience to accept.

Further accepting this supernormal contact erroneous knowledge of one thing as another (Anyathākhyāti) is accepted by the Logician in the case of invalid knowledge as already stated. The Śaṅkarite holds that in case of invalid knowledge, the Logician's theory is not correct as an indefinable knowledge of the mistaken object (serpent) is produced in the rope. This theory is called the Anirvacanīya khyāti theory. But the latter is too prolix to admit. It admits both a (mistaken) object and causal aggregate both as causes of the mistaken notion whereas the Logician does not speak of the object as a direct cause of the mistaken notion. Thus there is less prolixity in the Logician's view.

Even in the Śaṅkarite's theory the Anyathākhyāti theory has been admitted by some thinkers without which a mistaken notion of soulhood in the nonsoul cannot be established. Some hold that Anyathākhyāti is necessary to be admitted in a case of mistaken notion where the superimposed object is distant (not present). But the general opinion of the Śāṅkarite is that his theory of Anirvacanīyakhyāti is correct. They hold that in the mistaken notion of soulhood in nonsoul is only the relation between the two relata that is considered Anirvacanīya but not the relatum soul (as soul cannot be created by any Khyāti).

The arguments on the theory of error and dream are too complex to be discussed here. The interested readers' attention is invited to the attack on Jñānalakṣaṇā contact in the Advaita Siddhi (Prat. Bad.). The view of the Advaita Siddhi that the cause and effect-relationship (the contact between the eye and the cane-holder is enough for producing perception and not a knowledge of the qualification) appears not sound since a determinate perception of the cane-holder cannot arise without a knowledge of the cane (Daṇḍa) also though it is in proximity. Further if simple normal contact is enough for perception (without a desire to perceive some particular detail of the object) then its property, colour, intensity of the colour etc. also should be perceived which is not the case in actual experience. Thus though the cane-holder may have a pot also in his hand. We may not cognise him as a pot-holder when a cane alone is perceived. Hence we have to admit that mere contact (with the sense organ) is not enough for perception in the case of a qualified knowledge. Further it is not only the cane but contact (Samyoga) of the cane with the person also as an attribute is to be known earlier.

The view held by the Advaita Siddhi that even at the time of the perception of kitchen fire mere firehood is perceived is not tenable as (1) as already stated the knowledge of concomitance is different and the particular case is different (which cannot produce even inference) and (2) more smokehood, as the Advaitin argues, cannot be a distinguishing attribute (Prakāra) in his inferential consideration (Parāmarśa) unless it is known (unless it is a Visaya) and mere normal contact with the smoke (Cakṣus samyoga) by itself is not enough (just as a cane-bearer is known when only the cane also is known.[96] For the Logician in the indeterminate first perception mere smokehood has already been known and hence there is no difficulty for him to establish that mere smokehood already known is present in the second moment when the determinate knowledge arises in the percipient (as there is smokehood present in smoke) and this smokehood as a supernormal contact presents all the smokes (past and present) in a general way and in his consideration (Parāmarśa) (Dhumatva prakāraka dhumavān ayam paravataḥ) is rendered possible but in the view of the Advaitin mere smokehood is not known as an attribute (i.e. not a Prakāra) in his consideration as it (smokehood) is an attribute not perceived but is present in smoke. This is so because he does not accept indeterminate knowledge as preceding a determinate knowledge. That is why the Logician has boldly asserted that along with smoke smokehood is perceived by the knower in the determinate knowledge.

The Jñānalakṣaṇa Contact (Contd.)

The second type of supernormal contact called Jñānalakṣaṇa (one that is of the form of cognition of the recollection type) and is admitted by the Logician for the sake of a knowledge of syntactical connection of word – meanings of poets of old as also for establishing invalid or erroneous perceptions. Without accepting Jñānalakṣaṇa contact we cannot recollect the syntactical connections (Samsargas) between two words – meanings as experienced previously. This is also a case of a mental perception.

Now again in the case of erroneous perception (Pratyakṣa bhrama) also Jñānalakṣaṇa contact is necessary to be admitted according to the Logician. Take the case of a rope which is mistaken to be a snake in certain circumstances (of twilight or moderate darkness etc.). Here the large amount of similarity of the rope with the snake in its length, coils etc. makes it appear like a snake. It may be noted that the genus (snakehood) is not perceived as such by the cogniser but only some external properties as stated above induce the person to believe that it is a serpent. Unless this be admitted we cannot satisfactorily explain the rope-snake illusion.

It is not valid to argue as the Śaṅkarite does, that this is a case of erroneous inference and not erroneous perception. Probably his idea is that the person infers (falsely of course) that it is a serpent because of the presence of length, coils etc. in it. But this does not hold good as the perceiver knows full well that length, coils etc. are not a definite mark (Liṇga) inference of snake. Thus even before a false mark begins its inferential process, we have to hold that the snake which is already known to him and its impression in his mind (which is stimulated readily by seeing the length, coils etc.) is roused

(Udbuddha) and instant recollection of snake is produced in the percipient with the help of the prominent defect, length etc.) defying the reasoning process with the necessary mark (Liṅga) and its presence in the rope which have to intervene. We know that desire to infer from (insufficient) causal material is much more prolix than mere recollection which needs only arousing of the previous impression and thus a mental perception of the false snake is produced. We also know the maxim that with reference to the same object (of knowledge) when both the perceptive causal aggregate and inferential causal aggregate are both present, the former gets precedence.[97] This is a fact of psychology.

It may be noted that this type of supernormal contact (of the recollection type) (Smaraṇa) produces a supernormal perception of the same object with which it is in contact. That is to say if the recollection (as a contact) pertains to the object snake, the perception produced also is that of the snake. That is why this contact is defined as a knowledge (recollection) of an object which produces a perception of itself (of the same object).[98]

This contact is held necessary not only in the case of erroneous knowledge but also in the case of a perceptual cognition of the type 'Sandal is fragrant.' When one perceives sandal with the eye, its smell (fragrance) also is perceived as the Logician holds. This knowledge is a perception to him. A contact has to be established between fragrance, in the object Sandal and the eye. Such a contact cannot be the normal contact (Laukikasannikarṣa) as, though the object is in the normal contact with the eye and fragrance is inherent in it (in the object). The reason is that though the sandal is amenable to the eye (with its normal contact), the fragrance part of it is not negotiable with the eye (Ayogya). Hence the Logician urges a separate supernormal contact in the form of Jñānalakṣaṇā with the fragrance part of the object perceived. The idea of the Logician is that when the sandal is perceived with the eye, recollection (of the small part of it) as a supernormal contact (Jñānalakṣaṇa) intervenes and the object fragrance is also perceived. That is to say whereas in the case of sandal the contact is normal (Laukika contact) in the case of fragrance it is supernormal (Alaukika).

It may not be urged that by the earlier supernormal contact (Sāmānyalakṣaṇa) itself the fragrance can be cognised as fragrancehood (Saurabhatvam) of the form of a genus is present (by inherence in fragrance inherent in the object sandal) for though the causal aggregate of normal perception (in the form of) fragrancehood is not present, still the necessary (auxiliary) cause, the causal aggregate of perception wherein the object possessed of fragrancehood as a (distinguishing) attribute (Prakāra) is present. Hence it may be argued that by the Sāmānyalakṣaṇa contact itself fragrance is cognised and thus there is no need for the other Jñānalakṣaṇa contact.

But it may be noted here that though fragrance is somehow said to be possible to be known through Sāmānyalaksana, at least the fragrancehood part of the causal aggregate of the perception spoken of herein is to be cognised only with the help of the Jñānalakṣaṇa contact advocated by him. The reason is this. If by Sāmānyalakṣaṇa contact you try to perceive fragrancehood also you have to admit another property (genus or Akhaṇḍopādhi) in fragrancehood (of the form of fragrancehood or so) to establish a knowledge of fragrancehood.[99] We know this is not possible according to a maxim[100] 'Only those properties different from a genus or an unanalysable adjunct are cognised in a certain form.' In this case fragrancehood is a genus (Jati) and hence it cannot be cognised as possessed of a different property like fragrancehood etc. but is cognised in its own form as fragrancehood.

The objection raised by the Advaitin that if fragrance be stated to be cognised by perceptual process the intensity of the smell etc. should also be cognised is irrelevant as the fragrance of sandal is a case of mental perception with supernormal contact unlike the perception produced by the senses. Even in his mental perception the Advaitin must admit difference in intensity etc. are not perceived.

Even to hold that fragrance etc. can be inferred as does the Advaitin is not judicious as it is as already stated a more cumbrous process.

If it be objected by him that in case Jñānalakṣaṇa contact is admitted there is simply no case for the admission of a Pramāṇa like inference at all, it is not valid. The reason is that though (smoke along with smokehood) is perceived and all smokes are objects of (mental) perception in general, still the *particular smoke on the mountain* should be perceived in order that the *particular fire on the mountain* may be inferred. In the case of inference along with the general the particular (Viśeṣa) is necessary to be cognised. If the particular is not known the concomitance is not cognised; if the Viśeṣa is not cognised there is no objecthood (Prakārata) in the minor premise.

The Yogajalakṣaṇa Contact

The third type of contact is called Yogajalakṣaṇa contact; contact produced by the practice of Yoga as held by the Logician. This is not accepted by the Mīmāṃsaka. This contact has to be admitted since the long line of Yoga practitioners have shown since time immemorial their knowledge of things beyond their place and time. Even today we find certain practices of Yoga not amenable to the reason known to the best of rationalists. Hence we have to admit this contact. It is only a contact and their knowledge is only perception (as inference etc. are more cumbrous and more prolix to admit) and perception needs a contact and hence the admission of such a contact. With this contact a Yogin is capable of perceiving objects far away in time and space and objects too, subtle to be perceived by the naked sense organs.

Inference

Inference as a means of knowledge has been accepted by philosophers except the Cārvāka (the materialist). Why inference as a means is to be accepted has been discussed in the Logician's theory. No other philosopher has discussed inference in such detail as the Logician did and the credit of having established it as an important means of knowledge goes to him. The defects in the definitions of other systems of thought have been amply replied to in treatises on Tarka (Logic).

It may not be urged that in view of the Logician who accepts the supernormal contact of Jñānalakṣaṇa the acceptance of Inference as a valid means of knowledge would be superfluous for, by that contact from the smoke seen fire may be recalled not necessarily inferred. But this objection does not stand as the knowledge gained by supernormal contact is more immediate than inference as it produces the false notion of snake on the spot. Another point is that inference is not possible with a particular (object) recollected without a knowledge of the general.

The view of the Buddhist that the affirmative type of inference is only twofold (Tādātmya and Tadutpatti) is not tenable as we infer taste etc. from colour (e.g. in the case of a mango) which (inference) does not fall under either of the two types stated by him.

The several definitions of Vyāpti (concomitance) have been discussed in every detail and the final view established by the Logician.

It is very difficult to establish whether Pratyakṣa as a means of knowledge is more dependable or inference (regarding the same object of cognition), the defects of Pratyakṣa have to be removed only by a reference to inference. But it may be argued that even the removal of the defect (effected) by the inference is to be validated by Pratyakṣa but even if there is a defect in this latter (Pratyakṣa) inference has to come to our rescue – This goes on I think in an endless chain till the doubts are solved.

Just as Indeterminate knowledge is the result of Pratyakṣa for the Mīmāṃsaka or the Logician or Svalakṣaṇa for the Buddhist a knowledge of the object embracing not only Sāmānya (genus) but also embracing the particular (Viśeṣa) is produced from inference as inducement to action is not possible with the cognition of Sāmānya alone without the individual. Thus Sāmānya, by Arthāpatti, includes Viśeṣa too. The Buddhist is inclined to the view that a cognition of Sāmānya is the result of inference. Without accepting Sāmānya even the Buddhist cannot defend inferential knowledge.

The Syllogism

According to the Buddhists only two members (or even one, Hetu only) are accepted in a syllogism as against the five of the Logician or the three of the Mīmāṃsaka. His syllogism runs thus with two members. (1) 'Where there is smoke there is fire as in the kitchen' (Udāharaṇa) which speaks of concomitance (Vyāpti) and (2) 'This (mountain) has smoke' (Hetu) which speaks of the relation between the mark and the minor premises. Here we observe that the inference is not complete. The No. 1 member here is probably a perception and the No. 2 member is also a perception. Here we don't find the inferential knowledge strictly formulated. What we finally establish through inference is 'This (place) has fire' even according to the Buddhist. This is not achieved in the syllogism of two members. Both of them are what are apprehended already. If a person stops with those two pieces of knowledge where is the inference? Till the inferential knowledge is produced there is no completion of the syllogism. The Buddhist surely accepts that perceptual knowledge is of the Svalakṣaṇa type, the result of sense organ-object contact. On similar lines he has to accept here also the conclusion (Nigamana) as the result suppose the person's knowledge stops for some reason or other with the knowledge gained by the two members stated; inference is not produced. Thus at least three members have to be admitted if not the five of the Logician.

Further suppose there are the two members 'Where there is smoke there is fire as in the kitchen' and 'This (mountain) has light (Prabhā) (the mark).' Does this syllogism produce the required inference? No, It is because though light is also a mark (Hetu) of fire, still as it is not the same Hetu as is found in the earlier member (Udāharaṇa) where Vyāpti is cognised earlier the syllogism cannot produce inference. Hence the 'Upanaya' viz. This will has the same smoke which is pervaded by fire? Hence Upanaya also is necessary to be accepted. This argument has been advanced against the Mīmāṃsaka too by the Logician.

Thus all the five members of the Logician appear to be necessary so that there may be agreement among the statement (Pratijñā), the reason (Hetu) and the concomitance (Vyāpti). Without locating the particular place of the mark, smoke, it is not possible to infer fire on the mountain (in that place). Further the thesis propounded is required to speak about the mark and illustration. Hence Pratijñā also has to be accepted.

The Śāṅkarite also holds the same opinion as evidenced from the concerned portion of the Advaita Paribhāṣā.

The objection that since there is an order in Svārthānumāna, the same order should be followed in Parārthānumāna does not sound well since in the former the smoke is seen, then on the basis of the maxim that the relation of one relatum recalls to our mind the other relatum the concomitance 'where there is fire there is smoke' is recalled and then due to the person's desire to infer fire (which he probably requires for some purpose from the smoke already perceived fire is inferred. But in the case of Parārthānumāna the context is different and the procedure too. One who has not observed the fire on the hill desires fire for some purpose and he is probably in search of it and the other person asserts to the man concerned that the hill has fire. 'Why' is the question 'because of the presence of smoke,' 'If there is smoke should there be fire' is the doubt. To solve this the person says 'where there is smoke there is fire' and an illustration (kitchen) is shown. 'If fire be in the kitchen should there be fire on the mountain? Is the question or doubt.' Yes, it should be there as the (same) smoke pervades fire like the smoke in the kitchen and that is why the mountain has fire.' This is the order of the inferential material here. In the Buddhist view all of a sudden the Vyāpti is remembered or established. It is rather unpsychological. Further the Sāmānya-viśeṣabhava has to be maintained in the procedure between the general fire of the concomitance and the particular fire on the hill without which action cannot be induced later.

Hence the Logician's five member syllogism appears to cater fully to implement the inferential procedure.

The Jaina holds that two members Upanaya and Nigamana are enough for the purpose of inference.

The Mīmāṃsaka holds that either the former three or the latter three of the Naiyāyika's syllogism are enough. He thinks that the Upanaya function is performed by the Hetu and the Nigamana function is secured by Pratijñā. He argues that Vyāpti and Pakṣadharmatā are both secured with the help of the three members only. But the point to be noted in this connection is that though in the first three members all the necessary procedure is completed, still, in order to assert that 'the smoke, as the pervaded of fire' is present in the mountain, Upanaya is necessary to be accepted. Here it is not the ordinary smoke of the Pratijñā, it may be noted. Otherwise fire cannot be inferred. Nigamana is the final inferential knowledge which has been established beyond a shade of doubt (Tasmāt tathā). Though the Hetu is stated to have the three features Sapakṣe sattvameva etc. it has to be clearly shown by an illustration (as in Yathā mahānasaḥ) while stating the concomitance (Vyāpti) to prove that it is correct. If there is no illustration a wrong Vyāpti also may be cited. The Upanaya asserts, as stated above that the smoke, as pervaded by fire, is on the mountain (Vahni vyāpyadhīnavān parvataḥ). Without this statement fire cannot be inferred on the particular mountain. Finally in the Nigamana as the Vahnivyāpyadhūma is present on the mountain (for this reason) it is established beyond doubt, Abādha etc. that fire is present on the mountain leaving off the word (Vahnivyāpyadhūma) and retaining only Vahni (fire).

According to the Buddhist only three fallacies are necessary to be accepted. He is of the opinion that the valid mark (Hetu) has the three properties[101] and as such there is no need to accept the counterbalanced (Satpratipaksita) and the stultified (Bādhita). Asiddha, Viruddha and Anaikāntika are the three fallacies. The Jaina also maintains that there are three fallacies Asiddha, Viruddha and Anaikāntika. Akiñcitkara is also added of course.

The Vaiśeṣika also holds that the same three fallacies are to be accepted. Of course he names the Anaikāntika as Saṃdighdha. He is of the view that Bādha could be brought under the scope of Āśraya siddhi etc. or Anaikāntika.[102] Even Satpratipakṣa can be included under Anaikāntika etc. for in an inference like 'air is a percept' the counterbalancing inference is 'air is not a percept,' obviously those two inferences are not correct. One of them is wrong as one thing (air) cannot be both a percept and a non-percept. Hence it is brought under the scope of Anaikāntika etc.

The Mīmāṃsaka is of the opinion that there are three fallacies – Sādhāraṇa, Asādhāraṇa and Viruddha. Bādha and Satpratipakṣa don't find a place in Bhāṭṭa works also. The Sāstra Dīpika admits only these three. But according to Nārāyana there are four fallacies including Asādhāraṇa.

The Naiyayika's view is that there are five Hetvābhāṣas including Satpratipakṣa and Bādha. Bādha is a fallacy where the absence of the Sādhya is definitely known with the help of a different but more potent Pramāṇa like Pratyakṣa e.g. 'Fire is cold as it is a substance. This can be included under the Anaikāntika, as the Vaisesika holds e.g. when with reference to a horse an inference like 'This is a cow as it has horns' is made the fault is Bādha according to the Naiyāyika but Anaikāntika according to Vaiśeṣika. Of course in addition Asiddhi also is present as horns are not present in a horse.

As regards, Satpratipakṣa the Vaiśeṣika is of opinion that it also can be included under Anaikāntika etc. because two contradicting views cannot be expressed about the same object at the same time, (even with the help of a different Hetu as one of them, should be obviously wrong) e.g. 'Air is perceptual' and 'air is not perceptual.'

But the author of the Muktāvalī, is of opinion that Bādha is necessary to be accepted as a separate fallacy in order to include inferences like 'a pot at the moment of production has smell as it is earth,' where the fallacy Bādha is invariably and individually present. This appears to be a strong argument in favour of Bādha as a separate fallacy. The point here is that earthhood, the Hetu is present in the pot at the moment of production though smell, the Sādhya is not present.[103]

Presumption

In presumption when there is a knowledge of what is irreconcilable, some other fact is necessary to be presumed in order to reconcile it and it is the efficient cause (Karaṇa). Now the question that arises in this connection is whether presumption can be brought under the scope of inference i.e. to say whether, in cases of such a (presumptional) knowledge e.g. fat Devadatta does not eat by day,

Devadatta's eating in the night time etc. is arrived at by a knowledge of (invariable) concomitance or whether it is arrived at by a knowledge different from that of concomitance. Here the irreconcilability must be between fatness and not eating and this is set aside by presuming that he eats at night. This is what the Votary of the presumption-means holds. But he has to be questioned whether the irreconcilability is between fatness and mere not eating (Abhojanamātra) or between fatness and not eating in the day time (Divābhojana). Verily it should be the former alternative, for, there is the doubt 'how could he be fat without eating' – as the concomitance between eating and fatness is known to him. But as a matter of fact that is only part of the truth stated. The statement made is that he does not eat by day. Thus 'not eating in the day time' is stated in the sentence and not more 'not eating.' Hence we cannot maintain that there is actual irreconcilability (Anupapatti) in the statement made but only a seeming incompatibility and hence no presumption is possible. A second point against the theory of Presumption being a separate means of Valid Knowledge is that it admits the incongruity of concomitance (Vyāptyanupatti) that a man who does not eat cannot be fat, and in order to remove the incongruity an effort is made (Upapādakakalpanā). This effort is not different from establishing the property concomitance, by a negative inference. In removing the incongruity, however, the Mīmāṃsaka takes recourse to the full meaning of the statement made including 'not eating in the day time,' whereas he does not take notice of this (including the word 'day time' in considering the former incongruity.[104] This appears to be a vulnerable point in the Mīmāṃsaka view. This incongruity too is removed, only by the knowledge of a concomitance of the form 'where there is fatness despite not eating in the daytime, there is eating in the night.' Thus we have to admit in such cases as these, that, when there is a doubt regarding the fact how Devadatta could be fat as the well-established day-eating is not there, the doubt is solved by taking recourse to inference.[105] Further it cannot be urged that the concomitance of the thing to be presumed (Kalpya) with the instrument of presumption (Kalpaka) by its own presence (and not by its being known) (Svarūpasati not Jñāta) is the cause of presumption and as such presumption does not come under the scope of inference for, without a knowledge of the concomitance of these two it cannot be established that presumption is possible just as we see in inference that the concomitance between the reason and the object (of inference) is purposeful only when it is known (Jñāta).

Further, as previously stated, in the inference of fire from smoke, it can be urged that it is a case of presumption as fire is presumed by smoke, in which case, the Mīmāṃsaka will have to dispense with the means of inference altogether.

Regarding the other objection of some that a mere negative inference (Kevala vyatirekin) cannot be considered a means of valid knowledge, it may be stated that, though the negative inference is not capable of producing knowledge directly, it can be a means of valid knowledge when once the positive concomitance is formerly cognised and then applied in the case of new themes. Thus the validity of the negative type of inference also may not be doubted, though it is arrived at later than its positive type. It has already been stated how the Upapādakakalpanā of the Mīmāṃsaka cannot be something other than negative inference. 'Otherwise what is the means by which he has arrived at the particular Upapādaka' is a question here. How presumption cannot be a separate means is argued by Varadarāja on the lines suggested by Udayana. In the stock example of presumption 'Living Devadatta' 'is not in the house,' the Mīmāṃsaka presumes 'he is somewhere outside.' He urges that one cannot hold that there is no incompatibility other than being outside when 'he is not in the house,' for the Mīmāṃsaka rejoins that there can be no being outside without his not being in the house. What does the Mīmāṃsaka mean here - Is it that the one is not produced from the other which is purely absurd. If, on the other hand he means that one cannot exist without the other, then you have come to my point - Your stand is nothing else but 'not being without it' (Avinābhāva) which means that the major term is certainly not there without the Hetu which is a matter of concomitance and hence it comes under inference.[106]

It cannot also be maintained by the Mīmāṃsaka that there is opposition between the two means of Valid Knowledge 'not being in the house' and 'being alive' as the knowledge obtained by two valid means cannot oppose each other just as two valid pieces of knowledge (e.g. 'this is a pot' and 'this is black in colour'). Since both can co-exist. Here there is actually no opposition of two valid means of knowledge but a doubt regarding Devadatta's being inside the house or outside (when Devadatta's living is confirmed either by testimony or inference).

Hence it cannot be maintained that presumption is a separate means of knowledge.

The Means of Negation (Anupalabdhi) or Non-perception

Now coming to the knowledge of negation (Abhāvajñāna) we find it extremely perplexing to decide what the means of such a knowledge is. A theory of the meaning of 'not' is a knotty problem in every philosophy. We have already seen that some say that negation (Abhāva) is the means. That is to say that a knowledge of the negation of pot (Ghaṭabhāvajñāna) is produced by the negation of a knowledge of the pot (Ghaṭajñānabhāva).

Hence it is that it is called the means of negation (Abhāva-pramaṇa). Here the Votary of Abhāvapramāṇa is to be questioned whether the absence of knowledge (Upalabdhyabhāva) which he claims to be the means, serves the purpose as cognised (Jñāta) or otherwise (Svarūpasat). In the former case, even absence of knowledge (the Pramāṇa) itself is an absence (to be cognised) and hence needs another means i.e. another (Abhāva) to cognise it and so on and so forth and as such there is the fault of infinite regress. If it is a means as not cognised, then it is tantamount to holding that Abhāva (or Anupalabdhi) is nothing else but the means of Perception (Pratyakṣa) as (perception) has been defined as knowledge which has for its means something else but a knowledge (Jñānākaraṇaka jñānam pratyakṣam). Thus there is the possibility to treat Anupalabdhi as an auxiliary of the sense organ. This knowledge of negation (Abhava) is perceptual (Aindriyaka) since 'its means is not cognised as the other accepted one (Sampratipanna)' being the inference according to the Logician.

This cannot be a case of recollection of the pot as the pot has not been experienced before, as the Logician views. But the doubt is why an inferred pot or even any pot previously experienced capable of being recalled may not produce a recollection (when there is the desire to know whether a pot is there). But the apperception here is not 'I recollect the pot' but 'it is of the form' 'I see the absence of the pot.'

If the absence of the knowledge of pot be considered the cause not as cognised but as it exists (Svarūpasat) then there is the contingency of the absence of cloth, absence of mat etc. also being cognised as they too are present along with the absence of the pot and thus there should be either confusion of ideas or there should be no proof of a particular knowledge being produced. Further the negation of pot etc. should be continuously cognised.

That is why probably Gāgābhaṭṭa takes for granted that the absence of a knowledge of negation as cognised (Jñāta) is the cause and admits an inference as the intermediary activity (Vyāpāra).[107] This type of cognised absence of perception also may not be said to serve the purpose as the absence of the pot itself may be stated to be cognised just like the absence of knowledge (of the pot) in like manner since both are absences. Hence it cannot be established that absence of knowledge alone begets a knowledge of the absence of the pot.

Here negation cannot be the efficient cause (Karaṇa) of any knowledge as negation cannot produce a positive entity. Excepting the sense organ there is no other Pramāṇa different from knowledge. Even if mere Abhāva be considered one, still no activity (Vyāpāra) can be attached to it to produce knowledge in case the Abhāva is not cognised.

It may also be noted that simple non-perception of pot cannot by itself be the cause of a knowledge of the negation of the object (pot etc.) for, according to Bhaṭṭa, knowledge is supersensuous and is cognised only by the knownness (Jñātata) existing in the non-perception (Ghaṭopalabdhyabhāva). If the non-perception, therefore, on the other hand, is considered to be cognised (Jñāta) then as stated earlier there are faults of infinite regress etc.

The Logician's argument appears to be sound in this case since the absence of the pot is not cognised when the pot is cognised (by the eye) the absence of the counterpositive (i.e. pot etc.) serves as an ancillary cause of the sense organ. Hence Anupalabdhi cannot be called a means of knowledge. The sense organ itself is capable of producing a knowledge of the absence (of the pot etc.). Here it may be noted that, when non-perception (Anupalabdhi) that is non-cognised is the cause, only sense perception is produced (as in the case of the pot etc.), but when the non-perception cognised is the cause, then the knowledge of absence produced is only a case of inference.

Further as Udayana observes, non-cognition (strictly non-perception) as known produces only mediate knowledge (and not Pratyakṣa or perception). But non-perception by itself (as not known) with the help of the sense organ concerned as the efficient cause produces perceptual knowledge. He gives four reasons for his stand that the sense organ is the efficient cause of a knowledge of negation (of the object - one) that the knowledge of negation is immediate (and is hence produced by the sense organ), (two) that the sense organ's activity has not ceased, (three) that the efficient cause is one that is not cognised, and (four) all our external perception is produced from the mind as aided by the sense organ. He rightly argues that in a knowledge of negation (of pot etc.) three causes are essential – knowledge of the substratum (floor etc.), a knowledge of the counter-positive (pot etc.) and non-perception of that which is otherwise eligible to be perceived (Yogyānupalabdhi).[108] If this be not accepted the contingency is that when a black pot is perceived with the help of touch even a blind man should perceive the absence of redness in it as the Yogyānupalabdhi (non-perception of that eligible to be perceived) is there. Further if simple non-perception (Anupalabdhi) be the sole cause then a contingency arises that, when a man sees the object in front of him, he should be in a position to perceive the absence of the colour in it as the mere non-perception of the colour is present. If to avoid this trouble it is urged that contact with the eye also is necessary, then well said it means only that the eye aided by light is the efficient cause of the perception of negation. After various arguments and counter-arguments Udayana establishes that the negation of an object in the particular substratum is cognised aided by non-perception (Anupalabdhi) with the help of (perception produced by) the sense organ which can perceive the counter-positive (Abhāva pratiyogin) in the locus of the negation.

Another argument in favour of the Logician's stand is, as the Tārkika-Rakṣā, puts it, that just as the negation of inference, testimony etc. is cognised by the reason, verbal testimony etc. themselves, (so also) it may be held that the negation of pot etc. are cognised by the very sense organ which cognises the object pot etc. It is also pointed our that a qualified knowledge of negation must be produced from the sense organ and as such just as the Vieśeṣya floor is cognised by the sense organ, it is judicious to accept that the Viśeṣaṇa, negation of pot also is perceived by the sense organ itself. Another argument advanced is that though the 'substratum (floor) etc. is perceived by the sense organ, still there is no difficulty in arguing that the negation of pot also is perceived with the help of the rule because of activity (Vyāpāra) the activist (Vyāpārin) cannot be considered to be a superfluous cause.' Further it may be noted that it is a fault in the sense organ that is responsible for an invalid cognition in the case of negation. Further simple non-perception (of the object) (Anupalabdhimātra) cannot be the cause of perception of negation. Suppose a person does not see his wife in the house; will he then come to the conclusion she is not existent. If after a time she comes back what should happen to the validity of the cognition, when the previous knowledge of absence is negated by the presence of the object. Hence it cannot be urged that simple Yogyānupalabdhi is the cause of the perception of negation.

The Logician aruges that simple non-perception does not produce a knowledge of negation of the object but produces only a doubt regarding the object. How this argument can withstand further rejoinders by the opponent may be looked up in the Kusumāñjali.[109]

Verbal Testimony

Next we take up testimony. In a knowledge of testimony the means is stated by the Logician to be a 'knowledge of words' (Padajñana). But it appears to me that this is not a sound argument inasmuch as a knowledge of words (alongwith its operation 'knowledge of their meanings') may be means of mere verbal knowledge (Jñānakaraṇaṃ) but it is not a means of 'Valid' Verbal knowledge (Pramaṇa pramākaraṇa).' Then would it mean that verbal testimony is not a means of Valid Knowledge? Not so, it is one. How it is to be explained in the following way: In the knowledge gained by verbal testimony it may be asserted that the knowledge of (another) authentic person (whether it be his perception or inference) is the means of (our) knowledge (Karaṇa). It should not be doubted how the knowledge of another person constitutes a means of valid knowledge of another person for the validity of his kowledge in general (i.e. the validity of all his knowledge) is arrived at by an inference of the type 'This person's knowledge is valid inasmuch as it is the knowledge of a well-wisher who does not mistake one thing for another and speaks the truth' etc. When once with this inference the general validity of the authentic person's knowledge is decided there is no difficulty in particular pieces of his knowledge serving as means of valid knowledge to the other person. Thus when the mother states that such and such a person is one's father or brother there is hardly any doubt about the validity of the statement, for if not in all cases, the knowledge of a mother regarding the father or the brother could be relied upon. So also when once the knowledge derived from Vedic sentences is inferred to be valid in general the validity of particular sentences like 'one desirous of attaining heaven should perform sacrifice' etc. attain validity. Of course the general validity of the Veda is derived either by the fact of its being uttered by an omniscient or of its origination from a source which is devoid of human error.[111] Without this verbal testimony as a means of knowledge, I am sure, we would be left helpless in this world with the few things that are presented to us by the senses now and here and all past and all future including all distant and uncognised objects should be a sealed book for us in spite of our inference which also does not command a wide field of knowledge handed down to us from times immemorial and from places not traversed. This does not mean, of course that we should blindly follow what all the ancients have said; when there is a doubt about validity of testimony we should try to assess the truth of the statements, if possible (undertaking all the necessary trouble it involves) and then carefully criticise the facts; at the same time it does not also mean that we should go on criticising everything that the ancients hold for (I may go to the extent of holding that) after all the way in which we are trained to think, the words which we use, the impressions which we have, the objects with which we have to deal are mostly decided for us at birth by the influence of heredity.

Thus when the validity of the statement is once established, the meaning of the statement is understood through a knowledge of the words, next the meanings signified by them and then their syntactical connection. It is a different point altogether whether words signify meanings and then are syntactically connected or whether they signify meanings along with their syntactical connection.[112]

Thus even verbal testimony of the type stated above is a kind of valid knowledge where another person's knowledge is the indirect means of the validity part of the knowledge.

Analogy

Now with regard to analogy as a separate means of valid knowledge (Pramāṇa) we have to admit with the opponents of the means that verbal testimony is a potent factor in arriving at the resultant knowledge. Even in the first instance the resultant knowledge of appellation and its signification (Samjñā-samjñi-sambandha-jñāna) is arrived at by the means of testimony when the so-called transferable sentence (Atideśa vākya) is uttered, for the hearer, on hearing the sentence 'The gavaya is like the cow' gets a knowledge of the appellation and its significance and their relation. But this is a knowledge derived from Testimony and is of the general type (Samānyātmā). Why should the hearer go to the forest and see an animal resembling the cow? It is only to establish by perception the relation between the particular Gavaya (Viśeṣātmā) and the word 'Gavaya' and their relation. That is why probably the old Logicians were of opinion that the knowledge derived from analogy is of the type 'This (animal), is signified by the word Gavaya. In this view the animal in general is cognised with the help of Sāmānya lakṣaṇa sannikarṣa.

In analogy it is not necessary to accept an intermediary inference, as some philosophers suggest, as it is less cumbrous to accept, the recollection of the transferable sentence meaning (Atideśa Vākyārthasmṛti) and with this recollection the purpose of the means of knowledge is served. Really recollection (Smriti) is less cumbersome than Inference (Anumiti).

Thus if the relation between the appellation and its meaning (Samjña Samjñi sambandha) alone is considered to the result of analogy (in general) it is as well served by Testimony itself and there is no need for analogy. If, on the other hand, it is held that the particular animal is to be also perceived in the forest, there is no new knowledge produced by such perception except that the particular animal with its other perceptual details is signified by the word 'Gavaya.' Whereas in the former case the animal (as possessed of likeness to the cow) is known by Testimony and in the latter the animal (as possessed of likeness to the cow) is known through perception. The peculiarity of this means, as the Nyāyakośakara puts it, is that in this kind of knowledge of analogy the meaning of the word Gavaya embraces both the object qualified by Gavayahood as well as the word 'Gavaya' both–which is a peculiarity and hence its claim to be considered a separate means of knowledge.

Though the above argument appears prima facie to be sound, there are some serious defects in it as Udayana points out. The similarity with the cow of the Gavaya is only an external adjunct (Upādhi) and cannot be the determinant of conventionhood (Śakyatāvacchedaka or Pravṛttinimitta). Gavayahood (Gavayatva) alone which is more compact is the real determinant of the word (Gavaya). It may also be noted that if similarity with the cow is the determinant then there is the contingency of a person, not having seen a cow formerly, not being able to use the word Gavaya (as the determinant is not known to him). If on the other hand both similarity with the cow and Gavayahood both constitute the determinant then a forester who has not seen a cow but knows the

Gavaya will not be in a position to use the word Gavaya. Thus by the law of parsimony Gavayahood alone should be the determinant of a Gavaya. Otherwise there will be a perpetual doubt as to whether similarity with the cow is only a non-distinguishing characteristic (Upalakṣaṇa) or is the determinant of conventionhood. It may not be doubted how the same sentence serves two purposes giving two separate meanings for, as Udayana points out, there is a doubt about the import to the hearer whether similarity with the cow is only a non-distinguishing mark (Upalakṣaṇa) or determinant of conventionhood and by parsimony of expression the hearer confirms that the former is only an Upalakṣaṇa.

The Vaiśeṣika inference under which this means is brought is condemned by the Logician in the third Stabaka of the Nyāyakusumāñjali.

This analogy is of three varieties one based on similarity, another on distinction and a third on certain qualities.[113]

Thus analogy also has to be accepted a separate means of valid knowledge.

The view of the Mīmāṃsaka and the Śāṅkarite that a knowledge of the type 'the Gavaya is like the cow' is the means and a knowledge that his cow is like the Gavaya is the resultant knowledge, is not quite acceptable as no new knowledge is gained by this means since similarity is the same in both the means–knowledge and end-knowledge. By similarity is meant the presence of a majority of properties of one object in another.[114]

Inference

Inference is held to be a means of valid knowledge by all the schools of philosophy except that of Cārvāka. The Cārvāka himself, when he makes the first statement that sense-perception (Pratyakṣa) alone is valid knowledge, has to be intercepted how he has arrived at it. He has to maintain it by means of an inference. And even the validity of the knowledge is not perceived by him. He has to infer it. Then his statement that inference is not a means of valid knowledge also is to be maintained by another inference.[115] It is utterly difficult to get on in the field of philosophy without this Rama's arrow (Rāmabāṇa) which pierces into most intricate tracts of knowledge which cannot otherwise be arrived at. How are we to know the size of the Sun, the Moon and for the matter of that any astronomical fact? How are we to know things which we cannot reach to on the basis of a knowledge of the things within our reach?

How are we to know the subtle parts of our own body, objects too small and also objects too large to be conceived? In our daily life we infer such things and work upon these inferences which, as we see, generally give the required result.

I believe with the Logician that, as a matter of fact, the validity part of every piece of knowledge depends upon inference. Even the validity of perceptual knowledge depends upon inference though most often in our daily life, there is no necessity to go to the extent of assessing it. How inference can assess the validity of knowledge can be looked up in Book III on Validity of Knowledge.

If inference, then, is such an inevitable means of valid knowledge (Pramāṇa) what is its nature? What is inference, the means and inferential knowledge (or inference as it is also called) the end? Inference, the means is not different from a knowledge of concomitance (Vyāptijñāna) as the Logician holds. An invariable relation between objects is what is meant by concomitance (Vyāpti). This (Vyāpti) is based on the cause and effect relation (Kāryakaraṇabhāva) and the general and the particular relation (Sāmānyaviśeṣabhāva) as the Buddhist holds. That is why in every kind of inference from a particular knowledge previously cognised we arrive at another particular knowledge not previously cognised. Thus it is a very useful means of knowledge where, by a knowledge say, of the invariable concomitance (relation) of smoke with fire we are able to understand the presence of fire (though not visible) on a distant or unscaleable mountain. The distance of the Sun from the earth, the size of the Moon, the position of the Stars, knowledge, its means, the knowledge and feelings of others etc., are all cognised with the help of inference. Of course in the cognition made with the help of inference there may be many mistakes committed as when we try to infer the size of the Moon. We proceed from a knowledge of the proportion in which objects decrease their size when looked at from a distance and apply the same knowledge of porportion to decide the Moon's size. But sometimes it may be wrong to have the same proportion in all the spheres that intervene between the earth and the Moon–of course I don't know this, for certain. In that case the inference goes wrong. But we cannot help it we will have to ascertain it. Nor can we do without inferring. We have been inferring and trying our best to infer correctly (i.e. taking stock of as many facts known to us as possible).

Thus it is only a knowledge of invariable concomitance that can produce another new knowledge for there is the cause and effect theory etc. to guide us. There is no concomitance possible to be established without a knowledge of the cause and the effect etc. That is why it appears to me that a knowledge of similarity, incongruity etc. which are accepted by some philosophers as separate means of knowledge cannot be accepted as such, as they do not presuppose a cause and effect relation etc. by themselves. If it is admitted they do, then they are to be classified only under inference somehow or other. There is no escaping from it. Does a knowledge of similarity produce another new knowledge? No it cannot, for, unless there is some relation of cause and effect etc. no new knowledge can be arrived at. In concomitance (Vyāpti) there is the pervader (Vyāpaka) and the concomitant (Vyāpya); the knowledge of the one is produced by a knowledge of the other. In a knowledge of incongruity (Anupapatti) said to exist in the case of presumption (Arthāpatti) there is no possibility for cognising a new fact except with the help of concomitance.

What is the Means of Inference

Now what is the means of inference? All are agreed on the point that a knowledge is also the means. In case 'means' signifies 'the particular cause which has an activity or operation'[116] (i.e. the efficient cause) it should be a knowledge of concomitance only (Vyāpti-jñāna). If, on the other hand, it signifies 'that which is not devoid of the result'[117] the means should be 'consideration' (Parāmarśa). Taking the stock example of inference[118] the means in the former view is 'a knowledge of the concomitance of fire with smoke and its activity' is 'a knowledge (definite knowledge) of smoke on the mountain which (smoke) is the concomitant of fire' (Vyhnivyāpyadhumavān parvataḥ). In the second view the later is the means to aruge that consideration (Parāmarśa) is the knowledge of a relation to a qualified object (Visistavaisistyajñāna) is unnecessary to be admitted as does the Mīmāṃsaka, is untenable since the two pieces of knowledge - a knowledge of concomitance (Vyāptijñāna) and a knowledge of the mark in the subject (Pakṣadharmatā-jñāna) separately or jointly cannot produce inference. In case they are expected to do so, as the Logician objects, we should be able to infer fire from knowledges of the type 'where there is smoke there is fire (Vyāptijñāna) and 'The hill is possessed of light' (Pakṣadharmatājñāna).[119] Hence the necessity for a qualified knowledge like 'This hill is possessed of smoke which is the concomitant of fire' (Vahnivyāpyadhūmavān parvataḥ). It cannot be held that concomitance is necessarily of two kinds based on Kārya kāraṇabhāva and Identity (Tadutpatti and Tādātmya) as the Buddhist holds since it is possible to infer taste from colour which is not either of the above mentioned two. Taste is neither identical with colour nor is produced from colour. Hence the Buddhist view does not stand.

The Result of Inference

Now what is the result of inference? The concomitance (Vyāpti) is one already known. Hence fire is known in all the places pessessed of smoke. The hill etc. are objects of cognition (in the case of the mountain, sense perception). The major term (fire etc.) is something previously known (in the kitchen etc.) What then is the new knowledge gained by the means of inference?[120] It is, we have to admit, 'the major term (Sādhya) as related to the particular subject (Pakṣa).' The relation may be either simple contact or inherence or any other relation concerned. In the inference of 'God' with the help of the syllogism 'the earth, sprout etc. are possessed of an agent as they are products just like a pot (which is a product),' God is inferred as related to the activity of production by inherence (as the agent). Here though the agents of other objects are generally known, the agent as related to earth, sprout etc. is not known and it is that particular agent that is inferred; just as in the previous case 'the particular fire on the mountain is inferred.' A knowledge of presumption etc. are all products of the means of the knowledge (Vyāptijñāna). Thus we have to admit that, though smoke and fire are both things already known, yet the presence of the individual fire on the particular hill is something not known and that the object of inference.[121] Sometimes even the existence of a transcendental sense organ etc. is the object of inference. It may not be doubted how what is not known at all previously (sense-organhood or Indriyatva) (because no sense-organ is capable at all of being seen) can be inferred for the existence of an instrument in carrying out certain activities in other cases is cognised by us previously, as the axe in the case of cutting a tree. So also in the case of knowledge there should be a means (Karana) the eye etc. here, it may be urged, which takes the place similar to that of the axe in the activity of cutting. Thus we cannot dispense with inferences of such transcendental objects also.

Scope of Inference, Testimony and Perception

Thus inference and verbal testimony, we may hold are responsible for a wide range of our knowledge. Of these verbal testimony has an extremely wide range to cover. The knowledge we acquire from books, newspapers, magazines, from the statements of others, the teachers' lessons etc. is the most potent means of our knowledge and nobody can do without it. It is responsible for our knowledge of distant places and of distant times. Inference on the other hand, is responsible, through a knowledge of concomitance, for a knowledge of things which we cannot penetrate with our senses, objects which we cannot reach (in our own place and time also). In our everyday life also much of our activity is carried on with the help of inference. At every step we find its influene e.g. we start ten minutes before school time and we are sure to reach the school in time in normal conditions. We expect the bus to cross the road and leave room for us in a particular interval of time. We calculate and adjust our speed of walking according to necessity. All these are the result of inferences which generally do not fail us. But Inference and verbal testimony take a longer time to produce knowledge. Perception, however, is the most immediate source of knowledge and to some extent in ordinary life it is also exact. We see the pot and knew that it is a pot and get water in it (if once it is known, of course that it is for fetching water). No inference is necessary in this case. If there is a doubt about the validity of our knowledge and consequently about the object, however, there is the necessity for inference. That is why the Logician holds that with reference to the same object when the materials of perception as well as inference are present, the materials of perception are stronger and perceptual knowledge comes first.[122]

It may be noted that as between the causal aggregate of perception (Pratyakṣa Sāmagrī) and the causal aggregate of inference, both are simultaneously present the latter one is more powerful' in case both of them relate to only one object of knowledge (Samāna viṣaye). That is to say in such a case the knowledge of Pratyakṣa alone is produced disregardful of the other aggregate of inferential causes. But if it is the case of different objects of knowledge for the two (Bhinna viṣaye) the causal aggregate of inferential knowledge prevails as against that of perception. To make the point clearer an example may be given – when there is causal aggregate necessary for the perception of a pot (i.e. the eye, the pot, light etc.) and the causal aggregate necessary for Inference also (the form *of the pot,* itself its activity of fetching water etc.) then, only a *perception* of the pot results but not an inference *of the pot.*[123] But if the causal aggregate of the perception *of the pot* and the inferential causal aggregate of *fire on the hill* (Bhinne viṣaye) are both present in the cogniser only inference of the fire is produced but not the perception of the pot. It may also be noted here that if the desire for one particular knowledge is very strong the above rules will not operate.

Purpose Served by the Different Members of the Syllogism

The order of the five members of the Logicians syllogism is shown below alongwith the purpose served by them:

Statement of

(1) The proposition (Pratijñā)

(2) The mark or reason (Hetu)

(3) The concomitance (with the illustration) (Udāharaṇa)

(4) The mark as the concomitant of the pervader present in the subject (Upanaya)

(5) (Conclusion from the above) (Nigamana)

The subject having the object denoted by the major term (Sādhya) (Conclusion).

These five members accepted by the Logician appear to be quite necessary for us to arrive at inference for another's sake. The Mīmāṃsakas and the Vedāntins hold that either the former three or the latter three among the five members stated above are enough whereas the Buddhist holds that only two, No.3 and No.4 (Pakṣadharmatā) are sufficient for the purpose. The Jaina is of the view that No.1 and 2 above are sufficient but some of the very ancient Naiyāyikas accepted as many as ten members in their syllogism. Some Jainas also accept ten members but these are considered necessary to drive home the inference to a dullard. But the following will prove how it is necessary to have all the five members as each individual member has a particular purpose to serve in the scheme of inferential knowledge as the Logician approves:[124] The purpose served by the statements of Proposition (No. 1) the mark (No. 2) is that the person who is to be led through the inference should be introduced to the proposition without which he cannot proceed through the process of inference. All of a sudden to start with a statement of concomitance (item No. 3 above) and giving an illustration does not serve the purpose as what the speaker is driving at and why the concomitance is spoken of suddenly are not understood by the hearer. Thus the statement is necessary to declare the existence of a particular thing (Sādhya) in a particular object so that the reason can be tackled on to it without which the reason is irrelevant. If the mark or reason is not spoken of (item No. 2) the reason cannot be ascertained by the listener and an illustration cannot be given corroborating the concomitance. The proposition is different from the statement of concomitance (item No. 3) (Udāharaṇa) in that, in the latter, a knowledge of the major term (Sādhya) as existing in the subject (possessed of subjecthood) is not cognised but the concomitance indicates that the reason given in (2) is cogent. The illustration also serves to show the two (smoke and fire) as coexistent in the same substratum (kitchen). The Udāharaṇa is different from the Upanaya (Item No. 4) as the former does not produce a knowledge of the major term (as possessed of major-termhood) as existing in the subject. It is different from Nigamana (item No. 5) in that, in the former, the major term (Sādhya) has, as its attribute, only the determinant of Major-termhood (Sādhyatāvacchedaka) whereas in the latter it is further qualified (Hetu-jñānajñāptyatva-viśiṣṭa-sādhya-vān).[125] That is why the adjective 'not having as an attribute anything other than that determined by major-termhood' is to be added to the word major term in the definition of (4). Udāharaṇa (item No. 3 above) is the most important of all the five which establishes concomitance between the mark (Hetu) and the major term (Sādhya) without which no inference is possible at all. That is why every one of the philosophers (either the Buddhist or the Mīmāṣaka or the Vedāntin) admits this member as essential for inference. Here it may be noted that an instance (Homologue etc.) where concomitance is formerly noticed is cited. This serves as the statement of a general rule which applies to all cases of such concomitance and does not thus pertain to the particular subject (Pakṣa) on hand. This is the difference Udāharaṇa has with reference to Pratijñā or Nigamana. Upanaya (Item No. 4) is significant in that it declares that (in addition to the cognition of concomitance), the concomitant is present in the subject (Pakṣa). Thus Upanaya serves to denote the presence of the concomitant (as a concomitant of the pervader) in the subject without which there can be no relation between the two. As the third-time-reflection of the mark (Tṛitīyalinga parāmarśa) is not secured through any other member, this member also has to be accepted. Thus the theory that the first three members alone are enough is not satisfactory at all.

The purpose of Nigamana (item No. 5 above) is to state finally the major term as existing in the subject. Here, it may be noted that the major term is one that is established to be denoted by the denoter (mark). This member also serves thus to show that the inference is not either contradicted (Bādhita) or counterbalanced (Satpratipakṣita) as sufficient reason has been adduced in the syllogism.

Thus all the five members are necessary for a full-fledged inference.[126] But it may be noted here that while the first member denotes only the subject as qualified by the major term, the last member proposes to denote the same after being duly helped by the mark which is present in the subject and which is also qualified by concomitance.

The Fallacies of the Reason

Coming to the question of fallacy, we know that there is much divergence of view on the subject. The fallacy will have to be defined as the Logician does. A fallacy is one that is responsible for impeding or obstructing either inferential knowledge or its efficient cause (Anumititatkaraṇānyatarapratibandhaka).[127] Or it may be stated to be one that obstructs a knowledge of inference in one way or the other. Since inference is of the type "Sādhyavyāpya-hetumān pakṣaḥ sādhyavān" (i.e. the subject having the mark or reason as the concomitant of the object denoted by the major term, has the object denoted by the major term). Here four things are taken into account – they are the subject (Pakṣa), concomitance (Vyāpti), reason or mark (Hetu) and the object denoted by the major term (i.e. the inferred object) (Sādhya). Any one of the four cited above or its relation gets vitiated in one way or the other when fallacies arise. Thus I think we can classify the fallacies under the following heads:

(Faults of the reason or Liṅga and other faults of arguments)

1. Pakṣe sādhyābhavāḥ (This is called Bādha).[128]
2. Pakse hetvābhavaḥ (This is called Svarupasiddhi).
3. Sādhyābhāvabad vrttitvam (This is called Sadhāraṇā naikantikatva. This Hetu (mark) is present both in the homologue as well as the antilogue and thus is too broad).
4. Sādhyādhikarṇavṛttivam (This is called Asādhāraṇāndikāntikatva. This mark (Hetu) is absent both in the homologue and the antilogue (Asādhāraṇatvam).
5. Sādhyābhāva-vyāptatvam (This is called Virodha).

6. Dṛṣtāntābhāvaḥ (A fallacy having this is called Anupasamhāritva).

   Here the mark (Linga) is such that it has no illustration either affirmative or negative.

7. Vyāptyabhāvaḥ. Here the mark is called Anupasamharin (Vyāpyatvasiddhi or Sopādhikatva).

In this defective mark, due to the presence of an external adjunct (Upādhi), concomitance does not exist between the two objects stated. Satpratipakṣa or the counterbalanced cannot be different from what vitiates concomitance as otherwise each of the two can be counterbalanced by the other both of which however are not correct. The contradicted (Bādhita) cannot be considered to be a separate fallacy of the mark inasmuch as inferences itself is vitiated by the concomitance being vitiated. It is also not necessary that a separate means of knowledge (Pramāṇa) should contradict the inferential knowledge for inference itself could be shown to be incorrect due to the presence of incorrect concomitance in the syllogism. In addition to these fallacies (Hetvābhāsas) which are to be included under points of defeat (Nigrahasthānas)[129] the following may also be noted:

The four ineffective (Aprayojaka) Tarkas Ātmāśraya, Anyonyāśraya, Cakraka and Anavastha have been included by Varadarāja under Svarūpāsiddhi. But the Aniṣta Prasaṇgatvaka Tarka alone is brought under Vyāpyatvāsiddhi.[130]

It may be noted that Ativyāpti, Avyāpti etc., the defects in definitions (Lakṣanadosas) are the consequences of wrong inferences and hence are to be included under the different fallacies into which they fall.[131] Same is the case with names like Sādhya Vikasa Siddha Sādhāna, Bhagāsiddhi etc.

Do Objects Really Exist

Let us now examine whether we should accept a separate existence for the objects of the world as do the Sāṃkhya, the Mīmāṃsaka and the Logician realists or whether their existence could be denied as done by the Śaṅkarite and the Yogācāra, Buddhist. The idealist view is that it is not necessary to maintain an objective existence for the world apart from consciousness or cognition. It should not be however objected that the fact that a particular person cognises a particular object at a particular time cannot be accounted for as they atake recourse to a beginningless ignorance (Māyā or Avidyā or Karma) or even some unseen causes (impressions etc.) and try to explain it. But they will have to reply to a rejoinder as to how the same ignorance or Avidyā (or even form impressions without an objective difference) could produce differences in the experience of each individual. If they reply that it is the divergence in the ignorance itself, then they should be asked by why they should accept such a stand with a number of distinctions in ignorance, their rise, destruction etc. which are assumed and on the other hand deny what are actually cognised to be present in our life, the different objects which could be safely accepted. It is also necessary that, in the waking state, they should accept the presence of the object for sense-perception and a previous knowledge of the object for its recollection or for an inference in regard to it. In case objects do not really exist how can we account for a difference in the actual object which is capable of accomplishing some particular work and a recollected object or an inferred object which cannot really do so. Even if it be argued that even that work is nothing but knowledge, then why not its votary be satisfied with such a knowledge and satisfy his hunger etc. (without going in for the object, food etc.). If however, the external object also is required for such a purpose then why should we admit Avidyā etc. which we don't cognise and deny objects we practically cognise. Further we see that objects stand before us for a longer time than our cognitions stand. Even though we don't cognise the object for sometime the other person nearby cognises its existence much against the Dṛṣṭisṛṣtivāda. If each person, it be urged, has a separate object of his own, the stand is too cumbrous to be maintained and explained as one's pot is different from another's but water fetching etc. should be common. It cannot be urged, however, that the objects in the dream state are contradicted after waking up and so the objects in the waking state are also contradicted, when the final reality is realised for it remains to be experimented upon by each individual and if scripture has really laid it down so, we have to admit with the Śāṅkarite that there is a final reality which we here have not comprehended. Or it may be stated objects are transient. Thus it appears it is necessary to admit an objective existence for things of the world at least in the practical plane if not in the final reality. That is why probably the Śāṅkarite admits these objects in the Vyāvahārika empirical level. The Buddhists also (except the Yogācāra) accept the objective world. It may be noted that the Mādhyāmika also accepts something like this through his theory of Śaṃvritisatyatā.

Theories of Invalid Knowledge (Viparītadi-khyātivādāḥ)

Let us now examine the Theories of error or invalid knowledge also in a nutshell. It is very interesting to note that each school of philosophy has its own peculiar point of view with reference to invalid knowledge also and five such theories of knowledge of pertaining to five different schools are generally recognized though there are some others which accept them with slight modifications.[133] The five theories are (1) the Ātmakhyāti theory of the Buddhist (the Yogācārā school), (2) the Asatkhyāti theory of the Mādhyamika school, (3) the Anyathākhyāti theory of the Logician and the Jaina, (4) the Anirvacanīyakhyāti of the Śaṅkarite and (5) the Akhyāti theory of the Mīmāṃsaka. In addition to these the Sāṃkhya admits the Prasiddhārthakhyāti which is akin to the theory of the Śaṅkarite and the Rāmānujite also holds a similar theory but designates it as Satkhyāti.

Hereunder the illustration for the several theories of invalid knowledge taken is 'This is silver' with reference to an oyster-shell (Śuktirajata-jñānam).

The Ātmakhyāti Theory of the Buddhist

The Buddhist (of the Yogācāra school) believes in the Ātmakhyāti theory of knowledge and holds that the silver that is apprehended in the oyster-shell is not of the form of silver but of the form of knowledge alone (which has no object corresponding to it) and as such it is not an external object (Even according to the Sautrāntika the external objects blue etc. endow their form to the cognition and it is this cognition only that shines forth and not the insentient object which is only inferred). It is because of this fact that, later on, when the invalidity of knowledge is cognised the silverhood that is only of the form of knowledge is contradicted. In this way the soul itself (which is of the form of momentary cognition or knowledge) is apprehended to be an external object[134] having silverhood in it.[135] This is thus apprehended because of ignorance which is without a beginning.

A Criticism of the Ātmakhyāti Theory

But this theory of Ātmakhyāti is based on the argument that the silver cognised in the substratum of oyster-shellhood does not pertain to the object, in which case, on the one hand it should be experienced by one and all alike and not by the particular person alone that is mistaken and on the other, there hould be no case of invalid knowledge whatever as silver is considered to be present there also. In this way when the silver there does not refer to the object, (oyster-shell) it should have reference only to knowledge and the soul which is of the form of knowledge assumes that form. But this view is not acceptable as, in that case, we cannot account for different kinds of invalid knowledge as ignorance is only one as against the experiences of silverhood in an oyster-shell, yellow hue in a conch etc. which are many and there is no other external cause which can account for differences in invalid experiences.[136] Another defect in the theory is that, if silver is of the form of knowledge, how can we account for a valid knowledge of the form 'Silver is not knowledge,'[137] and again if silverhood were knowledge it (silverhood), like knowledge, would not be perceived at all by the sense organ (as knowledge is transcendental).[138] Further if the soul in the form of momentary knowledge is perceived as silver, then the cognition produced should be 'I am silver' and not 'This is silver.'[139]

The Asatkhyati Theory of the Buddhist

The Mādhyamika school of Buddhists maintain that in the case of invalid knowledge the silver that does not exist (Asat) is cognized.[140] The Mādhyamika objects that silver in an invalid cognition does not pertain to knowledge as the Sautrāntika holds, in which case of knowledge of the kind 'I have silver' (or 'I have a knowledge of silver') should be produced and not of the kind 'This is silver.' Nor does it pertain to the object in which case it should serve as silver.

This view also cannot be subscribed to as we cannot account for a knowledge of the non-existent silver with which the eye cannot come into contact.[141] Further, when you say silver is non-existent, does it mean that it is elsewhere in which case it may be admitted but then it would come under Anyathākhyāti (or mistaken notion) which the Logician holds; or does it mean that it is really non-existent in which case simple impression unaided by a stimulus (object etc.) cannot produce (that knowledge).[142]

Vācaspati Miśra also holds the Asatkhyāti theory on the ground that a false inherence (Alīkaḥ Samavāyaḥ) exists between the oyster-shell and the Silverhood presented in an invalid cognition like 'This is silver.'

The Theory of Anyathākhyāti of the Logician

The Logician maintains that, in an invalid cognition one thing is apprehended as another. That is why his theory is called Anyathākhyāti.[143] To take our stock example in the case of a mistaken notion of silver in an oyster-shell (signified by the word 'this' in the sentence 'This is silver') silver which is elsewhere (in the market) etc. is cognised. The idea is that the sense organ actually in contact with the pearl-oyster owing to some sort of defect (similarity etc.), perceives the pearl-oyster is silver which is present in a different place or time. It should not be urged then that even an object previously not experienced by the individual may be apprehended by the person, for it is held by the Logician that it is similarity and such other defects that restrict such invalid apprehensions.[144] Thus there is, in the Logician's opinion a qualified knowledge, in such cases, where the substantiveness (Viseṣyatā) subsisting in the object (i.e. pearl-oyster not cognised as such) is described by the attributeness (Prakāratā) existing in silver.[145]

Thus this qualified knowledge alone is capable of prompting one to activity and hence the theory of Prabhākara that, along with the perceptual knowledge of the thing in front (i.e. the pearl-oyster) and the recollection of silver, the non-cognition of difference from the desired object (Iṣṭabhedāgraha) also is responsbile for activity (Pravṛtti) is more cumbersome,[146] for he (Prabhākara) admits three causes as against the Logician who admits only one qualified knowledge (Viśiṣta jñāna) as the cause (of activity) which, latter, is more simple. It should not be objected, however, that the other two causes except the third one (in Prabhākarā's view)[147] are common to both the parties (Prabhākarā's and the Logician's) for even there, in the case of valid and invalid knowledge (taken together) qualified knowledge is one single cause commonly admitted for both by the Logician which is less cumbersome than three causes in the case of invalid knowledge and the first two causes in the case of valid knowledge as necessitated in Guru's view. On the other hand, by itself the third cause[148] given by Guru is mere prolix than the one qualified knowledge accepted by the Logician.

Now can it be urged by the Prabhākara, how, when silverhood is not in contact with the eye, silverhood is perceived[149] by the mistaken person; for it is rendered possible by the transcendental proximity in the form of Jñānalakṣana[150] which he (Prabhākara) also will be obliged to accept in certain cases.

In the case of the qualified knowledge (Viśiṣṭajñāna) producing activity the inference is stated to be like this: 'This activity is produced by a knowledge wherein the attribute is the determinant of the nature of the desired (object) because it is an activity just as the activity in the case of real silver.'[151]

The objection raised by the Śāṅkarite is that the error theory postulated by the Logician is more cumbrous as it takes four minutes to arrive at it e.g. 1. perception of Nacre, 2. apprehending its glittering nature, 3. recollection of silver and 4. a cognition of silver. But this objection may be met in this way: First it is only the glittering nature of the object in front (Cākācakya) (not nacre) is apprehended (with the help of the sense organ and the mind-soul contact), then due to the super sensuous contact (Jñānalakṣana pratyāsatti) silver is recollected (this recollection is the activity or Vyāpāra part) and silver is erroneously cognised. This theory of error is definetely less cumbrous than the Māyāvadin's theory of generating an indefinable silver from a (non cause) the pearl-oyster. Even in Ramanuja's theory a separate reason has to be given for giving prominence in the erroneous knowledge to a Guṇa not predominant by nature.

Defects in the theories of others may be construed on the lines of the criticisms already pointed out.[152]

The Theory of Anirvacanīyakhyāti of the Śāṅkarite

The Śāṅkarite upholds the theory of Anirvacanīyakhyāti. He is of opinion that, in an invalid cognition like the one cited above, illusory silver (Prātibhāsikarajata) is produced.[153] It cannot be stated either to be existent (Sat) or to be non-existent (Asat) or to be both (Sadasat)[154] – for if silver were existent how could an invalid cognition (Bhrānti) of silver arise, or how could its knowledge be sublated later (Bādhita). It could not be non-existent too as in that case it would not be perceived (Khyāta) on the one hand and on the other the knowledge of the non-existent silver could not later be sublated (Bādhita). Thus 'it' is a peculiar and indefinable silver that is produced at the time of illusion from the ignorance (Avidyā) attached to the Śuktī and later on is destroyed. It need not be doubted, then, how, even the real silver in the world is admitted by these idealists to be real, for to them Brahman is the only final reality (Paramārtha sat). Practical silver is a pragmatic (Vyavahārika) reality. But this illusory reality[155] is contradicted by a knowledge of something other than Brahman (i.e. here by a knowledge of silver); for they admit an empirical reality (Vyāvahārika satya) like 'silver' and perception of silver in the invalid cognition is later on contradicted by the empirical reality.

This theory of invalid knowledge swings neither to the side of silver being existent nor non-existent and it establishes that because it is neither, it can't be both. To admit such a peculiar and indefinable category is itself cumbersome for, each time the invalid cognition is produced we have to admit its production; later its destruction etc. which is too prolix. It need not be doubted, however, that, as silver does not really exist there, it cannot be an object of perception, as, by the proximity of Jñānalakṣaṇa, (supernormal) contact even real silver can be brought into the perceptual sphere. Accepting this proximity is not a concession granted by the opponent as it cannot be helped even by the Vedāntin, for arriving at a knowledge of fragrance or fragrancehood when Sandal is seen.[156] Another incongruity in the theory is that it cannot be explained how illusory silver is produced from a pearl-oyster as the required material is not present in it. On the other hand, if an infefinable silver is produced how is one prompted to activity (because it is not the indefinable silver that the person desires). If it be urged that the one is identified with the other then why not it be more safely and judiciously be identified with real silver itself (already cognised and elsewhere present) as it is less cumbersome to suppose.

The Ākhyāti Theory of Knowledge of the Mīmāṃsaka

According to Guru or Prabhākara, as we know, there is no invalid experience at all. All experience in his opinion is valid. In an invalid cognition (as accepted by others and not by him) of the form 'This is silver' the thing in front (signified by 'this' in the sentence) is the object of perceptual cognition (Pratyakṣa) and silver is the object of recollection (Smṛti) and not of perception[157] brought about by the impression of silver previously experienced in view of its whiteness, effulgence and such other similar characteristics which serve as the stimulus (Udbodhaka). The two, viz., the perceptional cognition of the oyster-shell (Śukti pratyakṣa) and the recollection of silver (Rajatasmṛti) are in themselves sufficient to prompt one to activity[158] and as such there is no necessity to admit a qualified knowledge as the Logician does.[159]

It is possible to hold the relation of the describer to the described (Nirūpyanirūpakabhāva) between the two objecthoods

(Viṣayate) presented by the aforesaid perceptual cognition and recollection,[160] and hence it is unwise to admit a qualified knowledge as does the Logicians, as it is more cumbrous.[161]

Nor can it be urged that a qualified knowledge is less cumbersome in the case of invalid cognition, as there is no normal proximity (Laukikasannikarṣa) of the eye with the silver (which is not actually present). Nor an one launch upon a scheme of supernormal perception (Jñānalakṣaṇa as already stated) says Guru, as it is not acceptable to him.

It should not be objected, nevertheless, that, in case there is no invalid knowledge, even when there is a knowledge 'This is silver' with reference to an oyster-shell, there should be activity; for (to this the Prābhākara replied that) it is not the perceptual cognition of the oyster-shell and the recollection of silver alone that are responsible for activity (in trying to seek for the object) but a non-cognition of the difference of the object desired (from the object in front) (i.e. Iṣṭabhedāgraha) also is another cause responsbile for it (activity).[162] Thus in Guru's opinion there is no knowledge of silver with reference to the oyster-shell and as such no invalid experience is recognised by him. It may also be noted that no distinction is made between the perceptual cognition of the oyster-shell and the recollection of silver and hence his theory is called Akhyāti (non-cognition) (of distinction).[163] On it is designated Akhyāti because there is the non-cognition of silver etc. by perceptual cognition.[164]

To hold that the cognition 'The conch is yellow' is invalid is not judicious, as Prabhākara holds, as a part of it (i.e. the conch part of it) at least is valid even in the opponents' view. How can even this experience be considered to be invalid; for the other part of the experience 'Yellowhood' (Pītimā) also present in the biliousness pertaining to the eye is also experienced by the man? Thus the two experiences gain a unitary general form and prompt the person to activity and in actual practice the object does not correspond (to the knowledge) and as such, though the experience is valid, it is said to be invalid, but where actually the thing corresponds with experience the designation, invalidity is not given. In this connection Śālikānātha quotes the example of hot water where actually the particles of fire are hot but not the water. But even the Logician, a votary of mistaken notion (Anyathā khyāti) calls 'hot water' a valid cognition though, in fact, the fire particles in the water (there) are hot. This experience of heat in water is similar to the experience 'The conch is yellow.'[165] Thus it is only with reference to non-correspondence with the object that we call cognition invalid and not because the experience is invalid (as the invalid knowledge is really experienced).

A Criticism of Guru's Ākhyāti Theory

This view of Prabhākara also is not sound inasmuch as it does not admit a qualified knowledge as he holds that it is not possible as a contact with the sense organ (with silver etc.) is not present since real silver is not there and as such there is no experience of silver possible with reference to the oyster-shell. If there be a rejoinder that by the Jñānalakṣaṇā proximity it is possible to have it, it is not so since such a proximity is not acceptable to him (to Prabhākara); and even without such a proximity he would be able to account for a knowledge of fragrance (when there is a knowledge of the type 'The Sandal is fragrant' when Sandal is only seen but not smelt) either by taking recourse to recollection or inference.[166]

If there are two cognitions in an invalid knowledge one should be of the form 'This is silver' and the other of the form 'I remember silver' and these would be two separate pieces of knowledge and not one as in our experience 'This is silver.'

Further "Is the cognition 'an invalid cognition is there' valid or invalid" Citsukha questions. If the Prābhākara replies that it is invalid then he would be admitting the existence of an invalid cognition against his own theory. Or, if he replies that it is valid he has to accept some invalid piece of cognition as its substratum which position is not safe for him.[167]

For further details of defects in the theory of Guru the concerned portion of the Tattvacintāmaṇi may be referred to.[168]

The Prasiddhārtha Khyāti Theory of the Sāṃkhya

The Sāṃkhya holds that at the time of invalid knowledge silver is produced. Silver which is known (Prasiddha) elsewhere but not in the place of the object of our perceptual cognition cannot be presented unless it is produced on the analogy of lighting which appears at the time of cognition and later on disappears when it is contradicted.

Rāmānuja's Satkhyāti Theory

Rāmānuja's theory is called Satkhyāti as the object of cognition 'Silver' is real even in an invalid cognition which may be stated thus: According to the process of quintuplication (Pancīkaraṇa prakriyā) all substances are created with the parts of all the five elements in some proportion or other.[169] Thus in an invalid cognition silver, though it is of the form of fire (Tejaḥ) mainly appears in the oyster-shell which is mainly of the form of the earth but also is of the form of fire in some measure. Then it may not be objected how invalidity is cognised, for there is the contradiction of the popular usage of the word 'silver' (Viṣaya vyavahārabādha) in an oyster-shell[170] where the silver part (or better say the fire part of it) is less prominent. Thus as the silver part is present in the pearl-oyster, the object of knowledge, however, is real but as the silver part of the same is small when compared with the other, there is no such usage of the word as 'this is silver.' That is the only reason why the knowledge is called invalid. In this way both the Anyathākhyāti and the Akhyāti theories also appear to be favourable to him.[171]

In the above two theories though the acceptance of another silver produced (or the presence of silver in some way in the latter theory) is justified, yet it is cumbersome, as already stated, to hold that another particular such object (whose properties have to be defined, produced (or cognised in the latter view) at the time of each invalid knowledge and destroyed later on. On the other hand it cannot be satisfactorily explained how (a different) silver is produced as the necessary causes inherent, non-inherent etc. are not present there for its production. Further the acceptance of more than one contradictory theory tends to prolixity.[172]

Madhva's View

According to Madhva there is no contact of the sense organ with the object inasmuch as there is the later experience of stultification as 'I have experienced the non-existing silver.' Thus Madhva establishes that the purely non-existent silver is experienced by the sense organ even when it is in contact with Nacre etc. owing to a defect. Though this looks as some kind of Asatkhyāti still it would be akin tc the Anyathākhyāti theory of the Logician when stretched further in its epistemological detail.

A Criticism of the Theories of Invalid Cognition

In the opinion of the Logician there is the perceptual cognition of the thing in front and the supernormal perception of silverhood by the contact called Jñānalakṣaṇā; but the Prābhākara admits perception and recollection. The latter does not admit a qualified knowledge (as does the Logician) which has the attributehood residing in that (silverhood etc.) represented by the substantivehood residing in the substratum of that (silver),[173] which is of necessity to be accepted as otherwise, there would be no activity prompted later. It cannot, however, be objected as to how the silver which is not actually present is cognised, for, by the Jñānalakṣana contact the perception of silver is rendered possible. The objection raised by the Śāṅkarite against this view is that in case the supernormal contact (Jñānalakṣaṇa) is accepted, the Logician might as well forego his theory that inference is a separate means of valid knowledge. For example since the smoke seen by the inferer signifies fire (through the remembrance of fire by the supernormal contact called Jñānalakṣaṇa) fire is secured easily and inference then becomes a redundance. But it appears to me that in the above objection, there is no case for inference as the Śāṅkarite holds as the minor term (Pakṣa) has no Pakṣatahood in it because as soon as the sandal is seen its fragrance is immediately remembered by recollection (instead of holding that it is inferred which is a more cumbersome process in these cases) and as such the Śāṅkarite cannot secure fragrance in the case cited with the help of inference as fragrance already secured by recollection (Jñānalakṣaṇa contact) bars the process of inference as Siddhi is present in the Pakṣa and not Siddhyabhāva as it should be (in the case of inference). It cannot be maintained that this assumption is cumbrous as its acceptance is obligatory even to the opponent in the case of a perceptual cognition like 'Sandal is fragrant' where Sandal only is an object of ocular perception. For obvious reasons fragrance need not be inferred in this case. Thus the theory of the Logician that the oyster-shell appears to be silver (or is mistaken to be silver) appears to be more sound dialectically and practically viewed inasmuch as it accounts for the unitary nature of the knowledge produced by an incorrect statement like 'This is silver' and also accounts for the later statement of the valid cognition 'I was mistaking the oystershell for silver all the while.'[174] The Digambara Jaina also holds the same view but designates it as Viparītakhyāti.[175]

How the other theories of Anirvacanīyakhyāti and Asatkhyāti are cumbersome has already been discussed. The Ātmakhyāti theory of the Buddhist cannot be regarded to be correct inasmuch as there is the unwelcome possibility of the cognition 'I am silver' etc. Further the theory that all objects are of the form of knowledge is itself open to a serious objection. The Asatkhyāti theory of the Buddhist also posits that the knowledge of the object that does not exist is produced which is contrary to experience. Even the protagonists of the other theories are obliged to accept the Logician's view when they have to satisfactorily account for the activity subsequent to an invalid cognition–for soon after one mistakes an oyster-shell for silver he resorts to activity and tries to use it as silver. Thus the Anyathākhyāti theory appears to be nearer to experience than any of the others mentioned above for as already stated, the cognition of a 'mistaken notion' is subsequently produced. This experience cannot be refuted.

References

1. That is to say as long as the knowledge is there it is only with the self.
2. Of course for the cognition of a cognition (apperception), cognition of pleasure, pain etc. the witness consciousness itself is responsible.
3. Pratyaksam kalpanapodhamabhrantam.
4. Vide Tar. Rak. VSS 8-11.
5. Ny. Ku. 3-VS7.
6. Yatparaḥ śabdaḥ sa sabdarthaḥ.
7. For arguments vide Tat. Pra., p.44.
8. Vide Ad. Sid. Ch. I. Dṛkdṛsyabhanga Prasaṅga.
9. The Advaitin accepts Vṛtti as related to the substratum-consciousness (Adhiṣṭhanacaitanya). Even if this relation be false what kind of relation can be established between them? Adhyāsa is not a relation.
10. Ny. Ku. IV VS 4.
11. For a clear treatment in English of the disputes on Saviṣayatva, Sākāratva etc. of knowledge vide 'The Concept of Knowledge – Indian Theories.'
12. Nirākāratayādhiyām Ny. Ku. Vs. 4.
13. Of course the Buddhist gives another explanation of the word 'Svaprakāsata' and this will be criticised later in this chapter.
14. Kartṛkarmabhāva.
15. Ajadarupata.
16. Vide Tat. Pra. (P-6 ll 3 et. seqq.).

17. Artho Jñataḥ.
18. Tadvati tatprakāraka jñānatvam pramātvam.
19. Tadabhāvavati tatpraḳārakam jñānam.
20. Tatprakārakatvesati tadabhavaprakaraka jñānatvam.
21. Ekasmin dharmiṇi viruddha nānādharma vagāhijñānam.
22. Viśesādarśanam kotidvaya smaranam dharmijñānam ca śamsaya matre hetuḥ.
23. Badhakalīnecchajanyam jñānam.
24. Mukham candraḥ.
25. Ajñātatattvāsrthe kāraṇopapathteḥ tattva jñānartha muhastarkaḥ.
26. Vyāpyāropeṇa vyāpakāropastarkaḥ.
27. Parvate dhumostu vahnirmastu.
28. Aniṣta prasanjanam.
29. Utkaṭānyatarakoṭikaḥ samśayah.
30. Samskaramatrajanyam jnanam smrtih.
31. Yat sattat kṣanikam.
32. Sosyam Devadattah.
33. Etaddesaitatkāla viśiṣṭa Devadattaḥ taddeśa tatkālopalakṣita Devadattābhinnaḥ.
34. This is the Sabdabodha of the sentence. Here it may be noted that place and time are viśesanas in the present time but are upalakṣanās in the past time and place.
35. Saṃṣkāramatrajanyam jñānaṃ Smṛtiḥ.
36. Saṃsargāsangidhīh or even prātipadikārtha.
37. Ghatosnityah (ghatatva visesana yukto ghatah anityah).
38. Smṛtibhinnam jñānam anubhavaḥ.
39. Ayaṃ ghaṭaḥ.
40. Samyoga, samyukta samavaya, samyukta samaveta samavaya, samavaya and visesana visesyabhava.
41. Pīno Devadattaḥ diva na bhunkte (Arthāpattiḥ Upapādya Jñānam).
42. Iha ghato bhaviṣyati.
43. Ghato naṣṭaḥ.

44. Yogyānupalabdhiḥ.
45. Ghatabhavaḥ bhūtalasvarūpaḥ.
46. Avinābhāva vṛttya sambaddhayoḥ samudāya samudayinoḥ samudayena itarasya grahaṇam.
47. Ajnatamula vaktrakah sabḍah aitihyam.
48. Ayamekaḥ, Ayamekaḥ, Imau dvau, Anekaikatvabuddhiḥ.
49. Ekona dvau.
50. Ekah dvau.
51. Śābdabuddhikarmanām dvikṣaṇavasthāyitvam.
52. Vrihibhiryavairvā yajeta.
53. Danḍi puruṣaḥ.
54. Viseṣane yidviśesaṇam tadviseṣaṇatavacchedakam.
55. Dandatvarupaviśeṣanatvacchinna pratiyogika sambandhaḥ samsargateya puruse bhasate.
56. Anekamukhya viśeṣyakam jñānam.
57. Svatyantabhavasamanadhikaranyam i.e. Co-existing alongwith its own negation.
58. N.B. 2-1-8. Pratyakṣādīnamaprāmāṇyam traikalyāsiddheḥ. Comm. thereon.
59. Vide Ibid, 1-1-16.
60. In the theories of course, where a knowledge (of concomitance) etc. are said to be the means the resultant, it may be noted, is only another knowledge and not the same knowledge.
61. Antahkaranopahitam caitanyam saksi.
62. Antahkaranavacchimam caitanyam saksi.
63. Saksi ceta kevalo nirgunasca.
64. For other definitions of Saksin vide S.S.L.S. pp. 149-157.
65. S.S.L.S., pp. 133-134.
66. The sentence means 'an order or a command demanding bringing which has for its object cow.
67. Ekamevādvitīyam Brahma.
68. Ekamevadvitīyam Brahma.
69. Saṃsargasangidhi.

70. 'Aparyayaśabdanamekapratipadikarttamatra paryavasayrtvam.'
71. Ekamevadvitiyam Brahma.
72. For details of the reputation of Aihandartha vide (Tat. Pra. p. 105 et seqq.).
73. For details vide (Tat. Pra., p. 111 para 2).
74. Here by reflection is meant only a subtle form of the object of experience making its impression on the mind whether the object be ocular, auditory or otherwise.
75. Nagrhita visesana buddhih visesye pravartate (Tar. Bh., p. 10 1.17).
76. Vide Ny. Sid., p. 496.
77. Ibid, p. 498.
78. Atitavastha-vacchinna vastu grahanam.
79. Vide Pra. Var. (Vṛ) - 2-333 onwards.
80. For the detailed Buddhists defence of his stand vide Pra. Var (Bḥ), p. 353 et. seqq.
81. Paryāya is what is produced and destroyed.
82. For arguments vide Pra. Mim., p. 29, para 124 onwards.
83. Vide Pra. Mim., para 130-131.
84. Yat sat tat kṣanikaṃ yathajaladhārapatalaṃ.
85. This is the object which I saw yesterday 'a poet etc.'
86. Neither Viśesyatā, Prakāratā nor Samsargata is present in this knowledge of pot or pothood for example.
87. Kṛta hāra kṛtābhyāgama prasaṇga.
88. Śabdetarodbhūta viśesaguṇā naśrayatve sati jñānasāmanyakāraṇa manassamyogāśrayatvam.
89. Ātmabhinnatve sati Arthasamyoga bhinnajñāna sādhāraṇa kāranibhuta samyogaśrayatvam Indriyatvam (By asādhāraṇa kāraṇibhūta samyoga' Mind-time contact etc. which are sādhārana kāraṇasamyogas are excluded.
90. For a refutation of the existence of objects Vide .... Vedanta Siddhānta Muktavali, Calcutta Edn., p. 72 et. seqq.
91. Sati dṛste kāraṇe Adṛṣṭakalpanāyā Anyayyatvāt.
92. In this opinion Pakṣatā is Sadhya Sandeha.

93. 'Yatra matānasīyadhūmaḥtatra mahānasīya vahniḥ' This should be the nature of Vyāpti in particular but not (Mahānasiya dhūmaḥ Vahnitvavacchinna) Vahni Vyāpyaḥ in which case the mountain fire also should be perceived in the kitchen itself.

94. Svaviṣaya visayaka jñānam.

95. Samāna viṣaya pratyakṣa sāmagrī anumiti sāmagrītah prabala is the maxim here.

96. Smokehood is said not to have been perceived in the Advaitin's view because it is not something known already for him like his smoke and thus his smokehood has no objecthood (viṣayatā) and hence no attributehood (prakārata) also in it.

97. Samāne viṣaye pratyakṣasāmagri anuniti sāmagrīto prabala.

98. Sva viṣaya viṣayaka pratyakṣa janako jñāna viśeṣaḥ.

99. Because Sāmānya lakṣaṇa is defined as 'Indriya sambaddha viṣayaka jñānaprakāribhuto dharmah.

100. Jātyakhandopadhyatiriktadharmāṇāmeva kincidrupena bhanam. Hence Sāmānyalakṣaṇa cannot operate in this case as the necessary fragrancehood is required to be cognised in fragrancehood. Thus jñānalakṣaṇa contact is admitted by the Logician.

101. Sapakṣe sattvam etc.

102. e.g. in a statement like 'This is a cow as it has horns' made with reference to a horse (vide Ny. K under Hetvābhasa).

103. According to the maxim 'Utpannam dravyam kṣaṇamaguṇam niṣkriyam ca tiṣṭhati.'

104. Because there is no incongruity between 'being fat' and 'not eating in the daytime' which may coexist.

105. Thus if the ordinary inference 'Devadatta eats in the night as he is fat without daytime meal' is considered not conforming to the rules of inference that Devadatta's eating is not a point of doubt which fact should make it a subject (pakṣa) of the inference, the following inference may be substituted in its place 'Devadatta's fatness is caused by night meal as it is not caused by day time meal.' Here the subject 'Devadatta's fatness' is doubted.

106. 'Yena vinā yadanupapannam tattasya vyāpyameva' is a rule.

107. Wherever there is a knowledge of the negation of pot, in spite of its being eligible for perception, there is the knowledge of the absence of pot' being the concomitance concerned. (In the previous view Abhāva is the auxiliary of the eye etc.; the sense organ which is the means of valid knowledge which need not be cognised. It is enough if the eye along with the absence of pot etc. is present for producing sense perception (The presence of the eye need not be known by the seer).

108. A knowledge of Yogyānupalabdhi is of this form. If a pot were here I would have perceived it.

109. Ny. Kus. Slab III Vs. 7.

110. Unless by Śabda (word) is meant the valid word (Pramāṇa bhūta sabda). The validity of the knowledge depends upon the authenticity (Āptatva) of the concerned person using the words. Thus validity is due to his Āptatva but verbal knowledge due to the words used by him.

111. This subject of verbal testimony as a reliable source of many types of useful information unknown or partly known, discussed in detail in the Hindu Śāstras needs to be deligently investigated by modern research scholars.

112. For details of the meaning of a sentence vide the author's "Philosophy of a Sentence and Its Parts."

113. Sādharmya, vaidharmya and dharmamātra as when we say 'The Gavaya is like the cow,' 'The horse is not twohoofed like the cow,' 'An animal with a long neck, hanging lips, eating thorn is a camel' respectively which are cases of analogy.

114. Tadgatabhūyo dharma vattvam (Sādṛsyam).

115. If the Carvaka would still persist that perception alone is valid and not inference the objector would quip "Does the Carvaka's wife observe widowhood when he is away from home since he is not to be seen the perception alone is valid for him.

116. Vyāpāravadasādhāraṇaṃ kāraṇaṃ kāranam.

117. Phalāyoga vyavacchinnaṃ kāraṇaṃ kāranam.

118. The hill is fiery as there is smoke on it.

119. Here *both* the vyāpti and the pakṣadharmatā (the one with *smoke* as the mark and the other with *light* as the mark) are

present but as the mark, smoke which is cognised in the vyāpti here is not the same as is found in the Pakṣadharmatā (where it is a different mark, light) and hence the defect in the Mīmāṃsaka theory.

120. "Viśeṣe snugamābhāvaḥ sāmānye siddhasādhyatā, Anumābhaṅgapanke sminnimagnā vādidantinaḥ." Is the popular objection raised against the efficiency of Anumāna as a means of valid knowledge.

121. It is to be noted that fire (determined by its general property, firehood present in homologues and absent in heterologues) (Sāmānyātmā) is related to the mountain and thus appears as a particular (individual) fire; though practically it is the Sāmānyātmā that is presented by the inference.

122. Samāne viṣaye pratyakṣakāraṇasāmagrī prabalā, bhinne viṣaye anumitisāmagrī prabalā.

123. Similarity the following may be noted:

(a) Samāne viṣaye Animite sābdasāmgryormadhye sābda sāmagrī prabala, bhinne viṣaye tu anumiti sāmagri prabala.

(b) Mānasa pratyakṣasāmagri is always less powerful it may be noted.

124. For several details vide concerned portions under Anumāna in the Nyaya Sutra and its commns. as well as Tattvacintāmani.

125. That is to say 'the minor term' (here the mountain) is one that is possessed of fire which is made known by a knowledge of the reason (smoke here) qualified by concomitance (vyāpti) and presence in the minor term (pakṣadharmatā here the presence of such smoke on the mountain) (Tasmāt tatha is the form of the Nigamana).

126. For details why the five members of syllogism have been admitted vide Nyāya Sutra 1.1.39.

127. For a detailed definition of the fallacy of reason (hetvābhāsa) vide Sāmānyanirukti of Gadādhara.

128. For examples vide Logician's theory of knowledge etc.

129. For 'Nigrahasthanas' vide Vātsyāyana Bhāṣya.

130. Vide Tar. Rak Vs 89, for other details vide 89 et seqq.

131. For several other details of hetvabhasas vide Man Mey, p. 69 et. seqq.

132. Tathā ca hetupratyayasāpekṣe bhāvānāmutpādaḥ pratitya Samutpada ityucyate - vide com. of Somasekhara Sastri on Madhyamika Kārika 24-8.

133. Ātmakhyātirasatkhyatiranyathākhyātireva ca, tathānirvacanakhyātirakhyātiḥ khyātipancakaṃ. (Sam Kan. Com., p. 454, 11.22-24) also Ny. Var. Tat. Tīkā 1-1-2.

134. Kṣaṇikavijñānasyātmanastadākārarajatādeḥ bāhyatvena khyātiranyathā khyātiḥ (Sam. Kau. Com., p. 454 last two lines).

135. Ātmanaḥ khyātiḥ–Ātmakhyātiḥ i.e. Ātmanaḥ bāhyatvena khyātiḥ. For details vide Bauddha Theory of Knowledge.

136. Vide Pra. Pat. (p. 27, 11.20-21).

137. Rajatam na jñānam (Sam. Kau. Com., p. 455, 1.4).

138. Vide Ny. Kau., p. 77, 11.10-11.

139. Vide Ny. Man., p. 77, 11.10-11.

140. Asataḥ. (rajatādeḥ) khyātiḥ–Asatkhyātiḥ (Sam. Kau., p. 455 1.8).

141. Asato jñānaviṣayatvasya Aprāmāṇikatvāt (Pr. Rat., p. 26 1.4).

142. Vide Ny. Man., p. 164, 11, 7-8.

143. Anyathā (prakārāntareṇa) khyātiḥ bhānam.

144. Vivādapadam śuktiḥ rajatajñānaviṣayaḥ rajatopēyabhinnatve sati rajatarthipravṛttiviṣayatvaṭ.

145. i.e. idaṃpadārtha (śūkti) niṣtha Viśeṣyatanirūpitarajataniṣṭha prakāratā śālibodhaḥ.

146. Lāghavena Pravṛttimātre tasya (Viśiṣṭajñānasya) hetutvakalpanāt (Muk. under Vs. 136).

147. i.e. iṣṭabhedāgraha (not noticing the difference between the object on hand and the desired one).

148. i.e. iṣṭabhedāgraha–Also vide T.S. Sar., p. 255 1.1.

149. Saṃyuktāsamavetatvarūpalaukikasannikarṣeṇa rajatatvasya abhāsāt.

150. Dharmabhānap rayojanikā jñānalakṣnapratyasattih (i.e. in this case silverhood is apprehended by jñānalakṣana contact).

151. Iyam Pravṛttiḥ iṣṭatāvacchedakaprakāraka jñānajanyā pravṛttitvāt satyarajatasthatīya pravṛttivat. (T.S. Sar., p. 255 1.5).

152. For further details on khyāti theories vide Sam. Kau., p. 454 onwards.

153. Na hi lokasiddhasāmagrī prātibhāsikarajatotpādika, kintu vilakṣanaiva (Ad. Par., p. 118 11.13-14). For details vide Ibid continuation.

154. Anirvacanīyasya (Sattvenāsattvena sadasattvābhyām ca nirvaktumśakyasya (Prātibhasikarajatasya) khyatiḥ Anirvacanīyakhyātiḥ.

155. Prātibhāsikasatya.

156. For when we see sandal (already experienced once as fragrant) we have the knowledge 'Sandal is fragrant' also. Here the normal proximity (of the sense with the object) is contact between the eye and the Sandal piece. There can be no contact of the eye with fragrance which also is apprehended (Saurabhāṃśe alaukika pratyakṣaṃ). So, in order to apprehend fragrance, in such cases, the Logician is obliged to admit this transcendental proximity called jñānalakṣaṇa (For details vide Muk. Prat. Vs. 64).

157. Netyucyate, rajatajñānasya smṛtitvāt (Mim. Bh. Par., p. 12 1.7). Idamaṃśa eva pratyakṣa viṣayaḥ na rajatāmsaḥ. Also 'Suktikāyām yadbhāsvaram rūpam cakṣusā paricchinnam tadrajatasmṛterudbodhakamityupapadyetāpi (Br., p. 13, 11. 5-6).

158. Asaṃ sargargrahakālina raṅga rajatādi jñānādeva . . . bhramasya visista jñānarūptvābhāvena akhyātireva bhramaḥ. (Ny. Kau., p. 78, 11.10-12).

159. i.e. tadvadviśeṣyakatvāvacchinna tatprakāratāśālijñānatvam.

160. Vide Pr. Rat., p. 229, 11.21-23.

161. 'Taddhetoreva taddhetutve madhye kiṃ tena' is the maxim followed here.

162. Katham tarhi viparyayaḥ, agrahanadeveti vadāmaḥ (Bṛ., p. 12, 11.22-23). Also Svantantropasthiteṣṭabhedāgrahasyaiva Sarvatra pravartakatvena (T.S. Sar., p. 252, 11.9-10). Also Pravṛttimātre bhedāgrahe sati iṣṭapurovartijñānasya lāghavena hetutvānna tu sadapi viśiṣṭajñānam gauravāt (T.C. Rah., p. 449, 11.1-3.)

163. Raṇgādeh rajatatvādinā khātyahāvo (a) khyātiriti tadvivaraṇāt (Ny. Kau., p. 78, 11.12-13). Also Vivekasya grahaṇasmaraṇa-

yorbhedasya Akhyātiragrahaḥ iti vadanti (Pr. Rat., p. 29, 11.26-27).

164. Vide Ny. Ko. under Khyāti.

165. Yatra tu vyavahāra visaṃvado nāsti tatra bhrāntirapi na vyapadisyate (Pra. Pan., p. 44, last line).

166. Surabhi candanamiti pratītistu yadi pūrva gṛhitasaurabha viśiṣṭādharmi viṣayā tadā viśeṣaṇamśe smṛtiranyathā tu anumitirupaiveti (Sam. Kau., p. 457, 11: 22-24).

167. Vide Tat. Pra., p. 63, 11.11-14.

168. T.C. (Rah), p. 431, onwards.

169. Śuktirajatajñānādāvapi vaidikapañcīkaraṇaprakriyayā rajatāvayavanām satvat tatra rajatajñānamapi pramāṇam. (Ny. Part., p. 37, 11.6-8).

170. The significance of the word 'Vyavahāra' here is to include the three kinds of Khyāti that are favoured by him 'Svabhımatā khyātitraya saṃgrahāya vyavahārapadam (Ākhyatiḥ, yatharthakhyātiḥ and anyathākhyatiḥ).

171. Sarvairapyanyathā khyātirdustyajatvāllaghīyasī, tadvādinapyavarjyatvāt tatopyakhyātilaghavam (Ny. Par., p. 39, last line). Also Svārasyamanyathākhyāta vakhyātau, laghavam matam, iti darśayituṃ bhāṣye dvitayam tadanuśritam. Ibid, p. 40, 11.2-3).

172. For a clear exposition of rival theories of Error and Their Refutation vide Pr. Rat. under Su. 445.

173. Tadvanniṣṭhaviśeṣyatānirūpita tanniṣṭhaprākāratāśālitvam.

174. Because a statement also decides the object for us 'Pratīti vyavahārabhyamarthasiddhiḥ'-is the popular maxim of the Logician.

175. Pra. Rat., p. 30, 11.18-19.

Glossary and Concordance of Technical Terms

Akhandārtha (vāda) - (the theory that the import of a sentence is one whole)

Akhyāti (a theory of error)

Ajñāna (ignorance) (also a positive veil that covers truth)

Atideśavakya (transferable sentence)

Ativyāpti (too wide an application (of vyapti))

Anavasthā (infinite regress)

Anaikāntika (the inconstant mark or reason)

Anukulatarka (a type of Tarka conducive to the Sadhya on hand)

Anupalabdhi (non-perception)

Anubhava (Experience)

Anekānta (vāda) (the theory of uncertainty)

Anumāna (inference on the means of inference)

Anumiti (inference or inferential knowledge)

Anuyogin (sub-stratum)

Anuvyavasāya (apperception or knowledge of knowledge)

Antarabhāsamanapadārthāḥ (categories which manifest themselves, in the middle)

Anyathākhyāti (a theory of error)

Anyonyāśraya (mutual dependence)

Anvaya vyāpti (positive concomitance)

Anvaya vyatirekihetu (a mark concomitant both affirmatively and negatively)

Aprasiddha (unknown or unestablished)

Abhāva (absence or negation)

Ayatharthajñāna (invalid knowledge)

Arthakriyā (activity carried out by an object (with a purpose)

Arthāpatti (presumption)

Avacchedaka (determinant)
Avacchedya (that which is determined)
Avastu (non-existent)
Avyāpti (too narrow an application of vyāpti)
Asaṃbhava (impossibility or inconsistency)
Asatkhyāti (a theory of error)
Asiddha (unestablished)
Avīta (negative inference)
Atman (soul, self)
Ātmakhyāti (a theory of error)
Atmāśraya (self-dependence)
Iṣṭabhedāgraha (non-cognition of the difference from what is desired)
Upanaya (application (of concomitance) to the subject on hand)
Upapādaka (proof)
Upapādya (to be proved)
Upamāna (analogy)
Upādhi (an external adjunct)
Upamiti (analogical knowledge), characteristic
Aitihya (hearsy or tradition)
Karaṇa (efficient cause)
Kevalavyatirekin (hetu) (a mark found only in negative concomitance)
Kevalānvayin (hetu) (a mark found only in positive concomitance)
Kṣanika (momentary)
Khyāti (-vāda) (theory of knowledge)
Cakrakāśraya (dependence in a cycle)
Caturdaśalakṣaṇī (a set of fourteen kinds of definition) (of vyāpti)
Cit (consciousness)
Citpratibiṃba (reflection of consciousness)
Citiḥ (consciousness)
Citta-(mind, momentary knowledge (Buddhist))
Caitta-(mental state)
Cetanā (consciousness)
Caitanya (consciousness)
Jñādhātvartha (meaning of the verb 'to know')

Jñāna (generally knowledge)
Jñānagrāhaka (sāmagrī) (the causal aggregate) which cognises.
Jñānalakṣaṇa (sannikarṣa) (a transcendental type of proximity)
Jñatata (knownness)
Jñaṇavāda (Theory of Knowledge)

Jaina
Bauddha
Tarkika
Mimāmsaka
Vedāntin
Sāṃkhya-

Jñeyāvyabhicāritvam (not straying from the object to be known)
Tatnātā (suchness)
Tarka (reductio ad absurdum)
Tṛtīyaliṅgaparamarśa (consideration of the reason for the third time)
Tripuṭīpratyakṣatāvāda (the theory that the triad of the knower, the known and the knowledge is perceived)
Dṛṣtānta (illustration example)
Dharma (property etc.)
Dharmin (substrate, the substratum of a dharma)
Dhārāvāhikajñana (cognition in a series)
Nigamana (conclusion)
Nigrahasthānāni (points of defeat)
Nirṇaya (ascertainment)
Nirvikalpakajñāna (indeterminate knowledge)
Nivṛtti (desistence from action)
Niśćaya (ascertainment)
Niṣkampa pravṛtti (unswerving activity)
Pakṣadharmatā (presence of the reason in the minor term)
Pakṣa (minor term) (the object denoted by the minor term)
Pañcalaksani (a set of five definitions of vyāpti)
Parataḥ prāmānyam (externality of validity of knowledge)
Parāmarśah (consideration)
Parārthānumāna (inference for another's sake)
Parokṣa (mediate)
Paramārthika satya (absolute or final reality)

Pūrvavat (a priori) (inference)

Prakāratā (attributeness) (objecthood)

Prakāritā (attribute possessorness) (cognitionhood)

Pramāṇa (means of valid knowledge, proof)

Prameya (object of knowledge)

Pratikarmavyavasthā–(the rule regarding perception of objects individually and at times only)

Pratibādhya (jñāna) (knowledge barred)

Pratibandhaka (jñāna) (knowledge which bars)

Pratyakṣa (perceptional knowledge)

Pratyāsatti (contiguity) (also sannikarṣa)

Prayatna (effort)

Pravṛtti (activity, urge to activity)

Pratijña (proposition)

Pratiyogin (counterpositive in the cae of abhava; the contained)

Pratītyasamutpāda (evolution from the causes available without the help of a sentient agent)

Prākaṭya (knownness)

Prātibhāsikasatya (illusory or hallucinational reality)

Prāmāṇyam (validity or correctness)

Bādhita (stultified)

Buddhi (intellect (Sāmkhya); cognition (others) internal organ of ascertainment (Vedāntin))

Bhrama (invalid knowledge)

Bhrānti (invalid knowledge)

Manas (mind, internal organ of doubt)

Matatrayasadhārana vipratipattiḥ (a controversy common to all the three views)

Mati (knowledge, a kind of knowledge (Jaina)

Mādhyamika (Nihilist) (a class of Buddhists)

Māyāvādin (the Sankara Advaitin here)

Yathārthajñāna (valid knowledge)

Yogācāra (Idealist) (Buddhist)

Yogajalakṣaṇā (Pratyāsatti) (a proximity called by that name)

Yogyānupalabdhi (non-perception of an object capable of perception)

Liṅga (mark, reason or cause)
Liṅgāparāmarśa (consideration of the mark or reason)
Liṅgin (the thing proved by the reason)
Vijñānavādin (the Buddhist who accepts the reality of cognition alone, the idealist)
Vipakṣa (antilogue, or a contrary example)
Viparītakhyāti (vāda) (a theory of error)
Viparyaya (invalid knowledge)
Viruddha (hetu) (the contradictory reason)
Viśeṣa (the particular, particularity, distinguishing mark)
Viśeṣana (attribute)
Viśeṣyatā (substantivehood)
Visiṣṭajñāna (knowledge of a qualified one)
Viṣayatā (objecthood)
Visayitā (object possessorhood) (cognitionhood, desirehood etc.)
Vīta (affirmative inference)
Vṛttijñāna (knowledge of the form of vṛtti)
Vaibhāṣika (a class of Buddhists)
Vyadhikaraṇadharma (a property existing in a different substratum)
Vyatirekavyāpti (negative concomitance)
Vyāpaka (pervader)
Vyāpti (invariable concomitance)
Vyapya (concomitant)
Vyāvahārikāsatya (pragmatic or practical reality)
Śabda (verbal testimony, word)
Śābdabodha (import of a sentence)
Śruti (scripture)
Śeṣavat (a posteriori inference)
Saṃvṛtisatya (dependent reality)
Sakampapravṛtti (swerving or doubtful action)
Samarthapravṛtti (action leading to the fulfilment of desire)
Sautrāntika (a class of Buddhists)
Sambhava (possibility)
Samūhālambana (depending on a group)
Sat (existent)

Satkhyāti (a theory of error)

Satpratipakṣa (the counterbalanced) (a fallacy)

Sandeha (doubt)

Sannikarṣa (proximity)

Sapakṣa (homologue or a similar instance)

Saptabhañginaya (the theory of sevenfold alternative of the existence of object)

Savikalpakajñāna (determinate knowledge)

Savyabhicāra (the inconstant reason)

Sādhya (the thing to be proved)

Sākārajñāna (vada) (theory that) cognition has a form.

Sādhaka (proof)

Sāmagrī (aggregate)

Sāmānyatodṛṣṭa (inference depending on a general observation)

Sāmaṇya viśeṣātmā (of the nature of the general and the particular)

Samanyalakṣaṇa (a kind of transcendental proximity)

Sūnyavāda (theory of voidness)

Smaraṇa (recollection)

Smṛti (recollection)

Syādvāda (the theory of the sevenfold alternatives of existence of objects)

Svalakṣana (the self-charaterised (object)

Svataḥ (prāmānyam) (internality of validity)

Svasam-vedanata (vāda) (the theory of self-cognition of knowledge)

Svarthānumāna (inference for one's own sake)

Hetu (reason or mark)

Hetvābhāsa (fallacy).

Index